Group-analytic Psychotherapy
A Meeting of Minds

Group-analytic Psychotherapy

A Meeting of Minds

HAROLD BEHR MBBCh, DPM, FRCPsych, M Inst GA

Training Group Analyst,
Institute of Group Analysis (London)
Private Practice: The North London Centre
for Group Therapy

and

LIESEL HEARST Dip Soc Sci, MAPSW, M Inst GA

Training Group Analyst,
Institute of Group Analysis (London)
Private Practice: The North London Centre
for Group Therapy

W
WHURR PUBLISHERS
LONDON AND PHILADELPHIA

© 2005 Whurr Publishers Ltd
First published 2005
by Whurr Publishers Ltd
19b Compton Terrace
London N1 2UN England and
325 Chestnut Street, Philadelphia PA 19106 USA

Illustrations © Harold Behr.

Reprinted 2005, 2006 and 2008

British Library Cataloguing in Publication Data

A catalogue record for this book
is available from the British Library.

ISBN-13: 978 1 86156 475 7 p/b

Contents

Foreword

Psychotherapy is at once an art and a science. The former is expressed through the intuition, personality and imaginativeness of the therapist, the latter through the discipline of interested participation in the ideas and work of others. Harold Behr and Liesel Hearst exemplify the combination of these two spheres of discourse in their extensive account of group analysis.

The text is the fruit of a long collaboration between the two authors in their roles as therapists, supervisors and teachers in the field of group analysis. The book is grounded in the theory and practice of the basic Foulkesian group model. With this as its cornerstone, the two authors have constructed a picture of present-day practice and taken us further into some of the new ideas which are rapidly developing in this field. It is, I believe, the most comprehensive and integrated clinical text on group analysis to date.

The major part of the book constitutes a narrative exposition of the vast array of issues and tasks to be faced in the practice of group analytic psychotherapy. The authors are well known for their ability to make use of clinical examples in the teaching and supervision of group therapy, and this is abundantly in evidence in the text. I particularly relished their lively dialogue on questions of technique in the important areas of assessment and preparation of patients for group therapy, and the early phases of a new group. A dramatic presentation of the group in action brings to life the craft of two experienced artisans in the field and is an inspirational reminder of the values, strength and therapeutic effectiveness of the Foulkesian model when the required conditions are carefully maintained.

This is a profoundly thoughtful book, compassionate and with many wise observations on clinical work. The writing is enlivened by the wit, colour and irony which will be recognized by the authors' many students and colleagues. It is a unique and substantial addition to the literature on group analytic psychotherapy and the widening scope of group analytic method and ideas. I am sure it will speak to all practitioners and become a valued reference text on groupwork trainings worldwide.

Tom Hamrogue
The North London Centre for Group Therapy

Acknowledgements

We would like to thank Mrs Sylvia Hutchinson, Professor Bryan Lask, Dr Steinar Lorentzen, Dr Malcolm Pines and Mrs Cynthia Rogers for their encouragement, support and sound advice. We are also grateful to Dr Ann Goldman for permission to use material based on a group for parents which she co-conducted with one of us. Finally, it is a pleasure to acknowledge the devoted labours of Mrs Lesley Behr, who transformed a mountain of scribble into print, guided us through some necessary computer skills, and nursed the manuscript through to its final form.

Introduction

About ourselves

The way we work as psychotherapists derives as much from our personal experience as it does from our professional training. In writing this book we have mainly trawled through professional waters, but the picture would not be complete if we did not add a few personal vignettes to give you a chance to judge our bias and compare it with your own. Of course these vignettes have been carefully chosen to serve as fig-leaves, but we hope that they will be sufficiently revealing to give you a glimpse of the social and cultural motivations which have formed our identities as group analysts.

Harold Behr remembers his group-analytic beginnings like this:

'I was brought up in the South Africa of the apartheid era. Aged eight or nine, I already knew that I was classified as 'European'. It dawned on me that I was lucky to be in this group because it gave me lots of privileges, by contrast with so many people around me who were classified as 'Non-European'. At the same time it troubled me to see children and adults from my camp, the 'European' camp, treating children and adults from the other camp so badly. I noticed particularly that the mocking gestures, insults and acts of violence of the 'Europeans' travelled in one direction only and were received flinchingly and with no sign of retaliation from the people at whom they were directed.

In those days I was allowed to wander freely around the streets of central Johannesburg. Crowds fascinated me, especially those gathered for political purposes. One scene in particular made a deep impression: Watching from the safe perch of an office block rooftop, I observed a seething crowd gathered on the steps of the Johannesburg City Hall. I learnt afterwards that this was an antigovernment rally being addressed by the Trade Union leader Solly Sachs. There was plenty of heckling going on, which I enjoyed. At the same time I was scared. From my bird's-eye view I could see another group forming. A line of police vans had parked down a side street, out of which spilled large numbers of khaki-clad police. They formed several circles, each circle surrounding a small bunch of spectators. The circles tightened and steered their contents, swaying to and fro, in the direction of the vans. A few people got hit on the head by truncheons. One by one they were pushed or thrown into the vans which then drove off.

A long shot in retrospect tells me that that scene planted in my mind the thought that groups were both exciting and dangerous. Like the crowd psychologists of the late nineteenth century, I made no attempt to distinguish between crowds and any other kind of group. It seemed that if you were in the wrong place, or on the wrong side, or if you spoke up and said the wrong thing, you were likely to get hit on the head and taken away to be punished. But what if you belonged to the wrong group through no fault of your own? I had no answer to this question.

Twenty years later I had my first experience of a therapy group. This was as a psychiatric registrar in Valkenberg Hospital, Cape Town. Valkenberg was a typical mental hospital, set well back from the main road in large grounds carefully tended by the patients. Here I joined an Occupational Therapist to take a group of four patients. Each patient had a different diagnosis, but what united them was a specified need to keep them in a locked ward. What I remember most about this group was my inability to match their concerns with their diagnoses, so meticulously formulated by the medical staff. In fact their diagnoses seemed largely irrelevant to them, since what they preferred to dwell on was the unfairness of their living conditions, their anxieties about an increase or decrease in their medication and the possibility of achieving promotion to an open ward. Lesson number two in groups: there appeared to be a gap between the objective world of the professional and that of the patient. When the two worlds came together in a group there had to be an adjustment of the professional lens before meaningful communication could be established.

Psychotherapy stood out for me like an oasis in this desert of alienation. In the Psychotherapy Department at the Maudsley

Hospital I had my first supervision in analytic group therapy from
Bob Hobson, Malcolm Pines and Heinz Wolff, people who actually
believed that holding conversations with patients in groups was a
respectable clinical activity. All roads pointed to the London
Institute of Group Analysis, where I was able to clothe my natural
leanings with a credible training. However, the feeling that groups
can be turned to ill effect, either in the fulfilment of an ideological
agenda or through a lack of professional understanding, has never
left me.'

Liesel Hearst's beginnings were very different.

'I was born in Vienna, into a family that held strong convictions of
what constitutes 'The Good Society', and how to behave in private
and public life in order to achieve it. Some of these convictions
turned out to be erroneous, others even dangerous. But they gave
me a clear sense of group identity and belonging, over and above
that usually acquired by the infant in a well-functioning family. With
it went the experience and realization of the influence one's social
environment has on the shaping of feelings, understanding of life,
and aspirations – in fact, one's whole personality.

I experienced just how strong and influential this group-belonging
had been when, during my teenage years, it was violently attacked by
a self-defined, powerful group which tolerated no diversity of race,
religion or ideology, and had acquired the means to impose its beliefs
on a whole nation. My family and I were among the fortunate ones
who escaped annihilation by emigrating. But the severance from my
country of origin was my first experience of exclusion from a group,
of becoming an outsider and of having to relinquish a cherished
sense of identity. I had to re-experience myself anew.

Eventually I joined another group – the British Army. Possibly
because this was a well-considered, voluntary act on my part, I did
not experience the army as Freud described it. I did not delegate
part of my ego to the High Command, the 'Leader' in Freud's terms.
I was well aware that my aims coincided with those of the British
Army at that time, to defeat Nazi Germany. It was literally a matter
of life or death for me, Britain and Europe.

When life as it normally proceeds for a young adult started again,
individual choices had to be made and responsibility for them

assumed. This led me to the decision to embrace Britain as my new home. It was there that I settled, studied the social sciences, married and raised a family. The original sense of belonging to a national group by right of birth can, in my view, never be replaced. But when this is lost, there is a gain: the element of choice, consciously and fully experienced.

After university came the seminal experience of psychiatric social work in war-scarred London. The courage and resilience of the people, and their immutable sense of belonging, helped me to get closer to my new world. As a 'foreigner' I stood outside the British class structure and was therefore able to make it accessible to closer scrutiny by my clients. I could help them to see what part of this group belonging had been given to them by society and what part was intrinsically theirs. This question has been a lasting interest of mine and has featured frequently in my professional life.

Before I reached my ultimate professional destination as a group analyst, there was a whole group which helped to shape me: the inter-disciplinary team of a Child and Family Psychiatric Clinic of which I was a member. One of the most satisfying group experiences of my professional life was working in a team which respected, indeed welcomed, a diversity of professional skills and orientations. It was this group which encouraged me to train, first as a psychotherapist and later as a group analyst at the newly formed Institute of Group Analysis in London.'

From these two divergent backgrounds there grew a professional cooperation of long standing and great variety. Our first work together was memorable as much for the mistakes we made and the resulting learning curve, as for its success and enjoyment. This was a training course in group psychotherapy for the staff of a mental hospital. The seminars were well received, yet there were mysterious hiccups: locked seminar rooms, lost keys, and participants being called out of the seminar. In the car on the way home at night we wondered about this unexpected and probably unconscious sabotage of the smooth running of the course. Eventually we stumbled on the likely reason: in putting together the inter-disciplinary group, we had omitted to include personnel from the hospital administration. This lesson stood us in good stead in our subsequent work on training courses in Denmark and Norway, where at our request the training groups had an inclusive inter-disciplinary structure.

In our many and varied training enterprises together, we have discovered that our early formative orientations, medical and psychiatric in the one case, and social and psychoanalytic in the other, offer a model for the synthesis of previously isolated disciplines. This is the essence of group analysis as we understand it.

Our work together continued with workshops for the Group Analytic Society and later with supervision courses for the Institute of Group Analysis. In keeping with our belief that one should practise what one preaches, we have got together with a group of like-minded colleagues and developed a base from which we practise and supervise group analysis, The North London Centre for Group Therapy. Our Centre also provides the setting for a yearly international summer workshop which gives us much professional interest and joy.

The authors

Harold Behr qualified in medicine at Witwatersrand University, Johannesburg, South Africa in 1963, and trained as a psychiatrist at the Maudsley Hospital and University College Hospital, London. From 1975 to 1996 he was Consultant Child Psychiatrist at the Central Middlesex Hospital, London. He qualified as a Group Analyst in 1975 at the Institute of Group Analysis, London. A former editor of the journal *Group Analysis*, he was the Convenor of the Institute's Training Programme in Oslo, and was awarded Honorary Membership of the Norwegian Institute of Group Analysis in 1994. He is currently a Teacher, Supervisor and Training Group Analyst at the Institute of Group Analysis, London, and conducts a private practice at the North London Centre for Group Therapy.

Liesel Hearst qualified in Psychiatric Social Work in 1949, and subsequently worked with the National Association for Mental Health (now MIND). After a break to raise her two children, she practised as a psychotherapist and group analyst in a Child and Family Psychiatric Clinic in Hertfordshire. She qualified as a Group Analyst at the Institute of Group Analysis, London, in 1974. Subsequently she worked on the Institute's training programmes in Denmark, Norway, Germany and Switzerland. She is an Honorary Member of the Institute of Group Analysis, Heidelberg, and the Training Institute in Group Analysis, Zurich. She is currently a Training Group Analyst and Supervisor at the Institute of Group Analysis, London and in private practice at the North London Centre for Group Therapy.

CHAPTER ONE

The social and cultural basis of group analysis

GROUP THERAPY BEFORE THE INVENTION OF THE CIRCLE

At the end of the nineteenth century the great pillars which supported the edifice of scientific learning – medicine, philosophy and the natural sciences – stood in splendid isolation from one another. The science of mind was in its infancy, but showing all the signs of an early identity crisis as it hovered uncertainly between the natural sciences and another newly emerging discipline, that of the social sciences. The Freudian revolution came like an earthquake to shake this edifice. Man stood revealed as a creature subject to irrational forces coming from the depth of his own mind, just when he was beginning to think of himself as a supremely rational being, liberated from the dark ages of mystical and magical thinking. Like Darwin, with his infuriating demonstrations of man's link with lower life

1

forms, Freud disturbed the world of science with his alarming theories of infantile sexuality and incestuous longings.

Despite challenges from the orthodox scientists of the day, the Freudian view gained ground. Neurologists and psychiatrists, perplexed by the bizarre and manifold presentations of their patients, turned for explanations to the new Freudian postulates on the nature of mind. The period up to the beginning of the First World War saw a proliferation of ideas based on Freud's premises and their application in clinical practice. A new form of treatment for mental disorder called psychoanalysis came into existence and caught the popular imagination. The science of psychodynamic psychotherapy had been born.

The old scientific order was crumbling, but so too was the old political order. The First World War saw the collapse of the great Austro-Hungarian, Tsarist and Ottoman Empires together with many of the kingdoms, duchies and principalities that had made up the jigsaw puzzle of Europe in 1914. In their place rose new monolithic ideologies: communism and fascism, each determined to dominate the world, if not by persuasion then by force. All eyes turned anxiously to Germany. The nation had been destroyed by the war but now, ominously, it began to rise from the ashes as the centre of a fresh conflict, this time between these forces of communism and fascism.

The Frankfurt School

The scientific community of Western Europe found itself propelled into the political arena. Those who looked aghast upon the menace of fascism and its ugliest manifestation, Nazism, worked assiduously towards the development of an antidote based on socialist principles and informed by professional insights. Many of them gathered in Frankfurt in Germany, where they established a network which became known collectively as the Frankfurt School. This was in effect a gigantic think-tank, devoted to the study and integration of different branches of the social sciences, psychoanalysis, psychology and neurology, and their application to the political and social issues of the day.

Many influential figures of twentieth-century social and political thought came from the Frankfurt School, as did some of the founders of the newly emergent disciplines of interpersonal psychotherapy and social psychology. Erich Fromm, Herbert Marcuse and T.W. Adorno were among a group of left-wing intellectuals at the Frankfurt Institute for Social Research who elaborated a new approach to Marxist social theory, the 'critical theory' of societal phenomena, which emphasized the importance of cultural and psychological factors in what had until then been a purely economic theory.

The inter-disciplinary culture of the Frankfurt School's network allowed ideas to flow across boundaries traditionally separated from one another, while the unifying ethos was an ideological one based on radical socialist principles. Their intention was to create a community of scientists and intellectuals as a step towards the achievement of a better society, but events overtook them. The rise of Nazism led to the dismemberment of the network and the dispersal of its members, some escaping to the United States and England, where they continued their work.

Foulkes, holism and gestalt psychology

S.H. Foulkes, the psychiatrist and psychoanalyst who gave group analysis its theoretical justification and developed it as a method of treatment, practised in Frankfurt between 1921 and 1933. It was there that he encountered the leading figures of the Frankfurt School and became intellectually and emotionally influenced by them. Foulkes was particularly influenced by the holistic approach of the neurologist Kurt Goldstein and by the ideas of gestalt psychology, whose leading proponent was Max Wertheimer. In the wake of the First World War, Goldstein had worked with brain-injured soldiers and had shown that they could develop remarkable powers of adaptation and recovery, contradicting the prevailing view that damage to the central nervous system inevitably resulted in irreversible loss of function. He postulated a holistic model of neural functioning, based on the premise that the organism as a whole could contribute resources which allowed new nerve pathways to open up and bypass traumatic lesions. From this model Foulkes developed his most creative metaphor, that of the group as a network of communication analogous to the neuronal network of the brain.

For Goldstein, the guiding principle of gestalt psychology was the concept of the whole organism as a 'gestalt' (literally an organized whole that is perceived as more than the sum of its parts). The healthy gestalt represents the whole organism coming to terms with the demands of the environment in which it exists. The observer has to consider all the phenomena represented by the organism and not give preference to the description of any special one. The system functions as a whole, therefore any given stimulus must produce changes in the whole organism.

Goldstein was thinking of the biological organism, particularly the brain. Foulkes incorporated these ideas into his conceptualization of the individuals in a group. He saw them as forming a network, analogous to the network of the nervous system. The group is seen to interact and react as a whole, and each individual contribution is understood in the context of this network. The group therefore influences and is influenced by each individual group member. The process has been graphically expressed by Gregory van der Kleij: 'It is as if the members of a group are the words of a sentence, none of which can express their meaning – except as objects – unless belonging to each other' (van der Kleij, 1982).

The concept Foulkes chose to express this process was that of a matrix, a dynamic network of interpersonal and transpersonal communication in which the individuals featured as nodal points, comparable to the neurones traversed by the interconnecting fibres of the neuronal network. The group itself represents this transpersonal network: it reacts and responds as a whole, and in the psychoanalytic sense, associates as a whole. All verbal and nonverbal communications occur within the developing group matrix, which is the operational basis of intrapsychic and interpersonal relationships. These two models, holistic and gestalt, came together in the Foulkesian conception of the group as an interactive and reactive organism within which there was a constantly changing constellation of figure–ground configurations.

The psychoanalytic contribution to group analysis

The third strand in Foulkes's model of group therapy came from psychoanalysis. Having trained as a psychoanalyst in the Freudian tradition, he believed that therapeutic techniques derived from psychoanalysis could be applied to groups, and that the main dynamic concepts of psychoanalysis were essentially compatible with a model of group function based on communication.

Foulkes began to develop his innovative ideas at a time when psychoanalysis was moving increasingly from the perception of mind as a mental apparatus made up of goal-directed instinctual drives and their vicissitudes, to mind as a dynamic system of object and part object relations, a system in perpetual flux. A wind of change was blowing through psychoanalytic thinking: Bion's container–contained model, Fairbairn's libido as object seeking, Winnicott's mother–child unit, Lacan's discourse between the subject and the self, Bowlby's attachment theory, and Kohut's psychology of the self.

Foulkes did not refer directly to any of these developments in the exposition of his own theoretical position. Asked once whether he did not think that object relations theory was especially applicable to group analysis, he replied, after a moment's thought: 'I don't need it' (Foulkes, personal communication). However, these new strands of thought in psychoanalysis later beckoned a number of group analysts and led to efforts at integrating them with group analysis. Dennis Brown and Colin James developed models of therapy which integrated the central concepts of Foulkes, Winnicott and Bion. Attachment theory and group analysis came together in the work of Mario Marrone, while the integration of self psychology with group analysis captured the imagination of a number of therapists including Irene Harwood, Malcolm Pines and Sigmund Karterud.

Foulkes considered himself a true Freudian, yet what he produced was a radical, almost revolutionary departure from what he had been taught and experienced in his training analysis in Vienna with Helene Deutsch and his supervision with Nunberg, a member of the *Kinderseminar*, the famous meeting place of young analysts which included Wilhelm Reich. Nor did his theoretical stance change after his emigration to England, during the course of his psychoanalytic practice as a training analyst with the London Psychoanalytic Institute.

Foulkes's dismissal of object relations theory sounded arrogant at the time. Yet he was saying something which is true of group analysis. He was pointing to the difference between the dyadic situation of psychoanalysis and the group-analytic situation in which a new therapy takes place. 'I don't need it' translates into 'I need different concepts to apply to this different situation'. Foulkes was referring to a situation in which the group itself becomes the frame of reference. All that goes on in it gets its meaning from this frame of reference, and within it. The term 'group situation' has a specific connotation.

It refers to all the people in the room, including the therapist, sitting together face-to-face in a circle. The circle encompasses both physical and psychological space and is bounded by the members of the group, who in the Foulkesian conception all share the same space (Pines, 1981).

While the group itself can be conceptualized in holistic and gestalt terms, it is also a psychoanalytic therapy. The individual benefits from an atmosphere in which reality and immediacy heighten transference experiences, and the perceptions arising from these experiences are held by the group, eventually to be modified, revised and used as reality-adapted new experiences of the self in relation to the others. In this way the analytic group can provide what Winnicott called 'the environmental essentials' of healthy development.

The role of culture in group analysis

The sociologist Norbert Elias is now being belatedly recognized for his seminal contribution to our thinking about groups. Belatedness seems to have dogged Elias. Most of his prolific writings were the product of his post-retirement years, and his earliest and best-known work, *The Civilizing Process*, though published in 1939, lay on the shelves for another 30 years before attracting the attention of scholars and group-analytic therapists. However, as his friend and chief exponent Stephen Mennell has put it, 'That was not the most propitious year for the publication of a large, two-volume work in German, by a Jew, on, of all things, civilisation' (Mennell, 1992).

Elias provides an element which is missing in Foulkes's psychoanalytic and quasi-systemic conception of group analysis: the importance of historical and cultural continuity to the interactions of people who meet face-to-face in a group. For Elias, the concept of interdependence was important: the notion that people are interdependent with others whom they have never met face-to-face. In his fascinating study of manners and the minutiae of human behaviour down the ages, Elias has shown how our psychological make-up has been shaped by a discernible evolutionary process in society. It is this process that has made us more aware of the effect that we have on others and of our identification with others, as expressed for example through advances in our threshold of shame and embarrassment and our ability to predict how others might react towards us.

Elias's spotlight on the socio-genesis and psycho-genesis of our behaviour – the chain of cultural events which links us to the past – inevitably raises questions about reversals and breakdowns in the process, and the part played in these by social trauma. This theme has been developed by Earl Hopper, a sociologist and group analyst, who has advanced a model of social regression in the face of massive trauma, and by Vamik Volkan, whose writings emphasize the importance of historical traumata in the perpetuation of inter-group conflict. Another group analyst, Farhad Dalal, has taken up Elias's theme of social relatedness and his concept of figuration, a notion intended to describe the inter-connectedness of human existence without having to cast people as either primarily individuals or primarily groups. Dalal points to the constraining effect of figurations on our thoughts and actions in groups, and links these to what he sees as a missing element in Foulkes's thinking about groups: the question of power relationships in groups and how this applies to the therapeutic process, for example through the imposition of racial and cultural stereotypes.

Leadership in group-analytic terms

Foulkes favoured the term 'conductor' to describe the group-analytic therapist, rather than 'leader', a term which did not sit comfortably with the socialist-minded fraternity of the Frankfurt School. The term 'conductor' was coined by T.W. Adorno, a leading social theorist whose later work on prejudice and the authoritarian personality earned him a place in the forefront of social psychology. Adorno's interest in the cultural superstructure of Marxism had led him to investigate the aesthetic and social functions of music and the relationship between conductor and orchestra.

The fluctuating location of authority between conductor and orchestra appealed to Foulkes as a model of leadership for his groups. He accepted that group members would initially turn to the conductor as the source of wisdom and insight, but saw these early projections of authority as based on omnipotent fantasies from which the group had to be gradually weaned. Only then could they discover their own collective authority and take responsibility for the therapeutic process. The conductor never relinquishes his own therapeutic authority, but remains largely in the background, allowing the different configurations and interactions to take their own course. From time to time, the conductor might have to 'nudge' the group, in Foulkes's word, when it seems to be stranded or veering in un-therapeutic directions; in other words, when communication is temporarily blocked. But for the most part the group as a whole is capable of moving the analytic process forward with little direction.

The group interacts as a whole, each individual contribution having to be understood in the context of the entire interpersonal network of the group – a network which both influences and is influenced by each person in the group. The Foulkesian view is therefore not one of eight individuals receiving psychoanalytic treatment in a group, nor is it the group conceptualized as 'the patient' in relation to the analyst. In other words, it is not a new psychoanalytic dyad. Psychoanalytic concepts such as the unconscious, defence mechanisms, repression, transference and counter-transference, projection and projective identification, do apply, however. But they are expressed and evaluated in the new context of the analytic group. To differentiate his approach from psychoanalysis, Foulkes arrived at the somewhat inelegant name of 'group-analytic psychotherapy'.

The group as a system

Foulkes's philosophy of groups accords well with a systemic view of groups, although he never overtly declared the affinity. The essential similarities between group analysis and systemic therapy lie in the importance attached by both to communication as the main agent of change, and the relegation of the individual to a less prominent role in the process than the interrelationship between individuals. There are, however, significant differences. In its attempt to bring human groups and biological processes into alignment with wider and larger phenomena, systems theory has played down the unique properties which make up the individual and his or her groups. The concept of an unconscious does not feature in systems theory, while it occupies a prominent place in group analysis, which moves fluently between the individual, in the depth of his or her unconscious, and the interpersonal field of the group with its social unconscious. Systems therapists have constructed models of therapy in which interventions tend to be confined to the immediacy of the present, the 'here and now'. The uncovering of individual histories is not seen as a therapeutic device in its own right, and the exercise is only justified if it can serve the purpose of changing the pattern of communication within the system of which it is a part.

These polarized views of systemic and psychoanalytic therapies have been reconciled through the efforts of group analysts such as Yvonne Agazarian, Helen Durkin and Robin Skynner, who developed models of group analysis which embody a synthesis of the two approaches. An integrated model of systemic and analytic methods is especially applicable to therapeutic work with families and organizations, both groups which face the therapist with a dense structure and well-established patterns of communication from the outset.

Meeting as a way of maintaining a group's identity

A group can be defined as a number of people united by a common attribute or outlook. The word 'group' can be used in an abstract sense, implying a category of people, whether or not they have assembled in the same physical space. Alternatively it can refer to a gathering of individuals for a specific purpose. Whenever a group meets it reinforces its identity, while a group which never meets, or meets only seldom, retains its identity as much through the attributions of others as through its own collective self-perception and is therefore prone to the vicissitudes and projections of the outside world in the shaping of its identity, and by extension, its destiny.

Groups which are specially constituted for therapeutic purposes have to provide enough time and space to allow for the emergence and repair of longstanding relationships through the process of communication and analysis. The conditions in which these groups take place are carefully designed to provide the atmosphere of safety which is necessary for the unfolding of such processes. In group-analytic psychotherapy, we expect people to entrust to the group their most personal thoughts at a time in their lives when they may feel least like doing so. The techniques of group analysis therefore have to ensure, as far as possible, that the people who choose to enter a therapeutic group will find it a safe and rewarding experience. Meetings have to take place frequently enough and over a sufficiently long period of time for meaningful change to occur.

The therapeutic group as a microcosm of society

Foulkes maintained that each individual is crucially determined by the world in which he or she lives. He challenged the dichotomies of 'individual and society', 'constitution and environment', and 'inside and outside world', maintaining that the only way these could be separated from each other was by artificial isolation, such as that occurring when a psychotherapeutic situation is set up, or by the construction of neurotic barriers. The task of therapy, therefore, was to allow these concepts to flow into each other through the process of communication, which has to become wider and deeper with the passage of time. When a therapeutic group meets, its members collectively represent the society in which the group is held and proceed to re-create it in microcosmic form through the formation of the group.

The group members, however, also bring with them into the group pockets of isolation, which represent their own unique areas of disturbance. This juxtapositioning of the collective normality which is the societal microcosm, with the different areas of individual disturbance, sets the stage for the process of therapy. The therapeutic value of the group is summed up in Foulkes's maxim: 'collectively they [the group members] constitute the very norm from which, individually, they deviate' (Foulkes, 1948).

Isolation as the basis of disturbance, and communication as its antidote

Within the wider society in which we live, we are born into a group. Throughout life we migrate through many groups. At any one time we occupy membership of several groups and each of these groups forms a psychological unit which contributes to the shaping of our identity. Neurosis, according to Foulkes, is a state of mind which develops when, as individuals, we get to be at odds with our group and become, to a varying degree, isolated from ourselves and others.

The neurotic position is by definition highly individualistic, and therefore works against the group. It acts as an irritant to both the individual and the group, and leads, if unchecked, to the isolation of the individual from the group. The individual's so-called neurotic symptoms are in fact an aspect of him- or herself which cannot be communicated in words, and which can therefore only gain expression in symptomatic form. For symptoms to become suitable for sharing, they must be translated into communicable language.

Communication is therefore a central concept in group analysis. Therapy proceeds by the translation of neurotic phenomena into shared communication, and this comes about through the verbal exchanges which form the currency of the group. An ever-widening and deepening pool of communication within the analytic group is the essence of the therapy itself. The group analyst's task is to facilitate this process by joining in, sometimes with his therapeutic authority, at other times more like another member. The analytic group is created as the space within which this communication can develop.

To sum up, body, mind and society come together in Foulkes's conception of therapy. The individual is seen as the basic biological unit, the group as the basic psychological unit and society as the unit which encompasses them both. The essence of man is social, and wherever possible, individual disturbance should be treated in its social context. This is created through the analytic group, a carefully designed therapeutic situation aimed at introducing society into the group, setting up a network of communication and making use of analytic techniques to reach areas of isolation which have become a focus of disturbance for the individual in his or her relationship with society.

CHAPTER TWO

A century of group therapy

'I HOPE THE GROUP ISN'T TOO AGGRESSIVE'

'History is bunk', said Henry Ford. Not so, say we. It is a helpful exercise for present-day group analysts to look back at the beginnings of their craft, and follow the process by which their concepts and clinical practices have evolved. What have they accepted, modified or discarded? And why?

Joseph H. Pratt: classes for consumptives

The first therapeutic groups were held in Boston, Massachussetts, during the first decade of the twentieth century. Joseph Hersey Pratt, a physician with an evangelical cast of mind and a prescient understanding of the interplay between body, mind and spirit, began a series of 'inspirational classes' for patients suffering from tuberculosis. In the pre-antibiotic era, the ravages of the 'white death' or 'consumption' could only be fought with an ascetic regime of isolation, dietary restriction and prolonged rest. Morale was generally low and the mood of the patients was apathetic or depressed.

Pratt noticed with interest that the atmosphere changed when his patients happened to congregate in corridors and waiting rooms while waiting to see a doctor. At such times they seemed to relish the opportunity to talk with one another about their illness. The tone of these conversations was unfailingly lively, and the conversations themselves seemed to have an uplifting effect. This led Pratt to a serendipitous thought: why not capitalize on a spontaneous phenomenon and turn it to therapeutic advantage? He organized his patients into groups of 15 to 20, which he himself led. Pratt gave lectures to the patients in inspirational style, urging them to take responsibility for their own health care. Pratt encouraged his patients to keep their own records, and to announce their progress to the group.

We can discern in Pratt's inspirational method many of the ideas which foreshadowed the practice of group therapy today. He recognized the therapeutic value of socializing his patients, infusing them with hope, discouraging secondary neurotic gain and giving them responsibility for change. He also harnessed the unifying power inherent in the process of bringing together people with the same problem and different strengths. He had some interest in psychoanalysis, but steered clear of its techniques. The unconscious dynamics of the group were left strictly alone, and his patients were not encouraged to think about their hidden conflicts. 'The class meeting,' he wrote, 'is a pleasant social hour for all the members ... made up as it is of widely different races and different sects, they have a common bond in a common disease. A fine spirit of camaraderie has developed. They never discuss their symptoms and are almost invariably in good spirits' (Pratt, 1907).

Curiously enough, some people today like to refer to their group therapy sessions as classes, an expression, perhaps, of the wish to destigmatize therapy and reframe it as the teaching and learning experience which it also is, in the broader sense of the analytic process.

Pratt later extended his method to groups of patients suffering from other physical and mental illnesses and the range of perplexing conditions which lie in the borderland between the two. Historians of group therapy have appointed him the founding father of group therapy, but he also deserves a place as a pioneer in the fields of psychiatry and psychosomatic medicine.

Edward Lazell: lectures for the mentally ill

Pratt's seminal paper on groups for the physically ill appeared in 1906. By the early 1920s, the lecture model as a form of treatment had migrated into mental hospitals. Here too, there were patients with rampant illness who languished with little hope of recovery. In Washington DC, Edward Lazell, a psychiatrist and follower first of Freud and then of Jung, began lecturing to his patients on the workings of the mind seen from a psychoanalytic viewpoint. It was a bold experiment, given the severity and unchecked nature of his patients' psychotic symptoms. Some were in a state of catatonic withdrawal, others distracted by their hallucinations. Yet amazingly, in the group climate created for them during the lectures, they appeared to absorb and retain the ideas which he imparted to them. The list of topics which formed the basis of his lectures would sit comfortably in a modern introductory course on psychoanalysis for the general public. It included such intriguing titles as: 'Usual Causes of Flight from Women', 'Inferiority', 'Daydreaming', 'Re-activation of Emotion' and 'The Fear of Death'.

Lazell laid particular emphasis on the importance of bringing the fear of death and 'the conflict around sexuality', as he put it, into the social arena. An added benefit of groups, he argued, was that they diminished the patient's fear of the analyst. He wrote that '[the patient] feels that there are so many others in the same condition as himself, he cannot be so bad', a view which resonates with current thinking on the importance of universality and mutual identification as therapeutic factors in group therapy. Like Pratt before him, Lazell was a forerunner of the holistic approach to medicine and psychiatry. In addition to his groups for the mentally ill, he held groups for patients with conditions such as hyperthyroidism, 'neurasthenia' and epilepsy, in which he emphasized the impact of emotional life on bodily functioning. He credited his patients with both the intellectual ability and the desire to make sense of their symptoms, a philosophy of practice which accords well with 21st-

century thinking on the importance of enlisting the active cooperation of patients in making decisions about the management of their
own illness. Lazell can be credited as the first group therapist to
bring the educational and analytic dimensions of group therapy
into harmony with each other.

Cody Marsh: the healing crowd

Lazell's contribution in the early 1920s was developed some ten
years later by the Reverend L. Cody Marsh, a minister turned
psychiatrist and cousin of the flamboyant cowboy showman William
Cody ('Buffalo Bill'). Like Pratt, Marsh applied a mixture of religious
revivalist and educational techniques to his group method. During
his lectures to large groups of inpatients at Worcester State Hospital
the patients were expected to take notes. He also instituted a programme of art and dance classes. Later he extended his lecture
approach to outpatient groups. His lectures, unlike those of Lazell,
had a populist social flavour and included topics like: 'People and
Social Customs', 'Adjustment to Hospitalization', 'Problems of Work
and Relaxation', 'How to Raise a Baby', and 'The Will to Balance
Serenity and Happiness'.

Cody Marsh drew on his experiences as a Morale Officer during
the First World War. The essence of treatment, in his view, was a kind
of revivalist conversion from 'introspection, phantasy, bitterness,
shame, inferiority ... to extrospection [sic], constructive planning,
cheerfulness, assurance, security', all laudable treatment goals by
modern standards. 'The motto on my psychiatric shield', he pro-
claimed with fine flourish, '[is]: 'By the crowd they have been
broken, by the crowd they shall be healed' (Marsh, 1933).

Louis Wender: small groups for 'mild' disorders

In the work of Louis Wender we enter the realms of small group
therapy informed more directly by psychoanalysis. Wender's ideas
became known in the decade before the outbreak of the Second
World War, mainly through his group techniques with borderline
patients in a mental hospital setting. He was at pains to differentiate
his psychoanalytic approach from the prevailing educational and

'orientative' techniques of the time. However, he did not break entirely with that tradition. Each of his sessions began with a lecture on the dynamics of behaviour and the significance of dreams. The patients met in same-sex groups, two or three times a week for one-hour sessions, in addition to having individual therapy, a combined approach which he encouraged.

Wender presented group psychotherapy as a method of treatment best suited to certain types of 'mild mental disease' where some affect was present and where there was no intellectual impairment. He made use of the transference, based on his view that the therapist functioned as a symbolic parent, and that the patients represented sibling relationships to one another.

Paul Schilder: coaching patients in the art of psychoanalysis

Paul Schilder occupies a place in the history of neurology and psychiatry as well as group therapy. His work on the mind's construction of body image and its development into a system of ideologies which affects the way we lead our lives started a chain of research into body image disorders which still continues. As a research professor of psychiatry at the New York University, he was well placed to raise the profile of group therapy, a method of treatment which he embraced with enthusiasm. He experimented with psychoanalytic concepts in groups, seeing his patients first in individual sessions, where he coached them in the art and technique of free association, dream interpretation, and the recovery of early memories. He was an exacting therapist who demanded accurate descriptions from his patients of their life histories, goals and interests, which he urged them to write down. Patients were then introduced into groups consisting of six or seven members, while being seen concurrently on an individual basis twice a week. He widened the scope of therapeutic intervention by encouraging group members to make interpretations to their fellow patients, a technique now regarded as intrinsic to group-analytic psychotherapy. He also broke with tradition in being quite open about justifying his own views and beliefs to the group, participating in this respect more like another member, in a way that his predecessors had not done.

Trigant Burrow: the social basis of consciousness

Trigant Burrow, like Schilder, was a medical scientist who became a psychoanalyst and then turned to groups. His defection from psychoanalysis came in a moment of Pauline revelation. One of his students who was in analysis with him challenged him to 'test his honesty' by reversing the roles of analyst and analysand. Burrow did so and became aware of what he saw as the authoritarian attitude inherent in the psychoanalytic dyad. But even this reversal of roles did not satisfy Burrow's criteria for reciprocity. Instead, he constructed a model of mutual analysis in small groups, coining the term 'group analysis' in 1925.

Burrow was a maverick who lost favour with the psychoanalytic establishment and antagonized Freud because of his radical ideas. He lived and worked in a commune in upstate New York, where he developed his vision of groups as the means of changing society. His methods of group therapy included the bold concept of introducing relatives, students and co-workers into his patient groups. In this respect he can be regarded as a progenitor of both the family therapy and therapeutic community movements.

Burrow set out his vision in a classic text, *The Social Basis of Consciousness* which received favourable reviews from D.H. Lawrence and Sir Herbert Read. The latter wrote:

> Only Trigant Burrow has suggested a method ... by means of which social aberrations can be corrected ... Essentially what Dr Burrow is proposing is not a psychological experiment, but new foundations for the next phase of human evolution   (Read, 1949).

Despite such encomiums, Burrow's contribution to group therapy has been relatively overlooked. His heroic attempts to unify the physical sciences, psychoanalysis and society into a single over-arching framework, coupled with his adventurous experiments in group composition, were more than the establishment of the day could stomach. However, his views on the social nature of man are germane to modern group analysis and there is a current renewal of interest in his writings.

Freud's aversion to groups

Despite his interest in the psychology of groups, Freud never saw them as a medium for his psychoanalytic method. He rebuked

Burrow for entertaining a vision of groups as a remedy for the ailments of society and endorsed the views of the French sociologist Gustav le Bon, who portrayed groups as dangerous entities capable of bringing out man's childish and bestial instincts. Le Bon was steeped in reactionary politics. He had been deeply affected by the riots and mayhem surrounding the Paris Commune of 1871 and believed that groups could only be controlled by the rhetoric of clever leaders or by the army, and then only to serve political ends. Caught up in a group, the individual slipped into a psychopathic state of diminished responsibility. Le Bon conflated the terms 'group', 'mass', 'crowd' and 'mob', thus undermining the idea of groups as a medium for civilized discourse, let alone therapy. The most influential of an emergent school of crowd psychologists, he was admired not only by Freud but by politicians as diverse as Theodore Roosevelt and Mussolini.

In his classic monograph, 'Group Psychology and the Analysis of the Ego', published in 1921, Freud concentrated on the dynamics of the large groups which society has institutionalized for itself, notably the church and the army. Such groups, he argued, are held together by their common identification with a leader, a symbolic father who is experienced as capable of dispensing both love and punishment. The group members relate to one another through this common identification with him. 'It is impossible,' he wrote, 'to grasp the nature of a group if the leader is disregarded' (Freud, 1921).

Freud was convinced that analytic therapy could not be practised in a group. In a letter to Burrow he wrote:

> I do not believe that the analysis of a patient can be conducted in any other way than the family situation, that is, limited to two people. The mass situation will either result immediately in a leader and those led by him, that is, it will become similar to the family situation but entailing great difficulties in the function of expression and unnecessary complications of jealousy and competition, or it will bring into effect the 'brother horde' where everybody has the same right and where, I believe, an analytical influence is impossible.   (Freud, 1926)

There is no evidence to suggest that Freud changed his mind.

Without Freud's imprimatur, psychoanalysts in Europe made few excursions into the field of group work. One of those who did was Alfred Adler, a student of Freud and an ardent socialist. Adler was interested in the problems of 'working class groups'. He employed educators and social workers to make contact with people in the community and established guidance centres at which group meetings were held. However, he did not use groups in his therapeutic work. His influence on the development of group therapy has been in its educational and social aspects.

Kurt Lewin: experiments in group dynamics

Though more of an experimentalist than a therapist, Kurt Lewin contributed to the development of group therapy in several important ways. First, he brought groups into the social arenas of industry, commerce, education and other non-clinical sectors of society. Second, he placed group dynamics on the map as a legitimate training and research enterprise. His involvement in social issues and his interest in styles of political leadership led him to design experiments which showed that groups run along democratic lines were more effective at problem-solving, and less likely to create a climate for bullying and scapegoating than groups led by authoritarian or *laissez faire* leaders.

Through Lewin's work, groups became a valid form of self-exploration and problem solving in non-clinical as well as clinical settings. His primary focus was the group as a whole, experienced in the present moment of its meeting, the 'here-and-now' as it came to be called. This focus set the stage for Sensitivity Training ('T') groups: intensely focused, short-term groups aimed at heightening people's awareness of themselves in a group context. The here-and-now focus also has some resonances with group-analytic psychotherapy, where the dynamic of the whole group emerges from time to time into the foreground, to command the attention of the conductor. Its main value, however, lies in the field of organizational dynamics, where the individual and collective histories of the group members do not generally feature.

As a scientist with a reductionist perspective, Lewin saw groups as subject to dynamic forces similar to those operating within a physical force field. Individuals were governed by primitive drives which propelled them through their life space towards emotionally determined goals until they came into conflict with the drives of other individuals. Progressive and regressive forces vied with each other in the struggle to achieve a civilized resolution. The dynamics of a group could be represented schematically by vectors plotted through the group space, to show how each individual negotiated his or her life space in relation to the others. Predictions and generalizations could then be made, based on the findings of carefully designed experiments.

Lewin's complex diagrams and formulae have been washed away by the currents of later research, but he was the first to place on record the view that groups, with all their attendant behaviours and emotions, could be governed by the same laws and principles which govern other natural phenomena, rendering them accessible to experimental research. He can be regarded as the founder of research into group psychology, and his aphorism 'there is nothing so practical as a good theory' still stands as a useful prompt to modern researchers.

Jacob Moreno: the theatre of spontaneity

Jacob Moreno was a charismatic figure who came from a background in medicine, philosophy and the theatre. It was the last of these which inspired him to introduce a new form of group therapy, which he called psychodrama. This was to have wide application in the field of the social therapies, including family therapy (through role play), gestalt therapy and the encounter movement. Psychodramatic techniques have also been adopted by some analytic group therapists who see no contradiction between an analytic approach and the use of action techniques based on spontaneity and catharsis.

The room in which the therapy takes place becomes, quite literally, a stage on which patients construct and enact the crucial dramatic scenes which form the basis of their problems. Moreno's imaginative method allows the patient to create scenes drawn from the past, the present, and even the future. The therapist, referred to as the director, pilots the patient, referred to as the protagonist, through the drama, drawing on the rest of the group to provide a supportive cast. Members of the group are chosen by the protagonist to play significant characters in the scenario being conjured up, or parts of the protagonist. The culmination of the drama provides a moment of profound emotional intensity, shared by the entire group. Like the analytic method, the psychodramatic method relies for its efficacy on the patients' ability to project aspects of their inner world onto the group, to experience the emotions liberated by the process, and to move on with a new awareness of themselves. The differences lie in psychodrama's recourse to action techniques and in the highly structuring interventions of the therapist, which call for an entirely different and specialized set of group skills. Psychodrama has burgeoned into a major school of psychotherapy, with a flourishing network of trainings and practices.

Wilfred Bion and S.H. Foulkes: analysis in small groups

Psychoanalysis was the first motor to drive the process of group therapy in the United Kingdom, and the two names most prominently associated with its development are those of Wilfred Bion and S.H. Foulkes. The contrasting backgrounds and influences of these two pioneers determined their different trajectories and resulted in the development of two very different therapeutic philosophies which are only now becoming reconciled. Bion, a Kleinian analyst with a supremely detached, almost mystical view of the world, had no great interest in therapy *qua* therapy and did not think of himself as a group therapist. He was occupied with the hidden configurations of the group and its unconscious life, and observed the group as a whole, rather than the individuals in it. His singular contribution to group theory lay in his discovery that groups are at the mercy of unconsciously determined attitudes, which he called 'basic assumptions'. These interfere with the manifest task of the group and have to be addressed by the group leader if the group is to function effectively. Bion identified three basic assumptions, each seeking a different kind of group leadership. In the dependency basic assumption, a nurturing type of leadership is sought, akin to that provided by a mother. A fight–flight basic assumption demands the type of leader who will either lead the group into battle with the enemy, or help it to flee to safety. The third basic assumption, which he called 'pairing', tends to arise when a group feels itself to be in need of rescue from a hopeless situation. The pairing behaviour might be expressed in overtly sexual terms, or in abstract terms, as in the pairing of ideas, the hope being that a new entity, a 'child' or 'messiah', will be born from the union, who will save the group.

For Foulkes, a psychoanalyst in the Freudian tradition and a German Jew who had left Europe for England in the year that Hitler came to power, society and culture lay at the heart of the analytic process. Group and individual were in constant interplay in Foulkes's scheme of things, with neither one nor the other in the ascendant. He was attracted to the ideas of the sociologists and holistic thinkers with whom he associated at the Frankfurt Institute in Germany and incorporated them into his theory of group therapy, which he called group analysis or group-analytic psychotherapy. His views on the theory and practice of group psychotherapy have had a wide influence in the United Kingdom and the continent of Europe, and are increasingly becoming known in other countries where psychotherapy is practised. The model of group therapy presented in this book is largely based on his ideas.

The Northfield experiments: groups for war casualties

To cope with the flood of psychiatric casualties returning from the battlefields of the Second World War, the British Army took over a large mental hospital, Hollymoor, near Birmingham. This hospital, renamed Northfield Military Hospital, became the main treatment centre in the United Kingdom for these patients, and it was there, given the opportunity that only war can provide, that a number of group-minded psychoanalysts set up two successive large-scale experiments in group and community treatment.

The first of these was the brainchild of Wilfred Bion and John Rickman. Bion was no stranger to battlefield conditions. A tank commander in the First World War, he had been psychologically scarred by the experience, and the award of a DSO for bravery had proved to be no compensation. He now applied his formidable mind to the task of helping his soldier-patients, who were not quite soldiers and not quite patients, to regain their morale. He came to the conclusion that the gloomy passivity of the men was being fuelled by their reliance on orders from above, and that this was chiefly responsible for the perpetuation of their low self-esteem. If they could be thwarted in their dependence on superior officers for solving their problems and telling them what to do, the stage would be set for the recovery of their morale. Bion and Rickman accordingly set about encouraging the men to take collective responsibility for the organization of their daily lives by forming task groups which they themselves ran. Recreational, social and activity groups flourished. But the design had a fatal flaw. The experiment had involved standing the existing military code on its head, and Bion and Rickman had failed to prepare the ground for this with the military top brass, including administrators who were neither psychiatrists nor psychotherapists. A snap inspection revealed a 'laxity in discipline' which to the military mind smacked of chaos and anarchy. The experiment collapsed and Bion left Northfield under a cloud.

Fortunately the second Northfield experiment fared better. Harold Bridger, Tom Main and S.H. Foulkes, who masterminded it, had learned from the mistakes of their predecessors and brought the hospital administration in on the decision-making process at an early stage. This corrective input saved the project and established as a principle the involvement of administration at the planning stage of any group therapeutic enterprise. This was to become a cardinal principle of later therapeutic community work.

The postwar era

Northfield proved to be the testing ground for community and group methods which were to be translated into civilian contexts after the war. Several of the psychoanalysts who had worked there went on to become prominent in the field of group therapy and therapeutic community work. In addition to Bion, Rickman, Foulkes and Main, there was E. James Anthony, who pioneered the use of analytic groups for children, and Joshua Bierer, who elaborated the idea of community groups into the concept of a day hospital. Another community-minded military psychiatrist, Maxwell Jones, who had worked in the army's Cardiac Syndrome Unit at Mill Hill, established the Henderson Hospital in Surrey as the first therapeutic community for civilians.

Bion went to the Tavistock Centre in London, where he established his reputation as an outstanding thinker in the field of psychoanalysis and group dynamics, and it was there that he ran the groups which provided him with the material for his classic work, *Experiences in Groups*. However, he did not pursue his practice as a group therapist, devoting himself instead to clinical and philosophical studies of the workings of the mind. His writings on the theory of thinking represent a conceptual leap forward in our understanding of psychodynamic processes.

Foulkes, who had been running a private group in Exeter before his posting to Northfield, went to the Maudsley Hospital, where his teaching on group analysis influenced a new generation of psychiatrists, notably Malcolm Pines and Robin Skynner, who collaborated with him in the establishment of a learned society devoted to the promotion of group analysis. From this base, and through the columns of a publication which he named *Group Analytic International Panel and Correspondence* (later to become the journal *Group Analysis*), he attracted a large circle of interested colleagues, especially in Europe. Foulkes also placed group-analytic psychotherapy firmly on the map of private practice with his establishment of the Group-Analytic Practice in central London. In 1971 he initiated the foundation of a training institute in London, the Institute of Group Analysis, which in turn has generated further trainings and institutes of group analysis, both in the United Kingdom and abroad.

Other models of analytic group therapy

In the United States group therapy had been born in the hospitals and clinics of a stable society, with religious-minded physicians serving as its midwife. The progression from educational to analytic methods had been helped along by academics who were able, through their positions in the medical establishment, to set up training programmes which integrated these approaches and made them part of the therapeutic culture.

By contrast, group therapy in the United Kingdom had its origins in the social ferment of a Europe devastated by the First World War and waiting apprehensively for the next one. Group psychotherapy established itself relatively slowly on the European mainland after the Second World War. German-speaking therapists in particular began to reconnect with their Freudian roots and from there developed a number of psychoanalytic models of group therapy.

Analysis of the individual by the therapist

Analytic group therapy in the United States retained a strongly individualistic flavour. The psychoanalyst tended to be seen as the
central figure in the group, as the repository of analytic expertise
and the sole source of interpretations. This was a model championed
by Alexander Wolf and Emmanuel Schwartz, two Freudian psychoanalysts who fought a polemical battle with the psychoanalytic
establishment to achieve credibility for the application of psychoanalysis to group therapy. Group members were clearly in role as
analysands, prone to all their individual defences, able to contribute
their free associations and dreams greatly enriched by their collective presence. This allowed multiple sibling-type cross-transferences
to arise as well as the 'vertical' transferences to the analyst as a parent figure. Wolf and Schwartz also introduced the notion of
'alternate sessions' – meetings of the group without the analyst – to
bring out additional material for analysis.

Samuel Slavson was another pioneer of the analytic small group
who strongly influenced its acceptance and development in the
United States. He treated children and adolescents in activity
groups, in which he offered himself as a parental transference figure,
while at the same time valuing the interrelationships between the
children as an important therapeutic factor. For this reason he set his
groups at a membership of no more than eight and no fewer than
five. Like Wolf and Schwartz, he did not take up group processes and
group dynamics as such.

Yet another concept of group psychotherapy has been developed
by Heigl-Evers and Heigl, known as the *Goettinger Schichten Modell*
(model of stratification). It follows the topography of psychoanalysis
in the sense of conscious, pre-conscious and unconscious. These
constitute the three layers in which the group functions and which
are separately addressed by the group analyst. In this model, norma-
tive behaviour regulation corresponds to the conscious in the group,
psycho-social compromise resolution to the subconscious, and collective group dreaming to the unconscious.

Analysis of the group by the therapist

Bion's ideas were taken up by one of his analysands at the Tavistock,
Henry Ezriel, who worked more clearly in a clinical context. Ezriel

evolved his own ideas on group process. Like Bion, he worked with the group as a whole, but he looked towards object relations theory for a working therapeutic model. For Ezriel the individuals in the group were its part objects, jostling one another at an unconscious level until they reached a stable position, the 'common group tension'. Driven by its unconscious fears and wishes the group passed through a series of relationships with the therapist before settling on the one which provoked the least anxiety. At any one moment, Ezriel believed, the group was in conflict over its wish to get close to the therapist and its fear of what would happen if that closeness were to be achieved. A compromise relationship was therefore settled on. In this model the therapist was to maintain an impeccable analytic stance in the 'blank screen' tradition, confining his interventions strictly to interpretations of the group's changing relationships to the therapist as observed in the 'here-and-now'.

This method of therapy, with its relative disregard for individual susceptibilities, lends itself in our view more to a training experience than a therapeutic one. It is at odds with Foulkesian group-analytic technique, although Ezriel's observations on the three forms of primitive relationship which govern group life offer an interesting perspective on the unconscious processes at work in groups.

In Germany, H. Argelander, influenced by Bion and Ezriel, has developed a model of group psychotherapy in which communication and behaviour patterns form what he calls a dynamic collective constellation. This process creates a gestalt – the group. Consequently he treats the group as an entity with an ego, superego and id. The exchange becomes bi-personal between the group and the group analyst.

Dorothy Stock Whitaker and Morton Lieberman provided a related model of group process in which the group was seen to pass through a series of conflicts arising out of unconscious wishes, each of which evoked a corresponding fear. The group members would struggle to find a solution to each conflict as it arose, as a way of moving forward. Some solutions, however, would restrict the group's development, and it fell to the therapist to steer the group towards the more enabling solutions and away from the restrictive solutions. Whitaker and Lieberman's method has found application in organizational settings and also provides useful insights into the functioning of therapeutic groups.

A very different conceptualization of the analytic group comes from R. Schindler, an Austrian psychoanalyst and group analyst who advances the view that group building comes about through the perception of an adversary, an oppositional entity (*Gegner*). The tension between the collective group aim and the perceived adversary stimulates and ultimately maintains the group. Theoretically, any other group formation outside one's own group constitutes an adversary. The interaction amongst the group members is determined by sociodynamic role distributions. Schindler calls them Alpha, Beta, Gamma and Omega, where Alpha represents the most assertive person in the group and Omega the most conciliatory. The role distribution changes as the therapy proceeds.

Analysis of the individual by the group

Foulkes broke away from the dyadic model of group therapy. Neither the dyad of analyst and analysand nor the dyad of analyst and group-as-a-whole satisfied him. Instead, he introduced a model of analysis based on the notion of a communication network, in which disturbance, but also normality and analytic capacity, was lodged in the group as a whole. In Foulkes's model the therapist is important, but not central to the analytic process. Group-analytic therapists have to accept that the group will invest them with analytic authority, especially at the beginning of the therapeutic process. However, one of the therapist's tasks is to help the group to recognize its own inherent ability to act as a collective therapeutic agent towards the members of the group.

Postscript

History flows alarmingly into the present. The pioneers of the early twentieth century have already slipped into the category of history, but what of the veterans of the mid-twentieth century? We believe that many of the classic writings on groups deserve to be revisited, or perhaps visited for the first time. It is always a rewarding exercise to study great minds at work, and there is a fair chance that new ideas can be discovered in old writings. This chapter has been in the nature of a selective tour, but we hope that it will stimulate further reading into the fascinating history of our field.

CHAPTER THREE

Planning an analytic group

MARCUS KNEW THAT IT HAD BEEN A MISTAKE TO INTRODUCE THAT TRADE UNION LEADER INTO HIS GROUP

The spark for an analytic group may come from a service need, a training requirement, the need for professional development or a private practice initiative. It is easier to plan the group when there is a pre-existing culture of respect for group therapy and analytic methods. But whatever the working context, much thinking and planning has to be done before beginning the assessment of prospective group members.

A therapy group, like any group, is part of a wider system. When planning it, one has to keep in mind the superior system in which the group will function. This can be an inpatient unit of a hospital, an outpatient department, a day centre, a child and family clinic, a private practice, a school or a community centre. Quite apart from the technical arrangements to be considered, there are the less tangible manifestations of the superior system which, if not included in one's planning, can throw a spanner in the works.

Envisaging the group

A group starts with a vision of its membership. If an analytic group for adults is being considered, we can begin by imagining a room with seven or eight people in it. This immediately highlights two separate tasks: choosing the venue and liaising with people who might have dealings with the future group members and whose cooperation will be necessary for a well-functioning group – potential referrers, professionals who share responsibility for the care of the patients in the group, administrators with responsibility for managing the premises housing the group, colleagues sharing the same work environment, and staff responsible for the secretarial work, reception, administration and security in relation to the group.

Different models of group therapy

The first decision is whether to run a closed or open group. The terms 'closed' and 'open' refer to the manner in which people enter and leave the group. In a 'slow-open' group, the members join and leave in their own time, while in a closed group all the members join and leave at the same time, at which point the group ends. In a truly open group, people come and go freely, with a minimum of attachment to the group.

Slow-open groups

The classic long-term analytic group is generally slow-open in character. The time-scale for such a group is open-ended, and the duration of therapy is measured in years rather than weeks or months. This is a prospect that sometimes provokes concern in would-be group members and referrers, until it is explained that group analysis is a process which addresses problems which have accumulated over a lifetime, and that it goes beyond the eradication of symptoms into the area of interpersonal reconstruction. The slow-open group is the group which models most closely the life groups from which its members come: the multi-generational family, school and work groups. The group members negotiate the time of their leaving in a dynamic context, and new members enter when it is right for them.

This pattern of joining and leaving creates its own set of tasks for the conductor. The emotional reactions evoked by exits and entries call for sensitive and skilful handling. The group has to deal with losing established, trusted, often loved group members. A departure may also evoke despondency or envy. Remaining group members may think: 'He has reached his aim. When will I?' Then there is the new member who re-awakens long-forgotten feelings of competitiveness towards a new baby in the family. In any event, newcomers have to be eased into the group and require special vigilance from the therapist for quite a while. Both arrivals and departures offer group members rich opportunities for working through psychic events such as loss and trauma. Group members also become more aware of the universality of their own life experiences as they encounter more of their fellow group members over time. The implication of a slow-open group is that the group itself has no end-point in sight, although the therapy of the individual is finite. The bringing to an end of a slow-open group is a therapeutic task in its own right, and will be considered in a later chapter.

Open groups

Groups are sometimes open in the sense of having a fairly rapid throughput of membership, with individuals attending for perhaps no more than one or two sessions before moving on. These groups are suited to some inpatient settings, for example a group for parents of hospitalized children, or a group for patients in an acute admissions ward in a psychiatric hospital. Post-discharge groups in psychiatric hospitals tend to have an open structure, with a core of regular attenders who help to maintain the group culture, and some more peripheral members who 'drop-in' from time to time when in need of support. This model also applies to groups for people with addictive disorders, who use the group to bolster themselves against a relapse.

Each session of a group in an acute hospital setting has to be regarded more or less as an event in its own right, with the culture of continuity being carried mainly by the therapist and other staff.

Therapists who work with these groups are involved in a race against time, and have to engage actively with the group. The sessions have to be tightly structured, with interventions predominantly taking an explanatory, supportive or psycho-educational form.

Closed groups

Closed groups are by definition time-limited, though this does not mean that they are necessarily short-term. A closed group can run for anywhere between six weeks and two years. The fact that the group is closed has dynamic implications for the therapeutic process. The shared beginning and ending imposes a cohesion on the group which can be put to therapeutic advantage. On the negative side, a closed group carries with it a greater risk of loss through attrition if some of the members decide, for whatever reason, to leave the group prematurely. This is likely to be more of a problem when the group is long-term. A closed group is also denied the opportunity to experience the fresh input of new arrivals. However, the bond which group members develop with one another from the outset, and the solidarity associated with a shared passage through the group, creates a powerful experience of group identification, often associated with a greater sense of safety in exploring deep and difficult issues. Closed groups tend to be homogeneous in composition; that is to say they have been put together on the basis of immediately discernible shared attributes or problems which give the group its specific identity. Homogeneous groups are considered in more detail elsewhere.

Short-term group therapy

When a group meets for only a few sessions, the focus of the group is generally circumscribed and the sessions are carefully structured in terms of content. For example, the therapist might include a psycho-educational component to begin with, or make use of 'warm-up' or 'turn-taking' techniques to accelerate the process of getting to know one another. A rounding off 'evaluation' may be held at the end, with structured interventions by the therapist, directing the group to reflect on its past and anticipate the future in the light of the group experience. Defining goals and setting exercises or tasks along the way can also form part of the process. These techniques can coexist with a group-analytic perspective, which is often called into play to manage group dynamic issues.

Short-term groups are of particular value in the treatment of the bereaved and those united by a particular traumatic episode, such as a natural disaster, terrorist attack or war-related trauma. William Piper, through his work with groups for the bereaved, advises the therapist to focus consistently on what the group members have in common rather than their differences. According to Piper, this facilitates the rapid disclosure of long-term conflicts and difficult relationships with the lost person, which in turn leads to an increased ability to tolerate ambivalent feelings and a corresponding reduction in the symptoms associated with bereavement (Piper, 1991).

Mental health services with long waiting lists are increasingly demanding time-limited methods, with treatment goals which are defined in advance. Psychodynamic therapists sometimes balk at this, in the belief that the imposition of a time limit does injury to the therapeutic process. The argument is that a time-scale cannot be stipulated in advance because of the very nature of the analytic method, which addresses the unconscious and is therefore unconstrained by 'real' time. However, the view that 'it takes as long as it takes' is likely to get a frosty reception these days from service managers under pressure from long waiting lists and budgetary constraints. The case for analytic open-endedness has to be reconciled with the case for the needs of the many to be met. Research into the efficacy of group analysis and which patients benefit from which therapy is one way of doing this.

Block therapy

Block therapy, meaning therapy delivered in blocks of time separated by widely spaced intervals, came about originally as a creative way of introducing group analysis to regions where there were no trained group analysts. It was logical, therefore, that the first excursions into block therapy would be in a training context. Expense and distance meant that several sessions had to be packaged into a few consecutive days, the blocks being separated by intervals of anywhere between one and six months. Block therapy is now practised outside a training context as well. It provides an opportunity for people whose lifestyles and work routines make it impossible for them to commit themselves to the weekly or twice-weekly model of group analysis. Block therapy also offers an avenue of therapy for people living in communities where neither the resources nor the requisite confidentiality for their own personal therapy exist.

The idea that group analysis can be delivered in this form has raised questions about the optimal frequency and intensity of the group-analytic process. It is argued that the weekly and twice-weekly model provides a greater sense of containment, which may make it the preferred model for people whose sense of attachment is more precarious, or those who need more intensive holding than can be provided by the block model. The corollary of this is that block therapy requires a stronger, more visible supportive professional network to be in place when it is offered to vulnerable individuals. This provides a cushion against psychological decompensation in the intervals between blocks. In the selection of patients for block therapy, the group therapist looks for greater ego-strength, and a resilient network at home on which the prospective group member can draw between blocks.

There is also an added stress on the therapist: the counter-transference arising from the group's need for 'the next block' is experienced as an intensified obligation of reliability as a provider of continuity, 'come what may'.

Vignette
In a block training course conducted abroad by five group analysts over 15 years, none of the group analysts missed a single block. Such statistically unlikely continuity of availability has to be seen as coming from the course structure and the needs of the participants – who assembled from a wide geographical area and always expressed a strong urge to be present at 'the next block' – whatever it might also say about the robustness and reliability of the group analysts themselves.

Those who have experienced block therapy, either as patients or therapists, believe that a deep and wide-ranging group analysis is possible with this method. The cluster of group sessions which makes up each block has its own rhythm of *crescendo* and *decrescendo*. Anticipation of the gaps between blocks forms an important part of the work during the blocks, and the fact that the group is held in mind during the long intervals is testified to by the instancy with which memories, associations and themes from the previous block are continued when the group reconvenes.

Co-therapy

Co-therapy in group analysis is practised predominantly in hospitals and clinics. One purpose of this is to provide a greater sense of containment in groups whose membership is likely to challenge the therapeutic culture. A second purpose is to extend the skill of group conducting to interested clinical personnel by way of a training experience. Paradoxically, the inexperienced co-therapist may have a more senior status in the hospital hierarchy than the experienced group analyst, a situation which is sometimes sensed by the group and expressed in the transference.

Whatever the reality, co-therapy results in the dispersal of the transference, with a tendency to split the two therapists into 'good' and 'bad', 'kind' and 'stern', or 'maternal' and 'paternal', irrespective of gender. This can be used in the service of the therapy, but only if the two therapists make the time to discuss the sessions openly, and with confidence in each other.

Some therapists prefer the model of a 'silent' co-therapist, the second therapist being more of an observer than a participant. This strategy should be told to the group well before it starts. Even so, it may evoke paranoid feelings of being watched or used for some secret purpose. If it is to become grist to the therapeutic mill, these anxieties have to be focused on by the therapist as soon as they become discernible. A contrasting model of co-therapy, which accords with our own experience, is that inexperienced co-therapists, even if psychologically naive, can often make useful interventions and bring fresh insights to bear on the group dynamic, provided they are given permission to bring themselves in spontaneously.

In all these cases, the very fact that there is a 'couple' influences the dynamics of the group. As well as being experienced as the parental couple, they may be seen as sexual partners, and fantasies will arise, and will need to surface during the sessions, about their lives outside the group, especially during breaks in the therapy. Group fantasies exert a strong unconscious power on the therapists, who may find themselves acting out some of the attributes assigned to them by the group. This is another reason to set aside time after each session to talk about the events and feelings which have been aroused during the session. Apart from being a useful 'de-briefing' experience, it promotes the professional competence, confidence and wellbeing of the two conductors.

The physical setting

Choosing the group room

The venue is encompassed by the group room, the building which houses it, the institution or agency which hosts it, and the wider environment in which it is situated. All of these are important in choosing the setting for the group. First of all, a venue has to be found which will be prepared to host the group. This may entail some energetic networking and questioning of colleagues in the know. Then, if the negotiation is successful, it is wise to inspect the proffered group room to make sure that it is spacious enough, suitably lit, well-ventilated, tastefully furnished, and protected from the gazes and sounds of the outside world.

Rooms which are used for more than one purpose or have multiple occupancy are prone to the unexpected materialization of clutter and post-meeting debris. More than one group analyst has been faced with the unrewarding task of moving heavy furniture around, sweeping away crumbs and coffee residue, and re-arranging the room minutes before the group is due to meet. It is also worth enquiring about safeguards against passing institutional traffic. Groups are too often subjected to random incursions by absent-minded staff, curious patients and wayward tea trolleys, and every seasoned therapist has a store of anguished memories about group sessions being interfered with by caretakers anxious to secure the building, cleaners, handymen and professionals intent on using the room for their own purposes.

The wider physical setting

There should be a convenient waiting room or reception area near to the group room. The room should be easy to find, and getting into the building after hours should not be in the nature of an obstacle course. There should be a way for patients to announce themselves if they arrive after the session has begun. Arrangements should also be in place for opening up the group room in good time and if necessary locking it or the building afterwards. There should be a clear understanding with the organization about the process of receiving patients, the need to see them individually as well as in the group, the mechanisms for getting messages to and from them, writing and receiving correspondence, and keeping their records securely. Finally, therapists should look after their own wellbeing and ascertain where in the premises they will be able to compose themselves before and after the group, make phone calls, attend to correspondence and keep their belongings safely while the group is in session.

Liaising with the administration

There should be a clearly stated contract with the administration. This sets the stage for a good working relationship and ensures that the administrative staff know of the group's existence, its time setting (including holidays) and the needs of the therapist. The therapist should supply the departmental secretary with the group members' names and contact details, and be clear how and when he or she can be contacted in case of an emergency. There should be agreed procedures on how phone calls, messages and correspondence will be handled, and everybody should be clear about where the records are kept and how they can be accessed. If all this is not carefully attended to, therapists may find their groups unintentionally sabotaged by curious acts of omission or commission.

Liaising with professionals

Good professional liaison involves enlisting the cooperation of professionals from related disciplines, both inside and outside the establishment where the group is being held. Where groups are held in hospital settings, colleagues in multidisciplinary teams like to know what therapeutic activities are being conducted on their premises, and are likely to be more supportive by way of referrals and more understanding when mishaps occur, if they are kept in the picture about the patients in the group and the group itself. In a very practical sense, the comings and goings of seven or eight people at the same time each week, not to mention their possibly loud carryings-on inside the group room, can be irritating to adjacent staff and patients. If this is tempered by an understanding of what is happening in the group, it is less likely to prove a bone of contention. Apart from the convenience factor, however, giving information to colleagues about the group is a good way of increasing awareness of group therapy. It is possible to do this without transgressing confidentiality.

Group therapists have to become acquainted with departmental procedures and practices and reconcile them with their own dynamic administrative perspective. There are sometimes mismatches between the two, such as the sending out of pre-formatted letters or questionnaires as a matter of routine, which call for delicate negotiations. If possible, group analysts should participate in clinical meetings, seminars and journal clubs, where they can contribute a group-analytic perspective, either by presenting aspects of their group or through a theoretical input.

Liaison with outside professionals involves making sure that they learn about the outcome of patients whom they have referred. Communication with primary care workers and mental health professionals who have a connection with patients in the group has to be regular and frequent. Psychotherapists are notorious for being over-inclusive in their initial report and then allowing the file to gather dust for anything up to a year or longer before writing again. Letters to outside professionals should be reasonably detailed, written on a basis of consent from the patient and mindful of confidential issues, but equally mindful of the recipient's need to receive a comprehensive opinion on the nature and origin of the patient's problems and the scope of the proposed treatment. Disturbing or unexpected changes in the course of the therapy warrant additional communications. Professionals such as general practitioners and community psychiatric nurses are often glad to receive a telephone call from the therapist. Apart from allowing for a fuller exchange of information, this provides a good opportunity for getting to know people in the network and becoming known oneself. This whole area of liaison applies as much to private practice as to public sector work.

Vignette

At a Child and Family Clinic, a group for mothers with severe personality problems was successfully conducted over several years, in no small measure due to the fact that the entire multi-disciplinary team, including the administrative staff, had been involved in its planning. Everyone had approved the choice of room for the group, and the timetable for the year, including the breaks, was known to all. The entire clinic staff had been briefed on the likely problems which such a group can cause to the running of a clinic and everyone was therefore well prepared for numerous lengthy telephone enquiries, arrivals on the wrong day, difficulties in leaving the clinic after a session, and various anti-social behaviours characteristic of the severely deprived and narcissistically disturbed patients who made up the group.

Getting referrals for the group

Interest in group therapy relies on a social and professional culture which recognizes the merits of psychodynamic psychotherapy in general and group psychotherapy in particular. Therapists who find themselves working in a region where psychotherapy is relatively unknown have their work cut out for them. A letter or leaflet describing the group in jargon-free terms goes some way towards raising interest and allaying the scepticism of professionals whose thinking might be geared more towards individual treatment methods or those focused on symptom relief as the ultimate therapeutic goal. The internet has opened up new and creative ways of publicizing groups. Psychotherapy services, practices, training organizations and therapists now maintain websites which reach potential referrers and patients alike. The distinction between one body of information aimed at professionals and a separate 'sanitized' body of information aimed at prospective patients has fallen by the wayside in today's era of psychological sophistication and open communication. Someone thinking of joining a group, just like someone thinking of undergoing surgery, will in all likelihood want to know what the process entails, and may well expect to receive explicit information before undergoing it.

The most time-consuming way of stimulating referrals, but also the most rewarding, is for therapists to make personal contact with key professionals in the network to inform them of their intention to run a group, and to describe the sort of person most likely to benefit from that particular group. In private practice, many referrals come in on the basis of word-of-mouth recommendations, after patients themselves have reported good progress.

The balance and composition of an analytic group

The referrals coming in from various sources may not afford the group analyst an opportunity to put together the theoretically ideal group with the widest possible span of personalities and diagnoses. This is a counsel of perfection and as such rather discouraging. Nevertheless, it is worth keeping in mind that the matrix is enriched by a diversity of ages, ethnicity, sexuality, personality attributes and symptomatology. The greater the mix, the greater the possibility for the group members to make use of one another, in the best sense of the word, for empathic purposes, and for undergoing the experience of mirroring, projection and projective identification, which are the group's specific tools. On the other hand, if the group has a preponderance of members with the same characteristic – say, a depressed or passive outlook – the resources available to its members will be correspondingly restricted.

The optimal number of patients

The threshold number for starting the group can be a problem if referrals are thin on the ground. Bearing in mind the traditional number of eight patients, can one start the group if one can only muster, say, three patients? This can be tricky. If one member is absent from a session, the therapist is left with the dynamic of a couple, not a group. It becomes less problematic if one thinks of a minimum of five members, to whom it can then be made clear from the start that the group will eventually have its full contingent of seven or eight members (Foulkes, 1948).

But the opposite problem also has to be considered: an embarrassment of riches. When the demand for places in a group is pressing, as in some public sector units with long waiting lists, the

question becomes: how big should a new group be? It is wise to resist
pressure to take patients into an already full group just because there
is a long waiting list. However, if a large number of patients is put
into the group at the outset, it is still possible to establish a group-
analytic culture. Foulkes, having laid down the size of the ideal
group, told his trainees that when practising in a hospital he would
put together a 'waiting list group' simply by taking the first twelve
patients from the list into a group. He maintained that after a short
while they would invariably 'shake down' to the ideal number of
eight. In effect, such was his trust in the group process, that he was
carrying out the assessment for suitability for group analysis during
the early sessions of the group itself, working therapeutically with all
the members until, by a process of self-selection, a minority withdrew from the group and a core of the membership persevered with
their group-analytic treatment.

Preparing information about the group

Let us assume that the intention is to run a slow-open, weekly analytic group for men and women with a range of psychological
problems. Preparation for this will involve the drawing up of a
detailed timetable of dates for the group sessions, showing holiday
breaks and any other dates when the group will not be meeting. This
is best mapped out for a year in advance, thereby giving a message of
predictability and showing that the time-scale of the group is an
important dynamic process in its own right. In addition to the
timetable, some group analysts give out a leaflet to people joining
the group, outlining the expectations and obligations involved.
Although this covers ground that may well have been gone over during preparatory sessions with the patient, many see it as a containing
and respectful thing to do, given that there is a lot of spoken information for the patient to take in during the early meetings with the
therapist. In addition to basic information about the time-structure
of the group, mention is usually made of the requirement of confidentiality and the importance of not socializing with fellow group
members outside the sessions. In the case of a group held in the setting of a private practice, details should be given about the
fee-paying arrangements. Some therapists like to include information on how to get in touch with them in the event of latecoming or

absence, and what is expected by way of notice when the time comes to leave the group.

In keeping with the move towards greater transparency about the nature of treatments being provided, there is an increasing tendency to include something about the theoretical foundations of group analysis. Other therapists, ourselves included, believe that this belongs to the early conversations with the group member, where it can be tailored to the interest and curiosity of the individual. A leaflet bristling with too many explanations and injunctions can also act as something of a deterrent to an already apprehensive person.

Keeping a record of the group

Two different sets of records should be kept: one of the group process, the other of each individual's progress in the group. The latter is destined for the individual's case-notes. A group register which marks the pattern of attendance of the group members, including absences and latecomings (notified and unexpected), provides a helpful adjunct to the understanding of both individual and group dynamics.

CHAPTER FOUR

Dynamic administration

PRoBLEMS IN GRoUP ANALYSIS . No 28 : GRoUP RAGE
Tony accuses Neil of pinching his chair

You come most carefully upon your hour.   *Hamlet* 1.i.6

Group analysis takes place within a carefully constituted setting which is the physical representation of the group-as-a-whole. The term 'dynamic administration' refers to the various activities which the conductor performs in order to create and maintain this setting. The concept includes such apparently mundane tasks as arranging the furniture in the room and drafting letters to group members, which on the face of it might be delegated to a secretary or administrator. The conductor takes on these tasks because they have dynamic significance and have to be woven into the material which forms the analytic process.

Division of tasks between conductor and group

Communications which take place outside the group belong to the same network as those which take place inside the group. This makes attention to dynamic administration as important as the analytic interventions which take place during the sessions. However, there is a significant difference in the way in which these two therapeutic tasks are distributed. While responsibility for creating and maintaining the setting is carried solely by the conductor, the analytic task is shared with the rest of the group. This allows for a creative interplay between the conductor as the guardian of the group's stability and the group as the agent of therapeutic change. The constancy of the setting often provides rich transferential material, which arises in such diverse forms as a challenge to paternal authority when the conductor insists on preserving the chosen setting, the experience of maternal containment when the boundary of the group is protected, and a parentified wish to be helpful through efforts to assist the conductor in preparing the room.

By the same token, the conductor does not enter into negotiations with the group members about the dynamic administrative arrangements for the group. Issues such the positioning of the chairs, the group timetable and the timing of a new person's entry into the group may be, and frequently are, talked about in the group, but these discussions have to be steered into analytical waters and not treated like items on a committee agenda. This leaves the conductor free to make all decisions needed to maintain the group in an optimal state. In fee-paying groups it is also up to the conductor to set fees and determine the manner of payment.

Handling messages

A further important area of dynamic administration lies in the handling of notifications of absence and messages to and from the group. All communications between the outside world and the group are negotiated by the conductor, who assesses their dynamic implications and decides when to contain them and when to bring them into the session. Some group analysts inform the group of any messages about absence or latecoming at the start of the session, others prefer to wait for the emergence of a dynamic which contextualizes the message before disclosing it. In this manner, all communications ultimately join the total network which makes up the group matrix.

The dynamic significance of the group room

Apart from the pragmatic considerations of comfort, continuity and protection from intrusion mentioned in the previous chapter, the room acquires a personal meaning for each group member and for the group as a whole. For instance, the group room can be experienced as the conductor's body, tacitly accepted as long as it remains unchanged, but anxiety-provoking and fascinating if change takes place.

Vignette
A group was invited by the conductor to meet for a session in her absence. An animated discussion ensued as to the place and time of such a meeting, and there was much excitement and interest: should the session be held in the pub next door to the practice? The park? One woman invited the group members to her home, but this invitation was ignored. Eventually the conductor drew attention to the group's unexpressed assumption that the meeting without her could not take place in the usual group room, on the usual day, at the usual time. It seemed that all these belonged to her, not available to them when she was not present. The possibility of possessing the room had raised the anxiety of possessing her body, and this had made them so anxious that it could not be contemplated.

The table in the centre

In the circle of identical chairs it is a good idea to place a small round table, of a size which allows a full view of each group member. This forms a symbolic as well as a real centre of the circle. It may have a box of tissues on it, and some therapists also like to place messages on it, such as notifications of absence, telephone messages or cards from a group member on holiday. These can then be picked up and read, or ignored, the responses being at once individual and available to the entire group.

Who sits where?

Group conductors vary in the way in which they regulate the seating arrangements. Some allow the group to position the conductor anywhere in the circle. Others indicate, explicitly or implicitly, that they prefer their own chair, which is left unoccupied until they arrive. Whichever seating constellation is arrived at has its own dynamic meaning. Who sits next to the conductor? Who sits facing the door? Why have all the men chosen to sit together? All these questions have a meaning, and constitute part of the nonverbal communication in the group. Their significance becomes clear only because the physical conditions in the room are being kept steady.

The dynamic significance of an empty chair

Should a chair be taken out of the circle if a group member has given advance notice of absence? Some conductors arrange the chairs according to the total number of group members, irrespective of whether an absence has been notified. Others remove the chair of any group member whose absence is expected. This allows any empty chair remaining in the circle to speak loudly of any group member whose absence is unexpected. The former arrangement expresses the concept of group-as-a-figure more accurately, since the group members belong to their group whether present or absent. By symbolically underlining this, the conductor prompts the group to talk about the absent person and express feelings of concern, anger or indifference which become grist for the analytic mill.

Vignette

In a group of eight men and women, one young woman invariably expressed unease when a chair in the circle remained unoccupied. She would ask the others whether they knew why the group member was absent, something she herself could never remember even when it had been made clear the previous session. At first she expressed disapproval, as if attendance in the session were a moral duty; as the session proceeded, she became aware of the high degree of anxiety which an empty chair aroused in her. 'It feels like something vital is missing ... it makes me unable to think and feel properly here ... as if I were a cripple ...' (in childhood, she had

experienced a fragmentation of her family, which was now reproduced by the empty chair).

Someone else said that it suited him well since there was 'more
left for me'. His need for more than his fair share of the group conductor and the group time contrasted strongly with the woman's
requirement of wholeness given to her by the complete circle. Both
these patients' unconscious emotional needs were expressed in and
through the circle of chairs.

Institutional intrusion

When the setting is in a hospital or clinic, the allocation of the group
room is not always under the control of the group analyst, despite
careful preparation of the optimal conditions before the start of the
group therapy. The room 'belongs' to the institution, and even with
the most careful planning, others' priorities may at times override
those of the therapy group, with unforeseen consequences. When
this happens, it is necessary to put the reactions of the group under
therapeutic scrutiny. Interference with the setting and any ensuing
tension between the institution and the conductor can result in an
extra-strong group cohesion by way of protecting the conductor.
Projective defences of the group members can be strongly employed,
so that everyone inside the group becomes good and loving, and all
hostility and destructiveness is experienced as residing in the outside
world, represented by the hospital.

Vignette
A new group of outpatients had been meeting weekly in the same
room of the hospital. Attendance had been erratic, group members
had been loathe to turn to one another, and interventions by the
conductor had been marginalized. Then one evening, shortly after
the start of the group session, the group room was claimed by a
staff member of the hospital who had been unaware of the group
meetings at that time. There was a heated exchange of words
between the conductor and the staff member, and eventually the
group was moved into another room, where the session proceeded.
The previous subject matter was taken up where it had been left

before the interruption as if it had not happened. In the following sessions, group attendance improved dramatically: latecoming and absences stopped and the group members talked to one another with much animation. A new urgency seemed to have gripped the group, and the conductor's interventions were eagerly sought and carefully attended to. Expressions of rejection and aggression within the group ceased. It was only some weeks later, after the 'expulsion' (as the incident became known) had been raised by the conductor and worked through in the group, that there was some return to the group of therapeutically important expressions of rejection and aggression.

The time boundaries of the group

The exact time of starting and ending the group session is a fixed, static, non-negotiable entity. Gregory van der Kleij has succinctly captured the need for an uncompromising stance on the part of the conductor:

> (all this) happens on that boundary between the actual interactions of the group members and the entire world around them. It is not that once started, at 5.30 p.m. the group members exclude that world around them. On the contrary, at 5.30 p.m. they begin their dialogue with it. And do so because so far they had failed to reach the results they wished for. They would not be there (in the group) otherwise. To facilitate that immensely complex dialogue, my task (as group conductor) is precisely to ensure that, for once, the world around them stops them moving around. I want it to stand still, as it were, pin it down, so that a proper dialogue can be held. (van der Kleij, 1983)

Fees

Many group analysts find no difference between the dynamic development of the groups of fee-paying patients and those whose members pay no fees directly to the conductor, maintaining that the therapeutic working alliance appears to be unaffected by the fee-paying factor. Others find that 'paying one's way' facilitates an adult working alliance, which in turn allows for deeper regression into infantile modes of experiencing. It is often observed that non-fee-paying groups remain demanding and angry for prolonged periods. The conductor in these groups is experienced as omnipotent, all-giving and all-withholding, wilful and autocratic. In effect, the conductor becomes the mother-figure of early infancy, whose authoritarian dicta can only be accepted or received with impotent rage or withholding actions. These states are a necessary and integral part of fee-paying groups also, but it would seem that the very act of paying one's fee preserves that part of the ego which is in the therapeutic working alliance with the group and the group analyst, alongside the regressed part of the personality.

Our own practice is to arrange for fees to be paid monthly in advance and distributed over the twelve months of the year. This emphasizes and symbolizes the steady, continuous belonging to a group which is there whether the patient takes part in the sessions or not, and whether the group meets or not, as during a break. It is desirable that all members pay the same amount, although it can also be argued that differential fees are acceptable if they reflect different economic levels in the group. The emotions generated from such a differential bring to the surface important therapeutic issues relating to favouritism, envy and the value which group members attach to their therapy.

Vignette

In a mixed group of eight, one member, a teacher, had expressed difficulty with what seemed to him the high fee which he had been told about at his initial interview. One month after his entry into the group, the group fee was raised, at which point the conductor suggested that his fee could remain unchanged. The patient accepted this without demur and continued to pay the lower fee for six months. The following month he presented a cheque for the full fee. When the conductor raised this in the group, the patient spoke for the first time of his rage with the conductor for having 'taken pity' on him. He spoke of his feelings of being different, less capable, an outsider who needed to be taken care of. This patient had been adopted at the age of eight months, and the feelings of excessive neediness and dependency on others belonging to that early period had emerged for the first time through the issue of fees. On reflection, although important therapeutic material emerged, it might have been a mistake to suggest the concession.

Contact between group members outside sessions

The group members will already know, from their preparatory sessions, that it is undesirable for them to meet up outside the group sessions. It is likely that this constraint will have been discussed in the group as well. The reasons for social abstinence are usually accepted by the group: that relationships in therapy groups are exceptionally close and confidential; that feelings such as attraction, love, hatred and dislike can only be fully expressed and explored in the group precisely because their expression remains free from the usual personal and social consequences which such expressions would have in the 'real world'; and that contact between some group members to the exclusion of others detracts from the shared experience which allows the group to work as a whole. When extra-group contact occurs, it is often an acting out of repressed or rejected emotions which are then lost to the group experience and to their analysis in the group.

Despite the culture of social abstinence, group members occasionally seek comfort, social support and confirmation with fellow group members outside the group following a difficult period in the group. The conductor has to find a way of bringing these outside communications back into the group when they declare themselves, and helping the group to analyse them. Group members discover that positive feelings can change into negative ones as the transference changes, and that a stable interpersonal relationship between group members is difficult to sustain outside the safety of the group boundaries.

Certain therapeutic settings, for example block therapy, encompass a degree of legitimate socialization which is not in itself anti-therapeutic. Encounters in the social milieu of such settings are frequently used therapeutically when they are brought back into the group sessions.

Vignette

In an experiential group which met for one whole week in a residential setting, it was decided to celebrate the last but one evening with a party. The group was to meet in the evening, in the room of one of the participants. Food and drink were provided, and someone produced a guitar. Soon a sing-song ensued, and people grouped themselves around two members in particular who seemed to have an endless store of traditional folk songs. People reminded one another of yet another song, and there was much excitement and animation. One man had been silent, busying himself with the food and drink. He left early, saying that he had a headache. The others stayed on together late into the night.

The following morning the group seemed to have difficulty finding something to talk about. Sentences were started and left unfinished. Communication was disjointed. When the conductor pointed this out, she was told that it was no wonder: the week was nearly over and everyone was thinking of the long way home to their families in different towns. The group then talked about the cars that would take them home in terms of their sizes and strengths. The early party-leaver sat in angry silence through all this. The conductor pointed out his anger and apparent isolation. She also remarked on the feeling of the group falling apart, into competing components of separateness. The angry group member then spoke in a bitter, hurt tone about feelings of isolation in the group, which he had not felt before. He had not known the songs that had been sung the previous evening; they were songs he had never heard at home; no one had had time to sing at home, and anyway he doubted whether his parents had known these songs. As for him, there had been no time for any of that sort of thing: he had had to work in order to get on. Others in the group then spoke about their family backgrounds and how these had been experienced in childhood. This seemed to enable the angry man to talk with feeling about the economic and social deprivation he had experienced as the child of a poor family in a well-to-do neighbourhood. He recalled with much emotion not having had gym shoes and not having been able to take part in sports for lack of the right clothing, or go on school outings for lack of the train fare. He could then speak of his current feelings of social isolation and his fear of poverty, in spite of his high professional, social and economic standing.

Contact with the conductor outside the group

All contact with the conductor outside the group sessions, even if momentary or casual, has dynamic significance. Not infrequently a group member tries to gain the conductor's attention before the start of a session, or after the session has ended. Most group analysts are familiar with the group member who arrives especially early and offers to help with the chairs, or the group member who takes his or her time gathering up possessions while the conductor waits patiently in a doorman-like posture, then seizing the moment to tax the conductor with a problem which could not be brought up during the session.

Sometimes a group member becomes profoundly distressed towards the end of a session. This is a situation which should not detain the group beyond the ending time, but may well call for flexibility on the part of the therapist by way of a containing intervention alone with the person. Although such 'foot-in-the-door' manoeuvres have unconscious roots, simply urging the person to bring the difficulty back to the following group session can sometimes tip the scales into some form of acting out behaviour, such as staying away from the group. This can usually be averted by rapidly exploring the problem area and suggesting a provisional solution, even to the extent of offering an individual session to explore the problem more fully as a prelude to bringing it back into the group.

Group members also sometimes seek out the conductor between sessions or during holiday breaks. Messages with varying degrees of urgency might reach the conductor in person or via a receptionist or another colleague.

Vignette

A group member regularly experienced separation anxiety at the approach of each holiday break, reproducing her original symptoms and complaining bitterly about the conductor's unavailability during the break. Just before one break, the group rallied around her with offers of their telephone numbers. The conductor discouraged this and asked the other group members to relate their offers to their own anxieties about the break.

During the first week of the break, the woman telephoned the conductor at home, crying and saying how desperate she felt. The conductor apologized for not being able to speak at that particular moment and undertook to call her back. When he did, a few hours later, he expressed concern at her distress and listened sympathetically to her for a few minutes. During the return phone call she sounded composed, and thanked the conductor for having taken the trouble to phone her. When the group reconvened, she said that she could not remember what the conductor had said to her, but added that she had felt calmed simply on hearing his voice, and that that had been enough for her. During subsequent breaks she felt no further need to contact the conductor, and her separation anxiety faded during the course of her continuing group analysis.

Contact between the conductor and a group member's relative

Relatives of group members, especially those in a close personal relationship with the group member, such as marital partners, have a keen investment in the progress of the therapy, as they would see it. Moreover they are not bound by the same therapeutic alliance and constraints as the group member, and sometimes instigate contact with the therapist or exercise pressure on the group member which brings him into conflict with the group.

If the point is reached where a relative seeks therapy in his or her own right, or if conjoint therapy seems to be indicated, it is best for another therapist to get involved. A negative view of the group by the group member's relative without the wish to participate actively in any therapy can usually only be worked on in the group as a dynamic issue for the group member. Occasionally, however, concessions to a particular social reality have to be made. Some groups, such as those composed of individuals with poor social support systems, or those whose defences are too fragile to sustain a tight group boundary, call for greater flexibility by allowing or even encouraging occasional contact with relatives.

Vignette
A young woman who had been in a group for several months reported that she was becoming more irritable and impatient with her husband. She had previously submitted to him and had allowed him to dominate her through her fear of being abandoned. With

the increasing confidence given to her by the group she found herself standing up to him, even threatening to leave him if he did not change his behaviour. This brought his dependence on her to the surface. He contacted the conductor, angrily complaining that the group was not helping his wife. However, he agreed to participate in conjoint sessions with another therapist, which proceeded to his own individual therapy. This brought him towards an acceptance of his wife's therapy and paved the way for them to work on their relationship in their separate therapeutic settings.

Contact with the professional network

There may be several professionals involved with a group member, including the referrer. Before a new member joins the group it is useful to clarify the basis on which any future contact might be made with key professionals, such as the need to keep a general practitioner or psychiatrist in the picture about a group member's progress. Most people joining a group accept the value of keeping lines of communication open with anyone who is actively involved in their care. Any doubts and reservations have to be explored, and a refusal to consent to contact with a specific professional has to be respected, although some group analysts regard permission to liaise with the patient's general practitioner as a *sine qua non* for embarking upon therapy.

The issue of liaison assumes particular dynamic significance when concern arises about the group's capacity for containing a group member's difficulties. If a group member becomes suicidal or develops psychotic symptoms during the course of therapy, the conductor may have to contact the group member's general practitioner or the local psychiatric service.

Sometimes the group analyst finds himself or herself in a dual professional role. As a psychiatrist, for example, there may be an expectation to take responsibility for prescribing or supervising a group member's medication. In a setting with limited resources this may be unavoidable. However, such a practice complicates the analytic process, and if possible the group analyst should enlist the support of colleagues to take on other aspects of the patient's care or treatment.

Queries are sometimes directed from outside professionals towards the group analyst, triggered by concerns of which he or she might have been unaware.

Vignette

Unbeknown to the conductor, a woman who had been attending the group for some three months consulted her general practitioner in a distressed state to ask for a more effective treatment for her depressive symptoms, which she felt were not being adequately addressed in the group. In the group she had been consistently helpful towards the other group members but conspicuously reticent about herself. The GP wrote to the group analyst, stating the problem and asking his opinion. The group analyst telephoned the GP, and during the ensuing conversation it became clear that the patient had been splitting the professionals involved in her care into those who were constantly there but ineffectual – the group – and those whom she idealized but who were unavailable and withholding – the elusive doctors. The contact between group analyst and GP symbolized a united parental couple for the patient, and put a stop to a professional collusion which could have resulted in the premature ending of her therapy. The therapist reported the conversation to the group. This provided both containment and confrontation, which enabled the patient to think about her difficulty in bringing her depression more openly into the group.

To summarize: dynamic administration is the means by which the conductor creates and maintains the setting of the group. The conductor alone performs its numerous tasks and accepts sole responsibility for preserving the group in its optimal condition, as a prerequisite for the transformation of individual disturbances into communicable language. Dynamic administration calls upon the conductor to structure the group physically in time and space, to mediate communications flowing between the group and the outside world, to guard the group's boundary, and to ensure that all actions are woven into the texture of the group dynamic. By continuously holding the setting at the very centre of the therapeutic process, the conductor imparts to the therapy its quintessential character.

CHAPTER FIVE

The assessment interview

There is a moment in the story of Frankenstein when the monster comes face to face with his pursuer, and begs him to listen to his sad story. The response of the pursuer encapsulates an essential dilemma of psychotherapy:

> You may easily imagine that I was much gratified by the offered communication, yet I could not endure that he should renew his grief by a recital of his misfortune. I felt the greatest eagerness to hear the promised narrative, partly from curiosity and partly from a strong desire to ameliorate his fate if it were in my power. Mary Shelley, *Frankenstein* (1818)

On the face of it, assessment for group analysis involves a conversation between therapist and patient about one of them: the patient.

The process of assessment is, however, a mutual one. The prospective group member is assessing the therapist as much as the other way round. The term 'assessment' implies the capacity to make a rational judgement. The would-be group member should be assisted in the process by being given an explanation of the method, purpose and rationale of group-analytic therapy. This explanation is tailored to the specific needs of the patient. It should include a cautionary account of the demands and complications of group therapy as well as its possible uses and benefits. In addition to giving an account of group therapy in general, some therapists like to give a flavour of the particular group which the person might join.

There are a variety of ways in which the assessment interview can be conducted. The two of us compared notes on this:

Liesel: How do you receive the person who walks through the door?

Harold: I extend myself in a friendly fashion. When it comes to receiving patients, I have known some psychotherapists to be like children in matters of etiquette. They forget to say hello. Or perhaps they omit it intentionally because they regard it as bad technique to indulge in any welcoming pleasantries. The principle of inscrutability is sometimes invoked in the belief that one shouldn't do anything which might cause a ripple on the pool of the transference.

Liesel: Like you, I believe that nothing is lost and much is gained by extending a warm, friendly welcome.

Harold: Let me now present you with a typical scenario. A 45-year-old woman has been referred to you by her general practitioner. She enters the room and you see before you a tired-looking, tense, worried, depressed woman. How do you begin your interview?

Liesel: Of course she is not quite new to me. I will have had some previous information about her, probably through a referral letter or some other form of communication from her GP. If she is one step ahead of the GP and has referred herself, there would have been some contact with my secretary, who would have told me who she is and what she wants.

Harold: OK, let's say you've had a letter from her GP describing her symptoms as depression and panic attacks – and outlining her family situation rather briefly. That's all the information you have.

Liesel: The file will be lying on the table between us and I would be introducing myself and telling her that I've had this referral from her GP. I would then invite her with words such as 'Let's talk now and see how I can be of use to you. Just tell me whatever you wish to.' I would ask a minimum of questions, in fact I would try to ask none at the beginning, and allow her to structure the interview. I would ask permission to take notes. To the best of my memory, my note-taking has only been queried twice, and in both cases it denoted a fear of misuse of the written information. If this happens it is essential not to jump to the conclusion that one is dealing with a paranoid personality. This may indeed be the case, but it is more likely that the fear is based on previous experience. One patient had actually suffered from the misuse of data given by him in a similar interview, and the request for information about what would happen to the notes I was making was, in the light of his experience, reasonable rather than pathological.

Harold: I have to say that I take it for granted that note-taking is part of the assessment interview, so I don't even draw attention to it. It is too much to expect the therapist to retain the wealth of detailed information and impressions in mind without making notes.

Now let's suppose that our patient begins to talk in a slow, hesitant way about her difficult relationship with her husband. Would you encourage this and allow this theme to develop with her?

Liesel: I would certainly listen very carefully. I would neither encourage nor discourage it. What I would try to do is to establish a relationship – in which she will take notice of me as well as I of her. In that sense I would make observations about her present state in the 'here-and-now' of the interview situation. I might say, 'You sound sad to me, you sound tired'. I would make some reference to the depressive state in which I experience her now. I would describe my experience of her in this session and see what she makes of it.

Harold: It's not uncommon for patients to begin to cry as they start to tell their story. Let's say your patient does this.

Liesel: That's difficult. I certainly would accept her tears for a while, but then I would intervene with a question. I might explore the tears. I would see them as a symptom – no, not actually as a symptom – I would see the tears as a defence against what lies below the tears, and I would make remarks which would encourage her to penetrate the tears and get down to a deeper layer of the exploration of her feelings and her existence. It would be very important in this first interview to get on to her relating more of what I would call her social history, which means, for instance, her culture and family of origin, and so on.

Harold: As far as the social history is concerned, I have in my own mind a sort of blueprint of what has to be covered during the first session. I think of two strands of dialogue which have to be woven together by the end of the interview. The first is a conversation about her symptoms: in other words, what she regards as the problem areas in her life, both interpersonally and in the way she feels. The second strand is about the rest of her life, the 'non-problem' to use Caroline Garland's phrase (Garland, 1982). I would try to find out whether she can imagine connections between the two. That's going to be important if she joins a group. I want to conduct a tour of her present and her past, in that order.

Liesel: That seems to me a little over-structured. It may be that this is unobtainable in the first hour of one's meeting a new person. If so, I would point out just how much we have left undone and how difficult it is to get down to her history and her problems, and I would suggest another diagnostic interview, which, in my experience, is gratefully accepted.

Harold: Yes, I also sometimes find that I have to extend the assessment process, but I still try to get a comprehensive history during the first meeting. I find it all too easy to get drawn into an emotionally powerful narrative before we have got anywhere near to working out a shared understanding of the next step. She is giving me a lot of information, but there is also a lot of information I have to give her, about the nature of group therapy, and my group in particular. I also want her to go away with some new thoughts about herself, and with a sense of hope.

Liesel: I can see that your approach is more complete, and therefore has to be more structured than my own would be.
Would you think that our patient can take all this in this
first encounter with you?

Harold: Maybe not, but I imagine that she will reflect back on our
meeting, and I would expect her to hold on to some facts
as a way of deciding whether she wants to come back at all.
I feel that I owe her an informed opinion of her predicament by the end of our first meeting. Or else I have to give
her good reasons for meeting again.

Liesel: In your scheme of interviewing, how do you lead from the
symptoms into the social history?

Harold: I usually find that I have to initiate a clear break between
the emotionally driven account of the symptoms and the
rest of the history. I might say something like: 'Let's leave
this area for the moment. It will help me to understand it
better if you can tell me something about other areas of
your life.' I would then probably follow that up with a specific question such as. 'Who are the other important
people in your life right now?'

Liesel: I probably do it differently and I am beginning to wonder
whether this has to do not only with our two different personalities, but also the fact that you are male and a doctor
and I am female and non-medical. It seems to me from your
description that I present a more receptive, maternal figure
in the first interview and that you present a paternal
demanding figure and that both are equally justified. They
influence the structuring of the first interview, but I think
the end result is probably the same, because I very much
agree that one has to get down to the practicalities of the
treatment situation of the 'here-and-now'. One should not
allow too much of the material to pour out in these interviews, if only for the reason that too powerful a transference
can be established in this first interview, when after all the
patient will eventually have to share you with seven others,
and if the relationship is too intimate and too maternal this
can result in difficulties when the patient is introduced into
the therapeutic group. This could give rise to resistance to
the group and a demand for individual therapy.

Harold: Getting the balance right between the patient's need to tell
her story and her need to learn about herself isn't easy.

And she also has to know what she is letting herself in for if she decides to join a group.

Liesel: I always keep in mind our analytic purpose, which is to develop a relationship in which needs can be expressed through the transference, initially towards the therapist and then towards the group as well.

Harold: OK, let's get back to our hypothetical patient. Suppose you conclude from her story that she idealizes her family. I might venture something to the effect that she might be seeing her parents through rose-tinted spectacles. She denies this, defends her parents and leaves you feeling that you have trespassed on sacred territory. Do you try to re-enter this area in another way?

Liesel: We are talking about unconscious defence mechanisms. I may be inclined to make a mental note of her defence, but I might leave it at that for the moment. There are various techniques for testing defence mechanisms. By the way, some of them are quite questionable. Many years ago a candidate for group-analytic training was invited to an interview by the training group analyst for his placement in a therapy group. As he came into the room the interviewer carried on writing and didn't look up at all. The candidate waited a few minutes and then said that he had limited time at his disposal, and could the interview please start. Later, the therapist told him that he had behaved like that to see how he managed his defence against rising anxiety. We would not proceed in such a manner ourselves, would we?

Harold: At what point do you begin to reflect your opinion back to the patient?

Liesel: I see this as happening all the way through the interview, whenever I offer trial interpretations. Collectively they form what you might call an opinion.

Harold: Again, I think we have a difference in emphasis. I also offer trial interpretations along the way, but I feel a kind of obligation to bring things all together near the end, with some kind of summation or formulation which I can deliver to the patient. Perhaps that's my medical training at work again.

Liesel: I would like to add to what you are saying about a formulation. When I sit with this woman in the room, I picture not only her but the group which she might or might not join. As I am experiencing her in the first session, I am wanting to see whether she fits in, in the sense that she will not be isolated in the group, whether some of her problems are presented by other patients in the group, whether she fits in age-wise and personality-wise. However, as one is inclined always to feel that a newcomer might disturb the group and not get what she or he needs out of the group, the first picture is usually a cautious one, rather than an over-optimistic one, in my experience.

Harold: As you continue to talk to this woman then, what factors would make you feel more optimistic about her potential to make use of the group? You note that she has already reacted rather negatively to your early tentative interpretation which attempted to link her symptoms to her tendency to idealize her family.

Liesel: The main factor would be whether I feel that we have managed some kind of working relationship, whether I can reach out to her and she can reach out to me, whether we can actually, in the deepest sense of the word, communicate. If we can, there is no reason why she should not be able to communicate in the group with other people. However, it could be that the group at that moment is in a depressive state, and depression tends to prevail over all other moods. In this case I would be very hesitant to introduce her at this moment to this particular group. I might suggest a number of individual sessions to prepare her and at the same time work to prepare the group for her entry at a time when it has got over the worst part of its depressive state. What I'm saying is that the timing of entry is almost as important as the personality of the new group member, and they have to be fitted one to the other. If a fit is not possible in the group which you have in mind, it helps to be working with other therapists in a network or practice which can provide a pool of groups, so that another group can be found for her.

Harold: So far we've talked about a prospective group member whose presenting problem lies in the area of mood. She wants to feel better. Let's think about another example, of a person who presents with a pattern of behaviour which is self-defeating. I have in mind a 42-year-old scientist, who is unable to complete an important research project. As the months have gone by he has become increasingly tense about this, but is unable to overcome the block and he has no idea about what might lie behind it When you meet him you get a sense of someone who is quite emotionally cut off.

Liesel: Despite the note of doom around that phrase 'emotionally cut off', he might very well be a suitable group member. He can communicate, but he has no idea why he fails in such a specific area, which at the same time is vital to him. The chances that he can come off the description of his symptom and slowly peel off the various layers and get to the bottom of it, are best served in a group, to my mind better than in individual therapy, because of the varied input and the free association of the other group members.

Harold: And now a third example, where the presenting problem seems lodged within a difficult interpersonal relationship: a 35-year-old man who is in a state of emotional turmoil because his wife has threatened to leave him. He is terrified of losing her and this has made him increasingly possessive. It is she who has urged him to seek therapy. She sees it as his problem and will have nothing to do with therapy herself. He expresses the hope that therapy might somehow save his marriage, but he also realizes that he needs therapy in his own right, regardless of the impact on his marriage. When you meet him it is difficult to get him to talk about anything other than his relationship with his wife.

Liesel: A presenting problem like this immediately calls to mind the possibility of couple therapy, but if, as you say, his partner will not lend herself to that, and it is clear that he wants therapy for himself, I would seriously consider him for a group. A positive feature of his presentation is that he sees his difficulty as being located within an interpersonal relationship, albeit a dominating and incapacitating one, but the very fact that he is experiencing his relationship in these terms bodes well for his group analysis. The group, by encouraging him to talk about his relationship and resonating to the emotional issues which it stirs in them, would help him to become more detached and less driven,

and therefore more able to think about the other relationships in his life.

Harold: What about a related problem, the case of a man who has
been given an ultimatum by his wife: 'Go and get some
therapy for yourself, or I will leave you'? His own preconceived view of therapy is highly sceptical, but he is
desperate and 'will do anything if it will help'.

Liesel: In such a case I ask myself whether the person will stay in
the group if for any reason the pressure from the partner
is off. One man comes to mind whose wife had actually left
him, and he came into the group and did good work. Then
she came back, whereupon he left the group. So, although
the motivation was urgent at the time, it was not strong
enough for him to gain the insight that it was his own personality that was deeply engaged in the interaction. So the
moment the pressure was off he actually withdrew from
therapy.

Harold: Would you test a person's capacity to make use of analytic
thinking by asking for a dream ?

Liesel: I might under certain circumstances. I'm thinking of a
patient who came for group therapy after prolonged individual psychoanalysis, and he already had knowledge of
the psychoanalytic process. There was no need to lead him
on to the royal road of dreams, it was a familiar route for
him. I might ask a less 'sophisticated' patient, 'Do you
sleep well, and do you dream a lot?' Often I then get a
dream. I do not directly ask for a dream to be related, but
I would show that I am interested in dreams and receptive
to them. To me, the relating of a dream implies psycho-
logical-mindedness. What do you think of that as a
construct?

Harold: The ability to see a dream as significant indicates psycho-
logical-mindedness to me, and I would regard this as a
good indicator of the person's ability to use an analytic
group. I would be more doubtful about someone who
stays with a very concrete narrative and seems unhappy in
the medium of symbolic thinking.

Liesel: How important do you regard it to find out about previous
therapy?

Harold: I like to find out what steps the person took to reach me,
and whether there is a history of previous experience of

therapy. I also have no compunction about asking how the therapy was experienced. I think that often a negative experience will have coloured this person's attitude to current possibilities. I particularly want to know on what note the therapy ended. If the therapy is still ongoing, I would want to redirect the person back to the current therapist to clarify the appropriateness of a transition, and to open up the possibility of an exchange with the other therapist. Let's now assume that you regard the person as suitable for your group. How do you begin to prepare that person for the act of joining?

Liesel: First of all, I make an effort somehow to make clear my belief that group therapy is the optimal treatment for that person. It's important, when one holds this view, to actually put this across, because often group therapy has an aura of being second-best, that is to say less 'deep' than individual therapy, cheaper, convenient for the therapist, and so on. I recall a supervision group where a supervisee, an experienced psychotherapist, replied to a telephone request for therapy with: 'I have no vacancy for individual therapy, but I can take you into a group.' The implication is that group therapy is being offered *faute de mieux*. It's important to dispel the myth of 'second-best', and to make it clear that in choosing group therapy for this particular person the therapist has given due consideration to other methods of therapy. It's then also necessary to talk about the therapeutic contract, which means regular attendance and all the other obligations attached to joining and leaving the group. I tend to give the person a written statement about what is expected. This is often mislaid or forgotten later on, but at least it is a bond between the therapist and the group member. It is, so to speak, a kind of 'transitional object' which the patient takes home and keeps. Having ascertained fairly early on in this briefing that the time and day of the group are convenient, I explain about the 'slow-open' nature of the group. I reply cautiously to questions about how long it is likely to take, but I make it clear that it is not a short-term treatment . On the other hand I do not overstate the time. I remember someone coming into the group and making it quite clear that she was certain that she wanted to stay only for a year. I felt at the time that it would be quite wrong to say that this was too short. This woman is now in her fifth year in the group. It was quite important to allow her to set her own targets at that time and change these targets while she was in the group. I am therefore not dogmatic about the time it takes, but I make it clear that this is a process aimed at deep and fundamental change. This also brings in a sense of hope.

Harold: I agree with all of that. I think the patient's first reaction to the suggestion of group therapy is important. Many patients say that they would like to think about joining a group, but they want some individual sessions first. Even if they don't put words to this, I sometimes propose it as an option, and I find that it is often readily accepted. Other patients are so keen to get on and join the group that they even want to dispense with the initial assessment meeting. This raises the possibility that they could be unconsciously devaluing the therapist or the opposite: an unconscious terror of being alone with the therapist, as is sometimes the case with people who have experienced childhood abuse.

Liesel: When would you not take someone into a group?

Harold: What you say about a particular group having to be right for a particular individual is the only way I can think about the question in general. Having said that, some patients are too narcissistic to be capable of identification with the other group members, others are too needy to be able to contemplate the sharing of attention which a group demands. Some individuals with too severe an ego-weakness may react negatively to the emotional currents in the group. Patients with poor impulse control may find the challenges posed by the group situation too much. I also think that people whose lives are dominated by rigid belief systems are unlikely to tolerate change. When I am in doubt I find that the therapy of choice generally declares itself to the patient after a few individual sessions.

CHAPTER SIX

The symptom in its group context

AND HOW LONG HAVE YOU HAD THIS FEELING
THAT YOU ARE A GROUP?

The person sitting in the group will have a story to tell, the opening words of which are likely to presage a tale of suffering and sorrow, misery and unhappiness, dejection and despair. But these ancient and emotive words have found no place in our modern diagnostic vocabulary. The professional language which has been handed down to us from medicine, psychiatry and psychology has given us a different vocabulary which, with its impersonal ring, impels us to categorize specific states of mind as things in themselves, to be explained to patients and colleagues with a degree of precision, like showing patients a slide of their blood under a microscope and pointing out the different cells.

One of these modern words from which we cannot escape is: 'symptom'. We can, however, broaden its context from the body to the mind, and from the mind to the group. What patients talk about when describing the particular problems which have brought them to the therapist can be thought of as the symptomatic area of their lives. An important task of the assessment interview is to tease out the symptomatic from the non-symptomatic areas. A second exercise, despite its alienating roots in medicine, is that of observation. While the patient tells their story we are forming an impression of the behaviour and personality underlying the story. In traditional medicine these two exercises are neatly partitioned into the 'history' and the 'examination'. Even though dynamic psychiatry has shifted the emphasis to an examination of relationships rather than individuals, there is still a value in distinguishing the patient's subjective experiences from the objective observations of the therapist.

A third strand has to be woven into this exercise, calling up more elusive elements: the therapist's emotional and intuitive responses to the patient encapsulated in the concept of the counter-transference, the dynamic negotiation of the psychological space which separates patient from therapist, and the formulation of the interpersonal relationship springing up between them. Finally, there is the prediction of the relationship which the patient is likely to form with the analytic group which he or she is to join.

The isolating nature of symptoms

The function of symptoms is to draw attention to a problem in the organism as a whole. A problem, or a set of problems, has been isolated and in some way rendered conspicuous. In interpersonal terms, a particular relationship, or even an entire network, such as a family, can be symptomatic.

The mind in isolation produces symptoms which the patient locates in one or other part of his or her network. Feelings demand thoughts, and thoughts attach themselves to specific relationships, or to the body itself. These become invested with symptomatic power which the therapist has to help the patient to translate into communicable language.

Distressing states of mind

Many patients begin their narrative by describing a state of mind
which troubles them. Commonly these are expressed as anxiety, fear,
depression, anger, shame or loneliness, each of which term has its
own multiplicity of synonyms and interpersonal contexts. In some
cases the root of the problem is located in another person or a group
of people, with whom the patient has, or has had, a meaningful relationship. In other cases, the problem is lodged, apparently without
meaning, within the self. The therapist's immediate task is to help
the patient to map out the symptoms in their interpersonal and
social context, present and past.

The following section describes some of the common starting
points for this encounter, and looks at how they express themselves
in the context of group analysis.

Anxiety in its many guises

> The prospect of being hanged in the morning concentrates the mind
> wonderfully.   Dr Samuel Johnson

Behind the dry humour of Dr Johnson lies a shrewd insight. The
emotion which we call anxiety helps us to concentrate on a sharply
circumscribed area inside the vast field of our consciousness, so that
we can mobilize a plan of action to deal with any unpleasant events
which might be stirring within it. The word 'anxiety' comes from the
Greek word for 'strangulation'. Like the related word 'angina', which
refers to the pain of coronary artery narrowing, it conveys a sense of
constriction, tightening, or cutting off. Some parts of the mind have
to be cut off to enable other parts of the mind, those concerned with
the function of alerting us to outside threats, to come into play.

The trouble with this deeply ingrained survival mechanism is that
it reduces our capacity for reflective thinking, an impairment which
works against the culture of analytic therapy, which relies on self-
reflection, contemplation of others and reverie as vehicles of change.
Extremely anxious patients often have to be guided towards a calmer
state of mind before they are ready to face a group. Some of the challenges to prevailing personal defences that occur during the course
of group analysis are intrinsically anxiety-provoking. The culture of

an analytic group is also one of containment, however, and this counteracts the processes which produce anxiety.

Are some people not anxious enough?

The absence of manifest anxiety can be deceptive. Some people who come for therapy appear, on the face of it, to be surprisingly un-anxious. The popular myth of the patient who is not anxious enough has arisen from a confusion between conflictual anxiety (or 'neurotic' anxiety, as it has been called) and organized anxiety, which is outside self-awareness. Confident and cheerful social facades are often flimsy and can belie deep underlying anxiety. When apparent lack of anxiety is coupled with violent or antisocial behaviour, the individual is often harbouring a state of great inner tension. Addressing this has to be the first port of call in a group.

Repressed anxiety affects the capacity to empathize, and may be associated with callous behaviour towards others. When this spills over into sustained patterns of antisocial behaviour which permeate the individual's relationship with society, the construct of a personality disorder is invoked, which has been called psychopathic. Such people appear to lack anxiety. The roots of this form of unacknowledged anxiety may lie in severe or prolonged traumatic experiences such as sustained abuse, dislocated attachments and catastrophic losses.

The question of whether these patients fall outside the recovery zone of group analysis is an open one. When anxiety has performed such a massive dissection of the psyche as to cut off empathic and identificatory functions, the reservoir of rage and shame which only finds expression in destructive behaviour may have to be tapped in homogeneous groups in special settings, if it is to be reached at all.

The group, by virtue of its function as a container, is a good medium for the reduction of anxiety. A person with high levels of anxiety is likely to pitch in with appeals for symptomatic relief and immediate, action-based solutions to interpersonal problems, but soon discovers the dissipation of anxiety in the calmly accepting way in which the group responds, and the discovery that he or she is not alone in this predicament. Sometimes, however, the level of anxiety is such, either inside the group or between group sessions, that the container function of the group may have to be complemented by individual sessions.

Phobias, panic attacks and obsessional thoughts

This triad of symptoms is grouped together because they are all accompanied by high levels of anxiety and because they often occur together in the same person. They baffle both patient and therapist by appearing out of nowhere, intruding into consciousness and capturing the attention of the patient despite efforts to banish them. Often there is no discernible connection between the content of the unbidden thoughts which accompany these high anxiety states, and the manifest reality of the patient's life. A caring mother will be assailed by the thought that she will stab her child if she comes across a knife, or a healthy man in the throes of a panic attack might be convinced that he is about to die of a heart attack. It is as if a part of the patient's mind has cut itself adrift from its roots in the unconscious layers of the mind and erupted into conscious awareness, threatening to overwhelm, or impelling the person to act meaninglessly and ritualistically.

The fact that there is often no immediately discernible connection between the symptom and the rest of the patient's life poses a therapeutic problem to the group. Phobic anxiety, panic attacks and obsessional thoughts all serve to isolate the patient from his or her interpersonal world. The very existence of these symptoms sets up a barrier between the patient and those with whom he or she is in a relationship, and imposes a secondary dynamic on these relationships, based on the need to control others. Through the symptoms the patient possesses a power that was previously lacking. There is an awareness that this is a spurious power which depends on the preservation of the symptoms and the preparedness of others to submit, but this awareness merely heightens anxiety.

These symptoms can be understood in terms of emotional paralysis, a powerful convergence of conflicting impulses riding on a set of conflicting attitudes. Anger and compassion towards a loved one, or fear of abandonment and rage against intrusion are frequent examples of dichotomous thought processes which heighten anxiety. In a group, such patients may at first make light of their interpersonal difficulties and focus relentlessly on their symptoms. The interpersonal culture of the group helps them, however, to define the conflicting assumptions underlying their fears and connect them with the relationships which generated them in the first place.

In the first few sessions the group usually succeeds in reducing the experience of isolation which plagues the highly anxious patient. Almost invariably, someone else in the group comes forward as a fellow-sufferer. Even those who have never been clinically labelled as suffering from conditions such as phobic anxiety or panic disorder confess to related experiences and show that they can empathize with the patient.

The reporting of phobic symptoms tends to diminish and the patient's interest and preoccupation shifts to the interpersonal arena of the group. While panic-driven, irrational thoughts can recede, obsessional thinking is probably less tractable, especially if it forms the pervasive amalgam of disturbing thoughts and actions known as obsessive compulsive disorder.

The interpersonal context of depression: melancholia becomes mourning

The word 'depression' is surrounded by an aura of acceptability which makes it easier to admit to than some of the more stigmatizing terms for which it serves as a catch-all. Professionals and patients often reach for it as a diagnosis which conveys (correctly) the notion of the suffering incurred by the need to carry a heavy burden. On the other hand, its connotations of vulnerability and helplessness impart to it a stigmatizing quality of its own, which makes many people reluctant to seek help.

Many patients who are depressed are suffering from a clinical entity which may also be amenable to medication, and it would be unwise for the psychotherapist to gainsay the marked relief provided in many instances by anti-depressants. Psychotherapy and anti-depressant medication are not mutually exclusive. Indeed, they are often complementary, although the group analyst who is also a psychiatrist should leave the prescribing to another colleague. Purists who argue that medication interferes with the delicate interpersonal operations which belong to psychotherapy may be overestimating the power of their own skills and underestimating the suffering inflicted by rampant processes which, though in part psychological, also have a chemical substrate.

Group analysts working outside a hospital setting are unlikely to encounter patients with the sort of profound depression which immobilizes mind and body to the point of stupor, accompanied even by hallucinations and delusions. Access to the thinking of such patients reveals a self-image which is at once grandiose and profoundly self-blaming. But this is only a caricature of the dynamics that underlie milder forms of depression. The condition in all degrees of severity carries with it a sense of guilt, an exaggerated perception of harm inflicted, and a difficulty in seeing the world as anything other than a place without hope.

The treatment of depression in the group

The first step in the group-analytic treatment of depression is to reframe it in an interpersonal context. Groups are particularly good at doing this. Even if there is a reluctance to accept that the depression has an interpersonal origin, the group member is likely to agree that it is having an effect on others. This moves the depression into an arena where it can be worked with as a dynamic process, not just a bolus of mental stodge crying out for something active to be done to it within the passive recipient.

Groups generally manage to walk the tightrope between accepting the group member's experience of depression and confronting the distorted thinking which impedes his interpersonal life. Repressed emotions are liberated by the group at a pace which the group member can bear. This is often a slow process. Like recovery from bereavement, it happens in waves, calling for the steady holding and containment which a group provides.

The predominant emotion underlying depression is rage. Yet to many people the idea that they might be harbouring anger, let alone rage, comes as a surprise. The interpersonal context of the group helps the patient to recognize these feelings and redirect them. There is a dawning awareness of an exaggerated sense of guilt and omnipotent responsibility as ultimately unrealistic and self-defeating.

By sharing their own experiences, group members show that it is possible to be angry with people to whom one feels indebted or compassionate – parents, for example – even though they 'knew no better', 'meant well', 'did their best', or 'suffered too'. The depressed person also discovers that it is possible to hate the dead. It is often the conductor's task to steer the group towards a reconstruction of the past, towards the retrieval of good and bad memories. This is an essential stepping stone to the recovery of true grief of which depression is often a pathological variant.

The effect of depression on the group

The depressed person provides a challenge to the group. The helpless posture often evokes frustration and annoyance, which can lead to a withdrawal of the attention initially lavished on the depressed group member. Some group members counter their own fears of destructive omnipotence by resorting to compulsive caring or infantilizing responses. The depressed person's gloomy outlook on life may spread a cloud of pessimism over the group and get them to question the very process of therapy. The therapist may become the sole repository of therapeutic optimism for a while, until other voices find their resonance with a belief in change.

The behaviour which most frustrates the group comes out of a state of narcissistic self-absorption into which the depressed person often sinks. This shows itself as withdrawal from group interaction or an apparent indifference to the troubles and concerns of the other group members. Two or three consistently depressed group members can provide a drag on the group, which calls for a strong counter-balance from group members with contrasting strategies for coping with life's adversities. This has to be borne in mind by the therapist when composing the group.

Suicidal ideation in a group

Suicidal thinking occurs commonly in depression. Both the thought and the act of self-harming or attempting suicide can well up in a number of different mind states. As well as in depressive states, it can arise from the promptings of delusional or hallucinatory experiences, or through a convergence of life events suddenly experienced as unbearable by people already sensitized by previous traumata. It can take place in a state of pseudo-calm dissociation, with premeditation, or in a state of arousal and disinhibition, with very little, if any, premeditation.

The threat of suicide, even if uttered repetitively or histrionically, has to be taken seriously. The group may become alarmed and look towards the therapist to intervene, and it may well be that when this happens, the container effect of the group becomes over-stretched. The therapist may then have to activate the outside network to provide the necessary containment. A group member who is under great tension, and harbouring suicidal or self-harming thoughts, experiences relief and even gratitude when the therapist recognizes the inadequacy of the group framework and the necessity for outside involvement.

Hypomania: the far side of grandiosity

Occasionally a swing towards the manic pole of the biologically driven mood spectrum comes upon the group unexpectedly through a patient who until then might only have experienced depressive episodes. Hypomania is distressing both for the patient (contrary to the myth that it is inevitably accompanied by a sense of wellbeing), and for the group. The hypomanic state is characterized by a heightened state of mental and physical activity, pressure of talk, irritable or aggressive responses to being thwarted, and a pattern of thinking known as 'flight of ideas' in which the person jumps from one idea to the next, the jumps being triggered by random associations or stimuli entering the field of perception. The patient might also tell of extravagant actions and grandiose ideas which are often put into practice with distressing consequences for relatives, and for the patient in retrospect. An emergent hypomanic state calls for the suspension of analytic work, and the conductor's energies may have to be directed towards guiding the person towards psychiatric help. If the conductor decides to introduce a patient with a history of hypomania into a mixed analytic group, it is important to ensure that parallel psychiatric back-up is in place from the outset.

Paranoia and paranoid mechanisms in groups

The words 'paranoia' and 'paranoid' have had a roller-coaster trip of usage through the last hundred years. Having started out as diagnostic terms for specific psychotic illnesses, they have now joined the vocabulary of disparagement and abuse which has been the fate of several other psychiatric terms used to describe disordered states of mind. It has been waggishly observed that 'I have been unjustly treated; you are too sensitive; he is paranoid'. However, paranoid thinking in its more precise clinical sense means that the person is attributing to some outside factor, whether a force, system, person, group of people, or an event, a significance which has a personal bearing, greater than is actually the case.

The diagnostic and descriptive senses of the term 'paranoia' are woven in with a third sense, the psychodynamic, without which it is difficult to make therapeutic sense of the concept. The great break-through in thinking about mental processes, which we now take for granted, came with Freud's discovery of the fluidity of the mind and its capacity to expel aspects of the self which, for whatever reason, cannot be borne at the time, and have to be located elsewhere.

Paranoid thinking has a less pathological aspect in the twin con-cepts of projection and projective identification, both of which find expression in the dynamic interplay of group analysis. Projection aims at eliminating intolerable aspects and fantasies of the self into another person, or group of persons, who are experienced as differ-ent in kind from oneself. Projective identification, on the other hand, seeks out a suitable 'Other' to receive the projections and hold them. It becomes a vivid and immediate communication of the emo-tional state of one person to another who will then experience congruent feelings to those of the projector. If it is the group analyst who is the subject of the projections, he or she will try to hold these feelings or fantasies and process them with the help of a more mature ego, to return them in an acceptable way, at the right time.

Post-traumatic stress disorder

The word 'trauma' derives from the Greek word meaning 'to pierce'. This is an apt metaphor for post-traumatic stress disorder. The con-dition develops when a psychological injury is suddenly inflicted, penetrates the accustomed personal defences and lodges deep with-in the psyche. The term originally had a more circumscribed meaning and was used to refer to the sequelae of massive and unusu-al traumatic events, such as exposure to acts of violence on a large scale, or being caught up in natural disasters. It has since come to be recognized as being much more widely applicable, and now refers to the aftermath of events such as sexual attacks, physical assault, road traffic accidents and muggings.

The symptoms of post-traumatic stress disorder cluster mainly around three protective mechanisms which the mind attempts to construct in the face of such overwhelming stress: avoidance of any context which resembles the one in which the trauma occurred, hypersensitivity to stimuli which resemble those associated with the trauma, and repeated experiences of the event itself, or fragments of it, as if the mind is attempting to expel the traumatic memories and images in the manner of dislodging a foreign body.

Group psychotherapy is applied in two different ways to the treatment of post-traumatic stress disorder. First, there is scope for bringing together people who have shared the same traumatic experience, either in nature (for example victims of domestic violence) or through having been there together (for example victims of a terrorist attack or train crash). This type of homogeneous group calls for specialized techniques which enable the members to reconstruct their experiences, attempt to gain mastery over the emotions, thoughts and images which flood them, and plan creatively for their future.

Second, a person suffering from post-traumatic stress disorder can join a mixed group, provided the condition is not so pervasive that it dominates the person's identity. If this is the case, it is difficult for the person to empathize with the other group members, and there is a risk of isolation, despite efforts by the group to draw him or her into empathic contact with them. If, however, there is some recognition of commonality despite the traumatic experience, good use can be made of an analytic group. The same processes that occur in a guided way in a homogeneous group occur spontaneously and gradually in a mixed group. The conductor should not hurry the process. The traumatic event itself may be surrounded for a long time by a wall of silence, and may only be brought into the group at a late stage through the chance associations of another group member.

Schizophrenia and related psychotic states

The group analyst who runs a mixed group is sometimes faced with a question: should a person be introduced into the group who has suffered a psychotic episode resembling schizophrenia, or who has at some stage carried that diagnosis? There are significant differences between bipolar disorder and the psychoses related to schizophrenia, which point to a more cautious approach towards the group-analytic treatment of the latter in a mixed group. In the case of bipolar disorder, the disturbance of mood, along with the thinking which accompanies it, can recede completely during a period of remission, which may be long or even permanent, with maintenance medication. This frees the person up to work analytically, able to explore the interpersonal context of the illness in the group.

Schizophrenic-type disturbance, on the other hand, is often characterized by progressive changes in the ability to think and feel, which disconnect the person from both the environment and from aspects of the self (the 'splitting' which gives the condition its name). A person afflicted in this way may be unable to pursue a train of thought, or may become preoccupied with inner experiences which cut them off from the social context. The difficulties in communication arising from these disturbances militate against the use of a group milieu designed for the robust interchanges of an analytic nature. There is also good evidence that heightened expression of emotion, especially in a context which might be experienced as critical, constitutes a very real stress for the person prone to schizophrenia, and may provoke a relapse. This should not, however, suggest a nihilistic attitude towards group psychotherapy. It is recognized that even severe or unremitting psychotic states are amenable to psychotherapy in homogeneously constituted groups, where the focus is on social and emotional support, enhancement of life skills, and psycho-education. If such a group is established, care should be taken that there are clear channels of referral and consultation open to a psychiatric network, identified and enlisted in advance.

Borderline states

The concept of a borderline state grew out of an awareness that some people have so precarious a hold on reality that they are easily plunged into profound states of catastrophic anxiety and distorted perceptions of relationships which carry them to the edge of psychotic thinking. In group-analytic psychotherapy this commonly shows itself as an exquisite sensitivity to perceived criticism or rejection from other group members, a proneness to expressions of rage, and repeated bids for the attention of the conductor. Destructive acting out, such as self-harming behaviour, is never far from the surface.

The defences which readily come into play are based on denial, projective identification and splitting, all of which stir the group into anxious efforts to contain and confront the person at the same time.

The conductor's task is to encourage the process of identification with other group members, at the same time protecting them from intemperate attacks. The inner world of the person with a borderline personality structure is in a state of flux. The group setting provides a contrasting framework of constancy and dependability which, over time, allows the person to experience the group members as strong enough to return each week, not having been annihilated, and supportive enough to challenge the persecutory fantasies which the person hurls at them through violent projections.

Therapeutic work with borderline patients is exhausting and challenging. An analytic group allows the person to receive attention both directly and indirectly. It frees them to observe the conductor in action with others and receive confirmation of reality-based experiences. Interventions have to be low-key enough to allow the person to retreat periodically without feeling overwhelmed or over-stimulated, an experience which for the borderline patient is tantamount to the infliction of psychic pain.

In a positive sense, borderline patients deepen the analytic process through their insights into the primitive defences of the other group members. By the same token, they push up the emotional temperature, and some group analysts are wary about introducing more than one such person into a mixed group.

Organic states

The mind reflects changes in the brain arising from pathological processes. These can develop subtly, as in the early stages of a physical illness, or they can declare themselves dramatically, as an 'event' which calls for immediate medical investigation. The group analyst has to be aware of the possibility that subtle changes of a physical nature can mimic psychological states of the sort that bring people into psychotherapy. Especially with older patients, it is important to bear in mind the fact that conditions such as dementia – a progressive and irreversible decline in memory and intellect (of which Alzheimer's disease is only one example) – can masquerade as depression. Patients with dementia go to great lengths to conceal their growing disabilities. They can be depressed as well, and the unsuspecting group analyst might construe their depression, memory lapses or emotional volatility as emanating from purely psychological factors. Once again, the co-existence of physical and mental disturbance, and the insidious slide from moderately to severely disturbed mind states, highlights the importance of keeping lines of communication open between psychotherapists, general practitioners and psychiatrists.

Psychosomatic states

Some group analysts find that patients presenting with persistent psychosomatic problems are difficult to treat in a 'classical' mixed group, and that they are best served in a homogeneous group made up entirely of psychosomatic patients. It is said that they hold back the group by being unable or unwilling to engage in interpersonal relations in the group or indeed to consider their own emotional states. They return time and again to their somatic complaint and insist on presenting it to the group repeatedly. They stick to it 'for dear life', as a group member once expressed it, and resist attempts at translating the somatic pain into its meaning.

However, it is our experience that such patients can do well if placed in the right mixed group. And far from holding the group back, they can contribute to the depth of the group's work.

Vignette
A middle-aged woman who had been in analytic therapy for quite some time had been told by her therapist that she might do better in an analytic group. In the initial interview with the group analyst she said that she had gained a lot from her therapy but that there were 'these persistent abdominal pains'. The group analyst established that these had been thoroughly investigated and no organic cause had been found.

The woman called them 'my pains' and described them at some length. The group analyst was doubtful whether this patient would be able to use group therapy, but she seemed eager to 'give it a try'. She said she trusted her previous therapist and would do as he had told her. After due preparation and well-timed notification of her entry into the group, she joined a mature, well-functioning twice-weekly group, where she was received with care and sympathy for her problem, the abdominal pains.

However, this store of sympathy began to wane alarmingly after her repeated and unchanging monologues about 'the pain', and the group analyst began to wonder whether she had done the right thing by her and by the group, by taking her into the group. Sooner or later the patient would notice that the group members were withdrawing from her and she would be confirmed in her sense of isolation from human contact, a feeling with which she was only too familiar.

Then, one day when she was once again talking about 'my pains', a man suddenly began to cry. He told the group of a childhood event which had come to mind 'from nowhere'. He described being alone in a dark room in his childhood home in a remote Scottish valley. The door was shut and only his mother came in and out. (It emerged later that he must have been kept in isolation with a childhood illness.) Then one day, probably to comfort him, his mother had brought him a budgie. He had got hold of it and he had torn out some of its feathers. 'I was in such a rage', he said, sobbing bitterly. No explanation or interpretation was given. Everyone in the room empathized with the little boy's despair at his isolation. The new patient seemed to be engaged for the first time with someone else's story and she listened with silent attention. The following session she spoke, not of her pain, but of her 'raging tummy'. Eventually the recounting of her pains became less frequent and she engaged more with the other group members. She became progressively in touch with an unhappy, isolated childhood and the resulting rage at what she had experienced as a preoccupied, uncaring family.

How had this been achieved? In group analysis, unconscious material gets stimulated and amplified through the pooling of associations: the condenser phenomenon. In this way, a man in the group had unconsciously resonated to the meaning of the woman's symptom, the repressed rage and aggression. This had enabled him to recall for the first time his destructive childhood rage, and later link it with unwelcome and self-destructive rages in later life. The woman had begun to translate her somatic symptom into its meaning: destructive rage and a deep sense of isolation. This resonance and its expression in the group was a much more effective interpretation than any verbal one could have been.

CHAPTER SEVEN

The start of a new group

The early sessions of a group imprint themselves on the collective mind of the group and influence subsequent communication in the group. Later in the life of the group, the conductor may be surprised or chastened to find him- or herself looking into a mirror which the group holds up, affording a glimpse of his style, manner and utterances during the crucial beginnings of the group. The return to the beginning happens typically when a new person joins. As if by way of an induction ritual, the group exchanges memories of the first session, occasionally with amusement, occasionally as a means of comforting or reassuring the newly arrived member. They frequently reminisce about their trepidation on entering the group and the reception given to them; they remind one another of people who were in the group 'in those days'; and they exchange recollections of what the conductor said and how he or she behaved.

These reminiscences form an important part of the working-through of the individual transference processes. Weeks, months, even years later, group members return to their earliest impressions of the group, as part of the integrative process. Associations may be made to the vivid impressions of a first day at school, or a new job. Family associations also come to mind: the metaphor and actuality of entering a new family, either as a parent or as a child. Emotions swirl around these important beginning moments, commanding analytic attention time and again.

Harold: Let's think about the first session of a new group. Here you are, the conductor, with seven or eight people sitting in the room, who have never met each other before. What are you going to be looking out for within those first few minutes?

Liesel: I would be expecting a circle of fairly worried, slightly frightened people, who don't quite know what to do with themselves. It's a new situation, different from any other social situation they have ever encountered. When people are not told what to do, not given directions, they very quickly fall back on patterns which they've learned throughout life.

Harold: Yes, on top of that there is the anxiety of not knowing anyone else in the room except the conductor. The first session is as close as you can get to the perfect conditions for 'stranger anxiety'. Add to that all the fears which go with a situation where you are expected to talk in a very personal way. It's amazing that people are prepared to put themselves in such a situation in the first place.

Liesel: It is important to remember that the conductor is the only one in the circle who has met everyone before, and has a good bit of information on everyone from the referral and the initial interviews. This gives the conductor a considerable emotional advantage, and therefore a degree of security, which is held for the others, as it were. There is also the security of being in at the very beginning of something, though every group beginning is a new one for the conductor also. No two beginnings are alike.

Harold: What does the conductor do at the very outset? My own inclination is to say something more or less right away, to lower the tension and offer an example of ordinary sociability. I might put words to the fact that while everyone in the room knows me, no one knows anyone else, and that it would be a good idea for people to introduce themselves.

Liesel: I have a slightly different approach. I wouldn't invite them to introduce themselves. I would expect them to do this themselves without prompting, because that is what one usually does in other familiar situations where people with no shared past meet to face a shared future. My aim would also be to reduce anxiety, but in a way which immediately sets up the very new situation where there is free-floating talk without a topic being imposed by any means whatever. Like you, I wouldn't remain completely silent. I would also say that the only one who is known to everyone is me and add that no one is known to anyone else, but then I would go on to make a virtue of this and say what a promising situation it is that we don't have to behave in the way in which we normally behave for the very reason that we don't know one another. I introduce the idea that we are coming to know one another in a very different and new way.

Harold: Perhaps you are quicker than I am to lead them out into analytic waters. I prefer to let them splash around in the shallows of social exchange a bit longer. Let's suppose that in the early moments of the session someone addresses a fairly basic question directly to you, such as, 'Have we begun?' or 'Is this all of us?' How would you respond? Let's say for good measure that this question prompts the rest of the group to look expectantly at you. The ball is in your court, now, isn't it? Or is it?

Liesel: If this is the very beginning of group therapy, during the first session, I would certainly reply to the question. It can be very injurious to self-esteem if someone asks a question and gets a stare back, or no reply, or if the conductor's gaze drifts elsewhere and the question is ignored. I would therefore reply, but in a manner which is slightly different from a direct answer. I would try to make it clear that I want everyone to relax, to observe what goes on inside their mind and body and try to put this into words. I would acknowledge that this is in fact a very difficult task but basically I would put this down as our aim. I would look at the person who asked the question, but I would then look round the circle, addressing everyone equally.

Harold: Yes, I see. You are responding directly to the questioner but tangentially to the question. I don't think anything is lost, though, by giving a fairly factual reply to the question in the first instance. But I wouldn't leave it at that. I would go on and try to find some way of turning the question round, such as: 'Yes, we started on the hour, but what were you wondering to make you ask the question?' I like the idea of following an answer with a question. I'm not fazed by the aphorism I once heard: 'if you ask a question, all you get is an answer'. Instead, I rather like a cartoon I once saw: the patient is lying on the analytic couch, blinded by searchlights. He exclaims in frustration: 'Answers! Answers! All I get is answers! How about a few questions?'

Liesel: Yes, an answer may be the right thing not only because it is the socially expected response, but also because it reduces anxiety to a manageable level. But this is not the usual social situation, and it might be important to demonstrate this so as to get the group going in the desired direction, in other words, the therapeutically optimal direction.

Harold: The first session of a new group generally proves to be less of an ordeal than the therapist expects, doesn't it? I've heard therapists talk of their relief when they see how, within the first few minutes, the group members begin to show curiosity and interest in one another and tell their personal stories. This is where I like to nudge the process along as a conductor, putting in the occasional question myself, addressed perhaps to an individual, perhaps to the group as a whole. I'm more interested in the process which this serves than in the content of the answers. I also think that if therapists join in this low-key way at an early stage they help to demystify themselves and the therapeutic process. I don't believe that this interferes with the transference, which I think will assert itself regardless.

Liesel: Part of the reason for the 'success' of the first session lies in the fact that people often come prepared with opening statements. With the strain of the occasion, people are on their best behaviour, which in this context means offering a socially acceptable version of their problem, one drawn from their repertoire of personal experiences, which is least likely to open them up to unwanted scrutiny. It is usually during the second, third and fourth sessions, when old patterns of introducing oneself, saying a bit of why one is here, have been tried out and have got somewhere, that a full-stop sometimes comes over the group and silence falls because there is no further development on the lines that are usual.

Harold: Yes, I think of it as each person bringing his or her own gramophone record to play in the group at least once That dates me, doesn't it! But I quite like it as a metaphor. After all, groups are scratchy and there's lots of surface noise at times, and they sometimes get stuck in a groove.

Liesel: Sometimes there are one or two group members who come with urgent problems, with great pain, with a family situation going all wrong, or a relationship having broken down, and there is a tremendous urge to unpack and see what the group does with it. This can be quite trying for a group. I remember a first session where a woman broke down and said she had just been told she had breast cancer. A dead silence followed. Clearly the group were overwhelmed by this major problem. So was I as the group conductor, for a while. It was very difficult indeed to deal with both this bombshell and, at the same time, make room for everyone else to feel that they had an equal right to talk about what they considered a much smaller problem. After the first five or ten minutes of this first session a young woman burst into tears and said that her husband had just told her that he was having an affair with another woman and that he wanted a divorce. I was concerned that the first speaker would feel neglected, but in fact that didn't happen. The other thing I was worried about didn't happen either: that everyone else would come up with their own horrific story.

Harold: This makes me think about the whole question of how to deal with a group in which a person, right at the beginning, discloses a highly charged event which takes the group aback. I can think of another example, of a woman who shocked the group by telling them, in graphic detail, about her husband's violent and abusive behaviour towards her. The group at once tried to empower her to take self-protective action. But I was concerned that she might become isolated by the very gravity of her situation and that other group members might feel that their problems could not stand comparison. How might you try to contain a situation like that?

Liesel: This is a difficult situation, but also a very promising one, in which one can actually introduce the group to the very essence of group analysis, which is putting the individual, each individual, into the centre without excluding the others, finding the common ground, not identical problems, but a linking one. For instance, take the abusive relationship. Not everyone in the group has an abusive relationship. Perhaps she is the only one. However, everyone has some sort of experience of violence done to him or her, of a situation in childhood, or at work, where the feelings are not dissimilar. I would therefore acknowledge this by the attention I pay to the one who relates this terrible experience, but would somehow try to widen it and acknowledge that we all know something about it.

Harold: That seems like a good example of converting an isolating experience into exchangeable currency. I sometimes do this by asking the person to suspend the narrative and talk instead about how it feels to tell the group about it. The other group members almost invariably respond to this by reflecting back how it feels to listen to such a terrible story. Suddenly we are all together in it, in the room, with the feelings, instead of a shocked 'audience' listening to an emotionally numbed narrator.

Another difficult situation that springs to mind is an aggressive challenge to the structure of the group early on. Is this common, in your experience?

Liesel: Not in the first few sessions. There seems to be high expectation and a kind of almost Messianic spirit, a trust that for once therapy will deliver the goods. The challenge to my mind is implicit in that there is also a kind of idealization of me as the group conductor. I am seen as knowing where I am going, as knowing what people are going to say and what to do with it. I think the overt challenge comes when, after a while, perhaps after ten or twelve sessions, it dawns on the group that I am not going to deliver the goods in the desired package. An aggressive attack might be made once certainty is reached that the conductor can 'take it', that this is a fairly safe place.

You talked earlier of the relief that therapists feel when group members talk easily during the first session. Do you share that relief?

Harold: Yes and no. I think that lots of talking at the beginning is better than long, sticky silences, which are unlikely to be reflective in nature. But I'm not lulled into complacency by the apparent comfort and ease with which people begin to talk during the first session. I don't see it as an invitation to start making interpretations about the content of the conversations. This is likely to act as a dampener, and I prefer to allow the group to find its own level of analysis in due course. At this stage, all my interventions are directed towards establishing the group as a place in which it is safe to talk and experience the commonality of the group.

Liesel: We seem to lay a different emphasis on the two important elements of group analysis in these early stages: the analytic and the social. You appear to be more cautious about the pace at which you introduce the free floating talk which defines the analytic culture of the group. I am more confident that a group can sustain this culture from the word go.

Harold: Another early concern is the risk of people not returning to the group after only one or two sessions. When I meet these people afterwards they sometimes tell of their experience of being different from the other group members. They have either held on to a position of superiority or they have felt overwhelmed by the enormity of the problems they have heard about. Another exit strategy is to take umbrage at a group member's comment, or pronounce the group unsympathetic.

Liesel: Related to what you say, I have found that some people can react badly to a disturbing disclosure, either because of a resonance to the material, or because they fear that such disclosures are setting a norm which will draw them into similar forced or premature disclosures.

We've talked about how we begin the first session. Let's now compare notes on how we bring the session to an end. How we do it the first few times sets a pattern which the group then follows.

Harold: I always keep a beady professional eye on the clock, especially if an emotional crescendo is building up in the group.

If necessary I start to sound a subduing note well before the end of the session. I don't believe that the session should spill over the time boundary to allow an agitated or distressed person to settle into a more contained frame of mind. On the other hand, I'm not in favour of robotic precision either. If a session ends on too abrupt a note, the group can be left feeling bewildered or frustrated, and someone is likely to leave feeling bruised. I try to find a bridging intervention as a way of linking the present to the future, for example: 'This is an important issue. I don't think we're going to be able to do it justice now, but let's put it on hold till next time.' Or: 'We need to think more about this one. Let's talk about it again next time'.

Liesel: The key concept for me here is containment, and I like your examples. Another way of providing containment towards the ending of the first session is to make some unifying pronouncement which sounds a positive note. I sometimes knit together the material of several group members to demonstrate a coherent theme. This affirms the group in its analytic task. However, I am careful to avoid obscure associations to primitive material for which the group might not be ready. I think of Foulkes's injunction to avoid 'plunging interpretations' – connections which stir such deep anxieties that the group either ignores them entirely or tries to grapple with them in an intellectualized manner without making true analytic headway. Such interventions are likely to puzzle some or all of the group members and usually have the effect of reassuring only the conductor. It is occasionally helpful to end the early sessions with a question directed at one of the more vulnerable group members. Examples might be: 'What has the session been like for you?' or 'How do you feel now compared with at the beginning of the session?' This helps the person to put into words any resistance which may be building up, and thereby render it accessible to therapeutic intervention. 'See you next week' is an encouraging parting note to the group as a whole, which reinforces the sense of belonging.

Harold: What clues would you be on the lookout for to suggest that a group member has not engaged in the group, or is thinking of withdrawing from the group at this early stage?

Liesel: I watch particularly for signs of disaffection, hostility or anxiety in relation to the group. These can be obvious, and there is a good possibility of averting a departure from the group if the non-engagement is expressed verbally. The group then works with the resistance behind the manifest objections and we stand a good chance of retaining the person in the group. But it is easier to overlook the more subtle, nonverbal features of disengagement: a downcast posture, preoccupied manner, or lack of interest in others, or an attempt to change the focus. The ambivalent group member often snaps the thread of associations and rebuffs invitations to join in.

Harold: I would add latecoming and absence to the list of premonitory signs of disengagement from the group. Persistent silence in the group is another sign, especially as a counterpoint to earlier lively involvement. I have noticed that group members who are going to leave the group badly will become emotionally absent even though they are still physically present. I suppose it is true that any of these warning signs can occur at any time in the life of the group, but I believe that they need special attention from the conductor in the early stages of the group because the other group members are simply not confident enough to pick up on them. The therapist may also have to show the way when there are strong expressions of affect such as profuse crying, prolonged outbursts of anger and conspicuous mutism. I prefer to engage directly with the protagonist, which may be necessary before the group can mobilize its own resources to deal with these emotions.

Is modelling part of our repertoire in group analysis? I believe it is.

Liesel: The analytic situation of the group is one from which the usual social props have been removed. We as conductors are going to be keenly scanned for clues on how to behave, because the group is new and bewildering in nature. I know that my reactions, what I show interest in, where I direct my attention, what I ignore, are going to be noticed, and to some extent copied. All this is grist to the analytic mill.

Harold: I think that the emotional style of the conductor is equally important. A conductor who shows curiosity and a spirit of enquiry stimulates those attributes in the group members.

Conversely, conductors who adopt a position of lofty detachment and confine themselves to pronouncing group interpretations which have the ring of finality, offer a model of leadership which sets them apart from the group, and I think this has an adverse effect on the group's ability to be spontaneous and confident.

Liesel: All that is true, but it is even more complicated than that. The therapist models not only styles of enquiry but roles. You as a male therapist and I as a female therapist will be closely observed in our interactions with the men and women in the group. And we will be scrutinized for evidence of our ethnic and cultural identity and our sexual orientation, not to mention where we stand on a host of social, political and cultural issues, and what values we espouse. Some of these characteristics are more visible than others, but all of them are heavily invested with transference projections, which sooner or later will come to form part of the analytic dialogue in the group. I find that I am anxious about excessive confrontation early on in the group. What do you do about that?

Harold: In general, I am inclined to step in sooner rather than later. Beginning groups are unsure about the level of confrontation permitted or expected. They may err either on the side of anxious avoidance, thus allowing an anti-therapeutic process to run rampant, or they may try to foster a culture of vigorous exchange ('tell it like it is') which rides roughshod over social sensitivities. This could alarm some members and produce aggressive and even sadistic exchanges which are anti-therapeutic at this stage.

Liesel: It is in the early stages of the group that the therapist has the greatest power to influence the culture towards a reflective and analytic mode. It seems to me that it is the manner and language of the confrontation that chiefly determines its success.

How would you summarize the main difference between the conductor's technique during the early sessions of the group and his technique once the analytic culture has become established?

Harold: I would see it mainly in terms of how active we are. We have to accept that at the beginning we are perceived as the repository of expertise in the business of therapy.

Or, to put it another way, we are on the receiving end of omniscient and omnipotent projections. We have to disabuse the group gradually of these fantasies, and at the same time we have to introduce them to the analytic culture. So I would hope that as time goes by we don't have to be so active, in the sense of making the connections, conducting the analytic enquiry, confronting and containing. The group members take over much of the analysing function, and the conductor slips more into the background, but never disappears entirely.

CHAPTER EIGHT

A newcomer to the group

LOW ON NUMBERS FOR HIS GROUP, DR STEIN CREATES A
NEW GROUP MEMBER, WHOM HE INTRODUCES SIMPLY AS FRANK

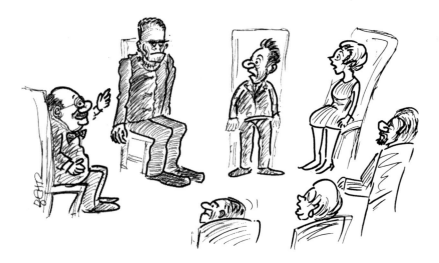

Successful entry into the group is helped by adequate preparation. The therapist shares with the potential new entrant the belief that group-analytic psychotherapy is the optimal treatment for that person. The therapist also owes the potential group member some information about the group which is being proposed. The days of cryptic injunctions to enter therapy and minimalistic instructions on how to behave in a group belong to another era.

Preparing the newcomer

The newcomer's preparation takes place in the individual setting. It begins during the first assessment interview, and if need be, it can be spread through a number of individual sessions. However, during this period, the patient may establish a strong transference relationship, which will have to be adjusted in the group if the patient is to share the therapist and relate to the others in the group. For this reason, some group analysts confine this dyadic relationship to a minimum. Our own preference, however, is to offer ourselves as a secure anchor in the turbulence of entry into an unknown situation. A significant proportion of the individual sessions is devoted to working with the issues which the patient brings. Eventually a way has to be found to weave into the dialogue a pattern of connections which link the patient to his future group.

What sort of information is given to the patient about the group? Much depends on the therapist's estimation of the patient's expectations and fears of the group and acquaintance with psychotherapy in general and group therapy in particular. Descriptions of the process of therapy are pitched at a level which can be understood and absorbed by the patient. This is another reason for staggering the preparatory process over more than one individual session.

Preparing the group

The new group member has been prepared for entry into the group, but what about the group itself? What does it mean to the group to receive a new member when it is working in full swing to its own and the therapist's satisfaction? The group also needs preparation for the newcomer's entry for, however often this event has been experienced in a slow-open group, it is new every time, and changes the group fundamentally.

What does 'preparation' mean in the context of a new person joining an established group? A group which has been disturbed by the unexpected or angry departure of one of its members will need a time-scale of preparation different to that which would apply to a group which has warmly said goodbye to a veteran group member whose leaving has been thoughtfully worked through and who has departed on a note of mutual acceptance. A depleted group which has been suffering from ragged attendance and fretting about its survival will have different expectations of a newcomer compared with a group which has been pulsing with full attendance and keen analytic activity. A group which has experienced a specific trauma, such as the death of a member, needs more time to work through the experience. The departure of a previous member, on whatever note, has to be worked through in its own time, a process which also continues after the arrival of the new member.

Vignette

In a mature, well-functioning group, a much loved group member had left after a long and successful period in therapy. His leaving was well-prepared – a process akin to mourning – accompanied by joyful reflections on this success story for the group. The date for the entry of the new member had been announced well in advance. When the new person entered the group room there were some polite greetings, after which the group all but ignored him. This induced the conductor, a woman, to turn frequently to the new group member, a man, asking him for his view on what was being talked about and encouraging him to join in with his own feelings, thoughts and information about himself.

This degree of intervention was unusual, and the group was puzzled by it. The group's reaction veered from mild reproach to envious anger: why was the newcomer being given so much attention and protection? Someone recalled that she had not been treated like this by the therapist on her entry into the group. Someone else observed how quickly one could be forgotten and replaced. The group spoke of the member who had left, implying that they wished he were here instead of the newcomer. The conductor became increasingly anxious for him: would he survive such a reception? Would he be back for the next session? She was also surprised to find herself angry with the group: how could they be so cruel and inconsiderate towards the newcomer? She had expected them to be receptive, helpful, working with her and not against her in her endeavour to fill the vacant place in the ranks of the group. The newcomer, on the other hand, was strangely unperturbed by this reception. He turned up for the next session and stayed on in the group to his and the group's benefit. When he was later asked about his first experience of the group, he said: 'It was what I was used to from my family. I wasn't shown any welcome there either.' When he revealed the roots of his resigned acceptance, he evoked an immediate empathic response and became a full member of the group.

If we consider this sequence, we can trace the unconscious impact which the entry of a new group member had on the group. In spite of careful preparation and a time lapse between the departure of one group member and the arrival of another, the process of separation, deprivation and loss had not yet been worked through. It never is, in the time given, and needs to surface repeatedly. It is a sign of a well-working group that conventional behaviour is replaced by the expression of real feelings, however uncivil and even cruel these may be. There was envy over the concern the therapist had shown the newcomer and the special attention she had given him. She had become the mother who devoted herself to the new baby in the family, to the neglect and detriment of the other children. The conductor, for her part, experienced unusual feelings of disappointment and anger, and a feeling of being let down by the group. Some of these feelings clearly belonged to her. She had, after all, acted carefully and professionally. But a good part of these feelings were put into her by way of projective identification. She was given a strong, irrefutable message by the group exactly how it felt in this new situation.

All this took place on an unconscious level. It had to be named and interpreted, linked with the group history as well as the personal histories of the participants. It may well be that the group had unconsciously reacted to the emotional state of the new member as it had been shaped by his previous experiences. This group had after all received other entrants very differently. Perhaps this is a case of having to trust the group, at least as much as one trusts oneself, to sense what is acceptable at a given time and what is not.

The timing of a new person's entry into a group

Time is one consideration. Timing is another. If ill-timed and ill-prepared, the introduction of a new member can be experienced as a disturbance and will be greeted with resistance. Even with careful preparation and timing, the entry of a new person is an episode in the life of a group which is charged with anxiety for everyone, often recalled subsequently by newcomers as a crucial determinant of their attitude towards the whole therapeutic process.

The point at which the new person joins may be close to a holiday break, perhaps too close to allow that person to feel grounded in the matrix of the group before having to step out again for a period. By the same token, group members need enough time to reach out to the new member, to help that person to make an opening statement, deal with any flurries of anxiety, outpourings of highly charged material, or unexpected firecrackers of the sort which can go off when strangers encounter each other.

In general, a new group member should have a run of at least four or five uninterrupted sessions in the group before any break supervenes. If the span is any less than that, it is better to postpone the person's entry until after the break, and if necessary, set up some individual sessions to span the extended interval. The question then arises: how soon after a break should the person join the group? Opinion divides here. The fact that the group needs to reconstitute itself after a period of separation and work through the inevitable ripples of anger and reproach which surround breaks before having to cope, as well, with a new face in the group, deters some therapists from conflating the two events. Other therapists, ourselves included, see no particular merit in separating out the two events, provided the group is judged resilient enough to remain on an even working keel. We would therefore be inclined to introduce the new person at the first group session after the break. The group and the newcomer can make a fresh start together, and there is even an advantage in providing the newcomer with space to listen to the 'old-timers' catching up: recapitulating personal issues and registering changes in their lives.

Vignette

Two members had left the group and had not yet been replaced. The group then developed a closeness and intimacy which was enjoyed by all. The conductor felt that the group was working well in an atmosphere of trust and empathy. There was a marked absence of dissent and aggression. Curiously, the talk often returned to memories of aggressive behaviour by one or other of the two departed members. This made the conductor aware of a deficit in the present group: a whole range of experiences in relationships had left the group along with the departed members. The group had delegated these unpleasant and unacceptable feelings to them, and had thus created an atmosphere of pseudo-consent and denial. When the aggressiveness of one of the departed members was mentioned yet again, the conductor voiced her thoughts.

This evoked the reply: 'Whenever we are happy and close, you come in to destroy it. You are happy only when we are at each other's throats.' A man said: 'My wife says that I have been nasty at home lately. She says I should take this to the group, not to our home.' Someone else said, 'We are only five people here. Perhaps we are afraid to attack in case someone else leaves.' The conductor realized that now was the time to bring in new members. She did not ask the group for permission, mindful of the important dictum that the setting to which the composition of the group belongs is entirely the responsibility of the group analyst.

Introducing more than one person into a group

If the group is open to the entry of more than one person, another situation arises. The advantage of bringing in two newcomers at the same time is that the period of turbulence created by the new entrants is foreshortened. An additional benefit is that a certain degree of companionship is afforded to the newcomers during the early, anxiety-provoking encounter with a group of strangers. Issues of mirroring, mutual identification, separateness and individuation frequently arise, often expressed through associations to twins. These offer interesting opportunities for working through in the transference.

A group which tries to exclude a newcomer

Attempts to exclude a newcomer are sometimes disguised as considerateness. A group so challenged may cite the wish not to intrude, offering, by way of justification, reminiscences of their own daunting experiences on joining the group. However, there is a difference between 'letting be' and 'ignoring'. The latter is frequently a resentful device, even a precursor to scapegoating, and deserves analytic attention. The conductor may have to judge whether this is the case, or whether the group's sense of timing is grounded in a genuinely welcoming attitude.

More difficult to manage is a group which actively rounds on newcomers, to put them in their place, as it were. The newcomer's well-intentioned efforts to suggest solutions or ask questions may be angrily received as showing a lack of insight or sensitivity, and any tentative personal statements may be given short shrift. This is another variant of the scapegoating mode which has to be treated accordingly.

The newcomer who is too obtrusive

Some new entrants into a group display a narcissistic obliviousness to the pre-existence of the group culture and seize the limelight, and with scant or no encouragement, set about delivering a dramatic or tedious account of their predicament. Attempts by the group to staunch the flow are frustrated, and the conductor may become aware of a general disengagement by the group. Here the conductor has to lead from the front in containing and confronting the obtrusive newcomer, or group monopolizer, as such people have been called.

The dynamic to be aware of is an all-or-nothing oscillation, between self-absorbed narration and uninterested withdrawal from the group. To bridge these poles the conductor may have to interrupt the narrative without withdrawing the focus from the person. This can be done by moving from the content of the material to the impact of its telling in the here-and-now. A comment such as: 'You've given us a lot to think about already; let's see how others feel about what you've said' changes the focus without inflicting too much narcissistic injury.

'We've met before!'

Although this might seem like an improbable scenario, it is not that uncommon, especially when the group is drawn from a pool of patients within a small community or locality, or when it is composed of individuals working in related professional fields. It is a dreaded scenario for most people entering an analytic group, who want to begin their therapy with a *tabula rasa* and who quite rightly expect watertight confidentiality.

The situation usually declares itself as soon as the new person enters the room, and calls for immediate clarification by the conductor of the context and nature of the relationship. Sometimes the connection is remote and tenuous enough to be sustained by the group, but the conductor has to be aware of anxious compliance on either or both sides, and if there is any sign of reluctance, the offer should be made to place the newcomer in another group. Failure to do this may result in one or other protagonist dropping out further down the line. Before introducing a new person, the conductor should scan the existing membership of the group pre-emptively, especially in terms of their professional, institutional, ethnic and religious affiliations, especially if the new person lives or works close to another group member.

Silence of the newcomer

A newcomer to the group frequently defers to the group at first, but sooner or later finds a way in, either through a tentative enquiry or opinion on another person's issue, or with a self-disclosing statement which hints at a willingness to introduce personal material. If it seems likely that the entire session will run its course without the new person giving anything other than a name, it is worth drawing him or her in before the end of the session. The act of speaking symbolizes engagement, and it does not matter too much what is said. The conductor only needs to ask one or two enabling questions of the newcomer, relating perhaps to other people's material, and then develop the dialogue if the rest of group is tardy or neglectful in its responses. By the second or third session, the new member should have found an opportunity to say something about the reasons for joining the group, and the group should have begun to resonate to that material. Persistent silence suggests a resistance to engagement, the basis of which is best explored sooner rather than later, with the help of a sensitively placed question or two. The answer to these may provide a clue to the nature of the underlying resistance to join in.

Opening gambits which antagonize the group

An established group has a culture of participation which is at once affiliative, analytic and challenging. This is a culture which has to be learnt by the newcomer. The group for its part has to be prepared to accept the new person's efforts to join, which may at first seem to jar on the analytic culture. These efforts can take the form of simplistic advice giving, interrupting someone's narrative with a change of topic, addressing the conductor to the exclusion of the group, or criticizing the group for what is perceived as a superficial or irrelevant conversation. Groups are generally good at leading the new member towards the realization that the customary social repertoire has to be suspended in the analytic situation. However, the conductor has to be on the alert for a group which has become precious and intolerant, and may have to protect the new person and even support well-intentioned efforts to bring a fresh perspective to the group. It is important not to send the new person away with the feeling of not belonging, and that their contributions are not valued.

Bringing the newcomer into the communication exchange

Some groups are adept at bringing a newcomer in with respectfully phrased opening questions or facilitating remarks. Most new entrants welcome an expression of interest in them which goes beyond the usual perfunctory exchange of names. However, if the group appears to be avoiding this, the conductor may have to show the way. The first session for a new person should not be allowed to go by without some intervention from the therapist which enables the new person to speak. It is probably better for the therapist to address the newcomer directly than to try and orchestrate a group response by interpreting their resistance or avoidance, although at some point these issues too will have to be addressed. The reticent newcomer may find it easier, in the first place, to be asked about their reaction to another group member's predicament, with a prompt such as: 'Does this ring any bells for you?' This serves the twin purpose of eliciting participation while maintaining a distance, and at the same time mobilizing the newcomer's native therapeutic skills from the very outset. The alacrity with which the group responds will give a good indication of the newcomer's social currency at the beginning stage of the therapeutic journey.

The successful integration of a new person

The therapist can breathe a sigh of relief once the new group member has begun to venture thoughtful observations about the other group members, and to ask interested questions about them and the group, especially if they are appreciated and taken up analytically. Another good sign is a positive report from the new member about their initial experience of the group. A critical moment for integration into the group arrives at the point where the new member brings the narrative of his life, the *raison d'être* for coming into group therapy.

This generally happens within the first three or four sessions of the newcomer's attendance. If it happens during the first session, the conductor may suspect that what is being presented is a well-rehearsed opening statement. The patient is sometimes impelled by an anxious determination to gain acceptance from the group, to secure a place, as it were, among the ranks of those with serious life issues. Or a new group member may be driven by a sense of urgency, a wish to 'get on with it', to get down to the business of therapy and claim the attention of the therapist and the group. The newcomer may come in spontaneously with their narrative, it may be prompted by the therapist or invited by one or two of the group members.

In whatever way entries and exits take place in ongoing, slow-open groups, one must keep in mind that these are seminal events for the group and for each member of the group. Beginnings and endings, arrivals and departures, are existential points in the life of the individual. Their negotiation throughout life will be influenced by the first experiences in the family of origin and subsequent life events. They are re-experienced in the slow-open group, re-arranged, re-evaluated, corrected, and metabolized to strengthen or rebuild the personality. Entrances and exits therefore deserve the utmost care in group analysis.

CHAPTER NINE

The group in action

" SHUSH! DON'T WAKE HIM — HE MIGHT BE
HAVING A GROUP DREAM "

A good group ... breeds and develops, creates and cherishes, that
precious product, the human individual.   S.H. Foulkes

Group analysis rests on a paradox: the conductor is the only person
in the group who carries the authority of a professional therapist, yet
it is the group as a whole which carries the therapeutic authority. In
order to embrace both wings of this paradox, the conductor has to
move adroitly between two positions: one which allows the group to
determine the flow of the therapy, and one which enables the conductor to assert his or her own therapeutic authority when
necessary, perhaps against the current of the group at the time. The
conductor also has to enable the individual members to do their own

analytic work. In the Foulkesian model the conductor is not the only 'analyst-therapist' in the group, and should not do the group's work for it. Instead, the conductor carries out a constant monitoring operation, sometimes verbally and actively, sometimes silently.

Analysis by the group

The conductor, in the capacity of dynamic administrator, has created the setting, and will maintain it in an optimal condition throughout the group's life. This situation provides the frame of reference for all processes, relationships and events in the group and on its boundaries (Pines, 1981). This is so because it is the group itself which is the active agency for change; the therapeutic agency, so to speak.

In one sense the conductor is simply a member of the group, penetrated and influenced by the group processes. At the same time he or she is also outside these processes, maintaining the free-floating attention which is needed to monitor them. Because of the professional role, the conductor is also a special transference object in the group, less 'real' and less open to reality testing than the other members of the group. This apparent contradiction creates a transference situation different from that of the psychoanalytic dyad.

How much of a blank screen can the group analyst be?

How 'real' should the conductor be for the group members? Being real could mean giving personal information, relating personal experiences, revealing emotional reactions, expressing curiosity or voicing personal, theoretical or ideological biases. The 'blank screen' concept lies at one end on a continuum of self-disclosure. The underlying intention is that the conductor should present him- or herself to the group in a manner which leaves the group undisturbed by any personal information. The argument is that, if transferential projections are to come the group analyst's way, the less personal information the group members have, the easier it is for their fantasies to emerge uncensored by reason or reality.

However, the technique which originated in a dyadic setting runs into trouble in a group setting. The setting in which group analysis takes place, the circle, influences all the phenomena that occur, including the conductor's transparency. As part of the circle, observable by the group members, it is questionable how much of a blank screen can be present under such conditions. The blank screen technique also comes into conflict with the modelling function of the group analyst, which calls for the open expression of interest in others through both verbal and nonverbal communication. A more or less inscrutable conductor inadvertently or intentionally attracts undue transferential attention and in so doing assumes an exaggerated importance in relation to the other members of the group.

So when does the conductor come into foreground, either as a transference figure or as a real person? One situation would be an undue focus on another group member, which represents a displacement from the conductor, such as might happen in an incipient scapegoating process. Another indication arises when the conductor is aware of being the centre of a powerful transference reaction, emanating either from an individual or from the group as a whole, which is blocking inter-group communication. In our view, transference interpretations which consistently put the conductor into the centre of the group tend to give him or her disproportionate weight and power, at the expense of the other members of the group and the group as a whole.

Negative transference distortions concerning the therapist can be voiced more freely in a group than in the dyad of individual psychotherapy. The presence of others makes such expressions feel safer. The imagined retribution from the therapist is diffused by an array of responses from others and by the holding function of the group itself.

In our own practice, we strive to achieve a balance between personal involvement and professional reserve. The dilemma is well exemplified when the conductor announces an absence for one or more sessions or cancels a session unexpectedly. Should the reason for the absence be given? And how should the inevitable questions be dealt with? A response of total silence in the face of such a question is only likely to increase the anxiety of the group or some group members to an intolerable level. We incline towards a more analytically 'neutral' approach in the first instance, replying with a question aimed at bringing out the fantasies, such as: 'I wonder what you think'. Having allowed the fantasies and feelings to emerge, however, it is respectful to give some explanation for the impending absence, accompanied, perhaps by a minimum of detail. The conductor must feel comfortable with the level of personal disclosure being offered. At the same time, he or she is governed by a professional judgement of what is best for the group at that time. However, it is a reassuring thought that whatever is done will be subject to transferential distortion.

Vignette
A therapist came to the group session straight from a hairdresser's appointment because she had to attend a formal reception that same evening. She was immediately challenged by two women. One said that the therapist looked younger – she liked her much better like this. The other said, with much emotion, that she hated the hairdo. On this occasion the therapist was content to remain silent. This allowed the varying transference reactions to emerge. The violently expressed dislike had been engendered by a memory of her mother, a socialite who would appear in the nursery at bedtime 'all dolled up with a different hairdo every time' and leave the child in the care of an indifferent babysitter. The woman who had taken pleasure in the therapist's hairdo spoke of her wish to have a younger therapist who, she said, would understand her lifestyle and her wishes better.

Self-disclosure on the part of the therapist also depends on the state of the group. A mature group which has taken in the language of therapy will be better able to move from the external to the internal, from reality to fantasy, and will be able to use both in the service of emotional growth.

Another aspect of the setting has to be considered in this context: anxiety which is heightened by the withholding of reality information may be sustainable and therapeutically productive for a group that meets weekly, but possibly not for a group that meets in block sessions with long intervals. In effect, the degree of conductor transparency, the withholding of information as opposed to its disclosure, depends on the state of the group, the time setting of the sessions, and above all, on the personality of the group analyst. This is an aspect often denied under the guise of professionalism. Groups are highly skilled at getting to know the person of the therapist behind the mask of the professional.

The nature and timing of interventions by the conductor

The ideal moment for the conductor to intervene is when someone in the group, or the group as a whole, seems very near to achieving an insight, a new way of experiencing – a translation from primary to secondary process thinking, from 'split-off' to integrated, from projected to accepted – but is not quite there. The conductor helps to bring it to life, as it were, rather like a midwife delivering a newborn infant. The silent monitoring of the conductor enables the group to experience rather than translate these insights into secondary thinking. In this way the conductor stays with the group instead of outpacing it.

The conductor should also be prepared to intervene – sooner rather than later – if the group is engaged in interactions which are unproductive or if the group is drifting in a counter-therapeutic direction. Here it falls to the conductor to lead the way, and if necessary change the direction in which the group is heading. The question of whether or not a group is veering off course is a difficult one. On the one hand, the conductor runs the risk of making a gratuitous intervention, distracting the group or pre-empting a therapeutic process which might already be in full flow. On the other hand, by not intervening there is a risk of allowing a counter-therapeutic process to run its course to a destructive conclusion, such as a sadistic attack by one group member on a vulnerable other. It is in the achievement of a balance between these two risks that the art of group analysis lies.

The concept of interpretation in group analysis

Interpretation in the strictly psychoanalytic sense occupies a less prominent place in the repertoire of the group analyst than it does in that of the individual analyst. Nor is it an activity confined to the group conductor. The contribution of every group member, as well as the collective voice of the group, can act as an interpretation in the broader sense of linking apparently unconnected phenomena in order to bring about a greater awareness of the origins and meaning of a particular utterance.

It is probably more helpful to think of interpretation as a process of translation. This is a concept which Foulkes invested with special significance in the therapeutic process. He saw it as an all-embracing term for the whole task of deciphering the code of the unconscious, the group equivalent of making the unconscious conscious (Foulkes, 1964, p.81). Interpretation, he argued, was simply one of the means by which the process of translation could be realized. A related concept in this exercise is that of location. This is a process of mapping out disturbance, behaviour and other events in the group matrix. In order to do this, the conductor has to be aware of the particular configuration of observable phenomena prevailing at the time. Once this has happened, it becomes possible to sense the level at which the group is communicating at that moment. To be understood, the conductor has to speak back to the group at the same level. With these tools at his or her disposal, the conductor is able to help the group to proceed from the symptom in its widest sense to the underlying conflict.

When the conductor does offer an interpretation, therefore, care is needed to use words and images which match the prevailing language of the group. Interpretations which boldly attempt to bridge the gap between the manifest content of the group's interactions and the group's primary process relationships, an underlying Oedipal struggle, for example, can sometimes perplex the group and provoke intellectualized responses or aversive silences. Foulkes referred to such interpretations as 'plunging' interpretations which ill-serve the group-analytic purpose of allowing the group itself to arrive at deeper connections in its own way and time (Foulkes, 1975).

The conductor's manifest behaviour in relation to the stage of the group

The conductor's interventions, behaviour and self-presentation in the group will be different in a mature group compared with, say, a beginning group or a group which is in the concluding phase of therapy. The demands on the conductor in this respect are simpler in a closed group, but become more complicated in a slow-open group, where members are at different stages in their therapy. In the early stages of the group the conductor is perceived as omnipotent and omniscient. Later in the life of a group, at moments of crisis, when breaks are imminent, or in the face of loss, individuals or the group as a whole might return to this fantasy.

The conductor's transformation from near-deity to real person cannot be accelerated, either by intentional reticence or by interpretation. One function of the conductor at this stage, therefore, and to a greater or lesser extent throughout the group's life, is to accept and hold the projections and projective identifications, and to feed them back, in a modified form, at the right time (Ogden, 1979). This applies to group projections as well as individual ones. The return of these projections is then used to widen and deepen the transpersonal and interpersonal communications within the group, as opposed to the fostering of a conductor-centred, heavily distorted transference relationship of each member to the conductor only.

Projective identification also occurs between group members, and requires sensitive handling. The conductor accepts and holds the projection, uncomfortable or even distressing as it might be. The group member who is the recipient will receive it as a confrontation, and is unlikely to accept it without a fight, not least because he or she has been unconsciously 'selected' by the projector, due to the recipient's repressed acquaintance with the expelled emotions or fantasies. A good example is excessive envy. The immediate reaction of the chosen member can be near-devastation, temporary withdrawal, or even dropping out.

The language of the group

Group analysis is a 'talking cure' in that it discourages action and encourages and uses verbal exchange as a means of therapy. The group analyst John Schlapobersky has described in depth the prevailing modes of the group's language as a progression from monologue through dialogue to discourse. Each of these modes of speech is being employed as a narrative of life events, or in what Schlapobersky calls the drama of the experiences in the here-and-now of the group. The group advances from the narrative to a reflective dialogue and discourse (Schlapobersky, 1994). It is this discourse that establishes what Foulkes calls the 'zone of communication' in which the group members learn to understand themselves and others (Foulkes, 1964, p.12).

The conductor joins the communication on all levels, for the most part as another engaged member, not giving ready answers or offering insights which the group itself might discover in its own time. At the same time, the conductor should not frustrate realistic expectations of leadership and insight. He or she plants a spirit of enquiry in the group and models a way of behaving.

Counter-transference in the group

The conductor also has to deal with the ubiquitous existence of counter-transference phenomena. In the group, these are multiple, criss-crossing among the group members, the conductor and the group as a whole. Freud observed that 'Everyone possesses in his unconscious an instrument with which he can interpret the utterances of the unconscious of other people.' In the group, the resonances from unconscious to unconscious are the most unadulterated form of communication one can reach. As such, they are a precious tool at the disposal of the conductor. But like all tools, they have to be skilfully used. The conductor has to decide whether what is communicated resonates to unresolved conflicts. If so, that is where it has to stay, to be handled outside of the group's ken. If the counter-transferential resonance responds to an unconscious message from a group member, or from the group as a whole, the conductor may decide to file it away for future use at an appropriate moment or present it to the group there and then in order to deepen and widen the group's capacity for feeling and understanding in the service of integrative growth.

'Trust the group'

Group therapists in training are sometimes urged to 'trust the group'. But what does this mean in practice? It is unwise to embrace this slogan in the innocent hope that somehow the collective wisdom of the group can justify a technique of neutral non-intervention on the part of the conductor. The trail of group therapy is littered with people who have dropped out or have been rendered more disturbed after having felt neglected or put at risk of being scapegoated by a well-intentioned but passive conductor nursing the belief that the group process should be allowed to run its natural course and that the wisdom of the group would prevail in the end. This caveat does not gainsay the fact that there may well be times when the group is one step ahead of the conductor in grasping a hidden dynamic.

Maintaining a balance between extremes

From time to time the conductor has to balance an over-emotional state with interventions aimed at restoring a more reflective mode of communication. Conversely, the conductor should be prepared to inject a note of emotional challenge if the group is experienced as coasting along in a rarified state of contemplative neutrality. The oscillation between reflection and turbulence is like the swing of a pendulum. The wide arc of the swing allows the conductor the freedom to observe and reflect while the group is actively engaged in the therapeutic work. When the group gets stuck in one or other mode, the conductor has the cue to intervene. The assessment of what constitutes a counter-therapeutic direction is not easy. The conductor holds a tentative stance, sometimes intervening robustly, but always open to self-reflection and challenges from the group. If an intervention is greeted with silence or open rebuttals and denials of its validity, it may be necessary to reflect on some personal wish or need in relation to the group.

Where in time and place does the group dwell at any given moment?

The terms 'here-and-now' and 'there-and-then' have become enshrined in group-analytic terminology. But there is also a 'here-and-then', such as the group's own history, and a 'there-and-now', for example, a group member's current life situation outside the group. Groups classically travel between their experiences of what is going on inside the room and events outside. Criss-crossing with these are the narratives of their individual pasts. When a group dwells excessively in one of these spheres, it is because some aspects of it are being denied or have not been worked through. One example of this is repeated rumination about low numbers in the group, which may represent an unspoken fear of the group disappearing. Another is the persistent attention paid by the group to one group member as 'the patient', a dynamic which effectively allows the other group members to avoid looking at themselves.

The 'here-and-now' of the group can also manifest itself as extremes of mood. For example, a group can remain steadfastly in a joking, light-hearted mode, a so-called 'manic flight', as a means of avoiding painful and depressing material. Conversely, a group can sink into a prolonged depressive state, determined to extract magical healing from the conductor, based on a transference perception of him or her as the omnipotent parental figure of infancy. Groups can also acquire a culture of a '*Katastrophenverschleiss*', a 'trading post for catastrophes', where only bad news and problems are traded.

The figure–ground constellation

Sometimes the group as a whole swims into the foreground of its own attention. At other times, an individual or a sub-group ('the new members', 'the men', 'the latecomers', for example) emerges into the foreground. This is part of the kaleidoscopic change in figure–ground constellations which constitutes the group-analytic experience. It is a process which the conductor follows rather than leads, unless the group appears stuck, in which case it becomes necessary to induce a shift in attention from content to process, from the material which is preoccupying the group to the fact of the preoccupation itself.

Groups which dwell exclusively on 'group-as-a-whole' phenomena generally do so under the influence of the conductor's theoretical orientation. However, this dynamic can also arise out of a specific situation in which the group finds itself, such as a perceived threat to its survival, a disturbing incident in the group, or a scripted event such as a long holiday break.

A group which dwells for too long on the problems or issues of one person may be caught in a process of active collusion between that individual and the rest of the group. Individuals with a capacity for dramatizing their plight, those whose psychopathology leads them towards excessive levels of disturbance or dysfunction, and those whose lives unfold in a horrifying spectacle of trauma and tragedy, are capable of riveting the group into a state of fascination, behind which often lies an omnipotent wish to heal. The individual should not be deprived of this attention too quickly. Eventually, however, the group has to be brought to a realization of its unconscious motivation in all its diversity. All these constantly shifting preoccupations require tracking, and if need be, intervention.

Ethnicity, language and culture in groups

Our society has undergone a radical change in a relatively short time in the diversity of the ethnic backgrounds of its citizens. Large numbers of people immigrate and emigrate, bringing in and taking out their cultural heritage – their languages, collective historical memories, customs, and behaviour patterns. These are usually well represented in an analytic group. The multi-faceted picture of humankind greatly enriches the group matrix, while at the same time posing challenges to communication.

In group analysis, communication proceeds mainly, though not exclusively, through the medium of spoken language. Group members are expected to speak the national language, but the emotional weight of words and sentences, which is acquired in childhood, can be lost in translation. Intonation, emphasis and manner of delivery differ from one ethnic group to another, as do idiomatic expressions, concepts of humour and cultural allusions. Attitudes to openness in the group are frequently coloured by a history of exposure to persecutory or traumatic experiences, such as the experience of having lived in a totalitarian or repressive society. There is also the transgenerational transmission of victimhood arising from a history of massive social trauma, at times going back centuries (Volkan, 1997). These are occasionally expressed through silence and secrecy in the group, phenomena which have to be understood in their historical, socio-political and interpersonal contexts.

How are ethnic differences received in the analytic group? And how can they be used in the service of therapy? Here the constitution of the group is all-important. A diversity of group membership in all its aspects – age, gender, social and cultural background and religious belief – creates an atmosphere in which new stimuli can be experienced in safety. The risk of isolation for any one member can be reduced by offering a 'group sibling', another group member who can be expected to understand and interpret the meaning and emotional content of what is said. This provides a subtle learning process that reduces fixed attitudes and styles of perceiving the world. The conductor's own ethnic identity and cultural background, subjected to transferential distortions as they are, should also provide a backdrop of counter-transferential scanning for cultural blind-spots and misunderstandings.

If alienation proceeds unchecked, a sense of 'not belonging' develops. The conductor should be alert to a dynamic which denies cultural and social differences, or the opposite, one which exaggerates them. In the former instance, the group labours under the myth that all in the group are socially and culturally homogeneous, and that any reference to difference is an affront to the egalitarian principle upon which the group rests. At the other extreme, differences can be seized upon as conspicuous markers of cultural identity, extinguishing commonalities and serving only to increase the individual's sense of isolation. People so isolated quite often collude with this dynamic in their wish to belong, and retire into a zone of silence around an important area of their identity. The resulting isolation may only yield after the conductor has drawn attention to the prevailing myth and has helped the group to find the words to challenge it.

Racism in groups

An optimally constituted group mirrors the society from which its members are recruited. The group members, including their conductor, inevitably bring with them the societal attitudes, assumptions, preconceived ideas, myths and fantasies about 'The Other' – those who are perceived as alien. A perception of immutable difference slides the group inexorably towards an emotional investment in maintaining an inclusion–exclusion dynamic and the construction of boundaries which become barriers and which offer a vehicle for malign projections. This is especially likely to occur when the difference from oneself is that of the colour of the skin. 'The structures of society are reflected in the structures of the psyche, and both are colour-coded' (Dalal, 2002).

The analytic group offers a safe environment in which deeply embedded ideas, including prejudices and racist attitudes, can emerge, can be verbalized and held up to scrutiny in the group discourse. But for this to happen, the group analyst must be in touch with his or her own, almost always denied, 'colour-coding'. Yet even when the group analyst is in touch, the notion that one is the product of a liberal, tolerant ideology which rejects the crudity and injustice of racism, militates against the recognition of racism when it does emerge.

Vignette

A white woman started the session in a state of agitation. She told the group that her ten-year old son had been mugged by two older boys on his way home from school. She paused, and reluctantly added, 'They were black'. She then turned to the only black man in the group with, 'No offence meant'. He politely replied: 'None taken'. After a tense silence, there was some talk about the rising crime-rate, how unsafe the streets had become, and the need for a stronger police presence. The group then turned to another subject.

The white conductor left the session feeling dissatisfied with herself, wondering why she had missed this opportunity to break the taboo on the subject of black and white, which had so far prevailed in the group. Was the subject of racism too hot for the group or for her? Not having pondered these questions until that moment, she had allowed an important societal phenomenon to be left untouched in the group and a resolution possibly lost to its participants.

Gender and sexuality in groups

Issues of gender and sexuality feature prominently in analytic groups, where they reflect the attitudes of the particular society in which the group takes place. In our experience, intimate sexual relationships and their attendant problems can be broached in a mixed group, although a language for talking about them has to be developed which mitigates feelings of shame, embarrassment and isolation. Groups can also evoke voyeuristic and exhibitionistic responses, eroticization of sexual issues and erotic transferential relationships, all of which phenomena carry a risk of acting out or 'acting in' if they are not recognized as such.

The transformation of societal attitudes towards sexual relationships and sexual orientations over the past 50 years is reflected in the diverse composition of today's analytic groups. Homosexual and heterosexual group members interact and identify with one another in the gamut of relationship issues which form the dynamic matrix of the group. As with ethnic and cultural distinctions, the conductor has to be aware of two extremes: denying the significance of differences in sexual orientation, or using them as a barrier to belonging and mutual identification.

At the assessment interview, a person may express a preference to join a mixed group, a same-sex group or a group comprising individuals with a shared sexual orientation. Such preferences may be founded on previously experienced lack of understanding, prejudice or abuse, or on the belief that the preferred group will help to resolve an identity problem. In all such instances, the first task of the group analyst is to help the person to arrive at an informed decision about the choice of group. The same principle applies to individuals who are unsure about whether they would like to join a group led by a man or a woman. Realistic and transference-driven fears and desires have to be unravelled and reconciled, but at the end of the day it is the manifest wish of the patient that must be respected.

Containment and confrontation: opposite sides of the same coin

For the most part, the conductor listens quietly and intervenes affiliatively, but sometimes he or she sounds a challenging note, either in relation to an individual or the group as a whole. Confrontation is a two-edged sword: it brings out into the open a process which is being avoided, and it increases the group's sense of containment by setting limits to an anti-therapeutic process. When confrontation occurs, the emotional temperature tends to rise, and the capacity for reflective thinking may be temporarily suspended. Nevertheless, confrontation may be needed as a first step towards highlighting transferential behaviour in which the 'as if' element has been lost sight of. Erratic attendance, latecoming, and intemperate attacks on a vulnerable group member or on the conductor are common indications for a confrontational intervention.

When two members of the group confront each other, the impact on the group is considerable. There is a fine balance between 'healthy' confrontation, which brings important issues out into the open, and the sort of confrontation which is predicated upon a basis of malignant mirroring (Zinkin, 1983) and escalates to the point of inducing the protagonists, or other, apparently neutral group members, to withdraw, perhaps even to leave the group. A group member's apparently robust response to attack can be deceptive, and a group member who attacks another may also be setting the stage for his or her own premature departure from the group.

Vignette

A woman frequently brought to the group accounts of her husband's selfish and abusive behaviour towards her. Despite concerned encouragement from the group to think about the possibility of leaving him, she steadfastly maintained her determination to stay in the relationship for the sake of their children. During one session another woman in the group directed an angry outburst at her, accusing her of failing to think about the effect of her husband's behaviour on the child.

The conductor reflected to himself that the angry woman had lived through a childhood marred by an abusive father and submissive mother who had stayed together. Before any such link could be made, however, a heated exchange broke out between the two women which left no room for anyone else to intervene, and which culminated in the first woman bursting into tears and saying that the second woman made her feel exactly the way she did with her husband.

The conductor confronted both women by urging them to stop the exchange and listen to him. In the ensuing silence he pointed out to each of them the unconscious repetition underlying their behaviour and the re-creation of a bully-victim dynamic in the group. The rest of the group swiftly reinforced this formulation, and both women were able to move on with fresh insights.

Working with dreams

The manifold therapeutic resources of the group are seen most clearly when we look at what it does with dreams. The dream is the Royal Road, as Freud called it, into the dreamer's unconscious. If the group members are to be enabled to get in touch with the content of the deepest and most inaccessible area of mental life, they will have to tread this royal road. They have to be encouraged to relate their dreams freely and gain some understanding of what they convey to them.

Group members are often unaware of the value of dreams. They may have to be invited to recover and capture their dreams. The popular belief that 'I don't dream', or that 'dreams don't make sense' has to be challenged. It may be necessary to explain that a remembered dream has a function: to make the dreamer aware of some hidden aspect which commands waking attention. The remembered dream knocks at the door of consciousness, as it were, demanding to be let in. In bringing a dream to the group, the dreamer opens another channel of communication into the social world at both conscious and unconscious levels.

Yet the dream, according to Foulkes, is 'particularly an individual creation, not meant for publication' (Foulkes, 1964, p.126). Also, the dream occurs in sleep, in a state of withdrawal from social contact. Group analysis, on the other hand, proceeds in a social context. How do we square this circle? We do so by carefully constructing the social context in which group analysis takes place. This enables the individual members to express themselves fully, and this includes their 'particular individual creations' – their dreams. The reporting of dreams is strongly influenced by the way in which they are received and handled by the group conductor, from whom the group will take its cue. Group analysts who value dream reporting and treat it with respect and sensitivity get dreams more often and in greater detail than those who see them entirely as individual properties, intrinsically unsharable.

When the dreamer relates the dream to the group, he or she engages the group in the process of decoding it. The group's reaction to the report is a clue to its meaning and has to be considered by the conductor in all its aspects. At what point in the session is the dream told? To whom is it primarily directed? – the group, one member or the conductor? How is the report received? The group may show interest, offer personal associations, or recall memories of their own or others' dreams. Or silence may follow, or apparent withdrawal.

These group reactions act like building blocks in the edifice of the latent content. They constitute interpretations in themselves. Often the meaning of the dream emerges without the conductor interpreting, as might be done in dyadic therapy. It is equally important that the contributions, both verbal and nonverbal, of the group members, make the dream relevant to everyone in a deeply individual sense. Far from the group acting as a backdrop to the dreamer, what takes place is a deepening and widening resonance through which members feel their own unique response. This makes it both a personal and an interpersonal experience. Some group analysts differentiate between 'personal dreams' and 'group dreams'.

Battegay, for example, defines a group dream as 'a dream of an individual in which a link to the group is apparent' (Battegay, 1977). We do not find it useful to make such a distinction. The fact that a dreamer relates the dream to the group makes it a shared preoccupation in which each group member as well as the conductor participates.

The attention paid to the timing and manner of delivery of the dream should be followed by attention to the affect remembered by the dreamer in relation to the dream, and to the dream content itself. To neglect such an intimate personal disclosure would be to inflict a narcissistic injury. The emotional colouring of the dream varies enormously. Tranquil detachment, terror and erotic arousal are a some of the affective states often reported by the dreamer, and these can be mirrored in the listening group. The dream context and its intrinsic personal meaning will emerge in a figure–ground constellation, the one complementing and deepening the other.

Vignette

A woman coming towards the end of her therapy tells the group the following dream: she is visiting her childhood home, but it is much changed, the rooms are large and cavernous. She finds a table set for a banquet, laden with food. Guests who seem familiar to her, but whom she does not recognize, are seated around the table. She feels that she is not entitled to be there. She goes deeper into the interior of the house, along a corridor. She comes to a tapestry partition, behind which shadowy figures appear to be engaged in some form of sexual activity. She wakes in a mixed state of excitement and fear that she has been discovered.

After a few moments of silence, a man in the group recounts a dream which he has just remembered. He is visiting his grandfather's farm, where he used to spend summer holidays as a child. His grandfather appears, looking like a much younger man, and tells him to feed the horses. He visits the stable and finds that the horses are not there. He suddenly becomes aware that there are wolves in the area and becomes frightened that one of the horses will be attacked and eaten by a wolf.

The group ponders this in a tense silence. Then another man says: 'Are you sure it wasn't a bear?' The group laughs at this pun on the conductor's surname. A woman says: 'I often leave the group feeling hungry. But I have a good meal at home.' Another woman says: 'I wonder what he (the conductor) does after the group. He probably has someone waiting for him at home to give him a bear-hug.' (laughter) A woman says: 'I still have my old teddy bear to hug. He's quite safe.' The woman who told the dream says: 'I don't have to "wolf" my food here.' She turns to the conductor: 'I feel quite safe with you. Anyway, the rest of you would protect me...'

The group carried on in this vein, 'dreaming' along with the two dreamers, resonating with personal associations, which vividly illuminated the rich content of the dreams. No interpretation by the conductor was needed; the associations themselves acted as interpretations, involving all members of the group in their own specific personal manner.

The use of metaphor and humour

'Metaphor', said Aristotle, 'is a mixture of the lucid and the strange'. We make use of it when we strive to express a truth which lies somewhere between the part and the whole, and which cannot be adequately stated by exclusive reference to one or the other. Foulkes's concept of the matrix as a web or network is the central governing metaphor of group analysis, and the language of metaphor provides us with one of the most powerful instruments of change in group-analytic psychotherapy.

Inevitably, some group members are more blessed than others with the ability to express themselves in metaphor. The dream can be seen as a rich supply of metaphoric thinking, but in waking life, too, there are opportunities for likening the events and experiences of everyday life to imagined conceptions. The objects which in childhood became personified to create symbols return in the group to become available for analysis.

The group as a whole can sometimes be expressed in metaphoric terms – the group as an island, a ring of fire, or a pool – and the personification of the group, expressed for example in the notion that 'the group is jittery,' offers the members of the group an opportunity to attach their own particular meaning to the term. Metaphors therefore have a unifying and centralizing role in group analysis, bringing together diverse personal experiences and increasing the sense of depth, intimacy and belonging.

Humour is another powerful instrument of change. The sharp juxtaposing of images or ideas, which, like the metaphor, are at once similar and different, can create a sense of surprise, sometimes even shock or outrage. The laughter which accompanies humour signals the release of tension which occurs when forbidden or unexpected thoughts suddenly enter the group. This can be enjoyed in its own right. The analytic purpose, however, is best served when the group goes on to examine the meaning of ideas which, though smuggled into the group in the guise of humour, may also have underpinnings of sadness, anger, sadism, discrimination or devaluation attached to them.

What is meant by technique in group analysis?

The status of technique in group analysis is sometimes downgraded. The myth is occasionally vaunted that technique does not matter too much so long as the virtues of empathy, warmth and impartiality are in place. The musicologist Grove points out that 'a player may be perfect in technique and yet have neither soul nor intelligence' – an observation as true of psychotherapists as it of performing musicians.

Yet without technique the group analyst is like a navigator adrift on the ocean without a compass or map. Technique derives from the theoretical framework internalized by the group analyst, combined with his or her personality. It is about how we sequence our interventions, to what we give priority, the language we use, and the timing of our verbal and nonverbal interventions. Foulkes aptly compared the process to the peeling of an artichoke, which proceeds from the outer leaves to the succulent heart. He maintained that the dichotomies 'horizontal–vertical' and 'superficial–deep' falsify the group-analytic process. The group is a field of activity in which all the members, including the conductor, interact constantly by communicating, translating their thoughts into words and redefining their individuality through a 'training' experience. It is this field that produces what Foulkes called 'ego training in action' (Foulkes, 1964, p.82).

CHAPTER TEN

Life events in the group

TRIUMPHS OF GROUP ANALYSIS:
HARVEY ASKS HIS BOSS FOR A RAISE

During their time in therapy, which may span a period of several years, group members are likely to be subjected to life events which have a profound effect on them. These have to be addressed in the group. Long-term group-analytic therapy is not a slide along the scale from some supposed position of abnormality (or 'disease') to normality (or 'health') but a deep and active process of reconstruction tailored to the individual personality.

A process which runs deep can sometimes be painful, so the group has to provide safety and pain relief as well as depth. The pace of exploration is gradual, and this means that a long duration is a prerequisite for deep and far-reaching change. The therapy of relationships is analogous to the management of chronic illness, the analogy lying in the notion of chronicity (literally a process extended in time). The group analyst frequently encounters interpersonal situations which remain intractable or even deteriorate. These are often punctuated by life events or crises which provide fresh opportunities for change.

The emergence of physical illness in the group

An illness can become manifest quite rapidly, or it can be harboured silently for some time before declaring itself. The group may become aware that a group member is not well before he or she is able to acknowledge it. A change in appearance or demeanour is sometimes picked up by the group, and symptoms which the group member makes light of can be anxiously focused on by the group. Groups occasionally act *in loco familiae*, voicing concerns which close relatives may be ignoring or downplaying. The group member's readiness or otherwise to seek appropriate medical attention can become a dynamic issue in itself.

Vignette
A 45-year-old woman told the group that she had been diagnosed as suffering from multiple sclerosis. Her husband was privy to this knowledge, but she was determined to keep her teenage children in the dark about it, and she had persuaded her husband to agree. The group explored her thinking around this, which was connected with her feeling that she was already a burden to her family because of her depression. She feared the effect which such knowledge would have on them, and she also held the hope that the diagnosis could be mistaken and that she might recover. The group helped her to think about the effect of concealment on the children's anxiety, given that her neurological symptoms were already evident. She responded thoughtfully to this, and accepted the possibility that her relationship with her children might become closer through a mutual process of sharing and support. The group in this case acted like a bereavement group, anticipating the loss of good health and the likelihood of increasing dependence and vulnerability.

Medical investigation of unexplained symptoms should proceed in parallel with psychotherapy. Groups sometimes collude with a group member's belief that physical symptoms are entirely psychogenic, which can result in delay in seeking appropriate investigation. When an illness does emerge in a group member, it carries resonances for the whole group.

The emergence of mental illness in the group

This can be as insidious as physical illness and more elusive, because of the wish to render all individual psychic manifestations into interpersonal and group terms. It is part of the required training of a group analyst to be able to recognize mental illness when it occurs in a group member. The question is whether it is within the capacity of the group to hold the afflicted group member, or whether it is to his or her benefit to leave the group and get more appropriate treatment. Mounting anxiety within the group is a useful sign that attempts to wrestle with the problem in the group may have to yield to outside professional intervention.

In either case, the shock to the group can be considerable. The emergence of mental illness engenders the fear that 'there, but for the grace of God, go I'. At the very least, it can result in a sense of helplessness and failure. It falls to the group analyst to recognize, acknowledge and take charge of the situation. Groups are usually relieved and grateful when this is done promptly. Such action can mean temporary or even permanent exclusion from the group. Outside the group, the group analyst may have to liaise with primary care services, relatives and mental health professionals on questions of hospitalization or medication. Sometimes re-entry to the group after a period in hospital is possible and right for the patient and the group.

In any case, the whole episode will be registered as a traumatic event in the life of the group and will have to be worked through time and again, in all the various meanings it will have had for the individual group members and the group as a whole. The group might come to be experienced as a dangerous place which can produce psychosis, or as not strong enough to cope with it when it occurs. The group analyst might also react to the event with self-doubt, guilt at having brought the patient into the group in the first place, or worry about the group members' reactions. This is an occasion when contact with trusted colleagues by way of peer supervision can help to clarify which element of the group analyst's reaction belongs to him or her, and which is experienced by way of projective identification from the group, and is, as such, a valuable message about the group's psychic reaction to the trauma.

The experience of bereavement

A slow-open group with a steady membership over a long time span is likely to have to deal with bereavement befalling one or the other of its members. In our experience, groups tend to deal with such events with sensitivity and compassion. Time and space is given to the bereaved group member to put into words the pain at the loss, but also to voice the negative feelings which often emerge early in the long mourning process. Again, it is important that the group should offer the bereaved person an opportunity to voice and work through the event, while at the same time the experience should be made relevant to all the group members, each at their own level of psychic reality. When this is accomplished, the group will emerge strengthened in its ability to empathize and not be taken over.

Bereavement can also occur in the group itself, through the death of one of its members, and most traumatically, through a suicide. In the latter instance, the experience of devastating loss is accentuated by feelings of guilt at not having prevented the death, and by anxieties on the part of the conductor about the professional repercussions. The feeling of shock is all-pervasive and tends to live on in the group for a long time, whatever the interventions of the group analyst.

When a death occurs, the group may ask for facts and details, such as the links being made with the family, contact with outside agencies or funeral arrangements; one or more group members may wish to attend the funeral. The group analyst too is likely to be deeply affected, both personally and professionally. He or she may wish to attend the funeral, and as dynamic administrator, should accept responsibility for conveying condolences to the bereaved relatives and representing the group at the funeral, if appropriate. The first analytic task is to keep the group intact by allowing the necessary time and space for the event to be digested. This is another indication for supervisory contact with a colleague. If the event is given the time and space it deserves, it will become available in all its aspects to each group member, enabling everyone to face and interpret the existential experience of loss and death.

Becoming a parent

At the other end of the continuum that constitutes the life of an analytic group is the event of parenthood. The group will have participated in the run-up to the birth of a baby in all its ups and downs, the joyful anticipation as well as the doubts and fears that accompany it. A group member's pregnancy is an occasion to experience the unique character of an analytic group, which allows for, even invites, the socially unacceptable expression of feelings such as anger at intrusion into the group's preoccupations by outside events, or envy of the prospective parent. The group member who is to become a parent may have to be helped to cope with such negative feelings in the group.

Vignette
In a group in which two of the women were unable to have children, their pain and envy towards the prospective parent were strongly felt, and after some hesitation, expressed. This made for a stressful atmosphere in the group, which when repeatedly voiced, eventually changed into a pained acceptance, and then joy for the parent-to-be. The envy was symbolically compensated for by the decision to greet the birth with flowers and a present collectively chosen by the group members. The conductor did not regard this concession to social convention as an impediment to the analytic task.

The group may have to cope with a degree of emotional withdrawal by the mother, due to a process of 'draining interest from herself on to the baby', as Winnicott put it (Winnicott, 1965). This can evoke feelings in the group reminiscent of those felt by siblings at the birth of a new baby. Memories and associations of being sidelined, neglected, or displaced in affection come to the surface. If these can be voiced and explored, they can bring about a therapeutic regression in the group to long-forgotten early childhood experiences, which can then be re-experienced and incorporated into the mature personality.

When the new parent is a father, he may need the group's support to cope with a shift in the relationship with his partner, the establishment of a new relationship with the baby and the subsequent reclamation of the adult relationship with the mother. This can usually be achieved without excessive friction, but it is a hurdle to negotiate, the significance of which is only too often denied. In a group with a wide span of ages, there will be echoes to the event from one or other of the older group members. This can range from advice to empathy and identification, all of which facilitate the expression of feelings over such emotionally charged events as the loss of the undiluted attention of his partner, fear of added financial strain on the family and the assumption of responsibility for the baby's welfare.

The question sometimes arises whether the newborn baby should be brought into the group. The wish for this may come from both the mother and the group. This provides the conductor with the chance to explore the interface between the realistic pleasure in sharing the arrival of the baby and the powerful symbolism invested in the transition from the mother as a single being into the mother–child dyad. The conductor might sanction a single 'ceremonial' visit, but even then he or she should be prepared for some negative fall-out, expressed either at the time or later. A mother's wish to attend the group regularly with her baby, if gratified, probably has more of a disturbing effect than a therapeutic one.

Changes in personal and family relationships

Difficult couple and family relationships frequently provide the incentive to enter therapy. The ensuing changes, experienced as progress by the group member and the group, can sometimes disturb an equilibrium in a dysfunctional relationship at home. The other partner of the couple can come to regard the group as a force undermining the relationship and put pressure on the group member to leave the group. The group analyst should be open to the possibility of referring a group member for couple therapy or family therapy, which can proceed in parallel with the group. Separate therapy for the partner is also an option.

Groups are frequently faced with the breakdown of a group member's special relationship, the dislocation of a family constellation, the forging of new relationships and the problems of adjusting to a reconstituted family. These are generally highly charged interpersonal situations which set up powerful resonances within the group. Group members sometimes develop strong identifications with one or other partner of a fractured relationship, and the conductor has to rely on the group as a whole to provide a constructive diversity which accurately mirrors the conflictual situation. Relationship and family breakdown can all too easily offer themselves as a voyeuristic spectacle, and the conductor has to be prepared to name this process should it occur.

Traumatic life events

Sometimes a group member suffers a traumatic life event, such as an assault or burglary, or involvement in a road traffic accident. The first priority is to assess the emotional state of this group member. If the incident is fresh, he or she may still be in a state of shock, which is not always easy to detect. A traumatized person can remain strangely composed for some time, perhaps talking in a rational, detached way, and it is only much later that affect will be released. The person may then collapse, shaking and immobilized, or may be taken over by spasms of weeping. Distraught behaviour can manifest itself in the group, and warrants active containing. Group members freely offer spontaneous comforting expressions of a gentle physical nature – holding, soothing and touching. The group member's shock can sometimes send repercussions through the group. The therapist listens to the narrative with one ear and scans the group for signs of vicarious shock, making a mental note of anyone whose verbal, but more especially nonverbal, communication is a signal for special attention.

The discovery of a family secret

People often enter therapy harbouring a secret which they both hope and fear the group will discover, and to which the conductor may or may not be privy at the outset. It is not uncommon, during an assessment interview or in the course of preliminary individual sessions, for the prospective group member to disclose the secret but to exhort the group analyst to respect their wish to withhold it from the group. The conductor works with this along an extended timescale, recognizing the isolating nature of secrecy, but accepting the powerful feelings of shame and guilt which attach to secrets. The moment of disclosure in the group has to be piloted by the group member, secure in the knowledge that the conductor will be there when the time comes.

A different order of secret is one which becomes known to the group member while he or she is in therapy. For example, one group member learnt that his father had committed suicide when he was a small child, another that he had a half-sister of whose existence he had been unaware, another that her father had been a patient in a psychiatric hospital for many years. Group members often feel emboldened by their participation in the group to embark upon a quest to discover information about themselves and their families. Those who were adopted as children sometimes use the group as a safe base from which to seek information about their biological parents and face the difficult task of meeting with them. The confidentiality and containment of the group makes it a first port of call when disturbing or shocking information is unearthed.

Vignette

A 40-year-old man who had been estranged from his family since the age of 15 struggled with his ambivalence about seeking out his parents. He retained a vague memory of his father, who had disappeared mysteriously when he was about four years old. His mother and her family, whom he had experienced as uncaring and rejecting, had never spoken of his father, and had gone to the lengths of excising his image from family photographs. With the support of the group he contacted one of his father's relatives, who told him that his father had died in prison, where he had been serving a sentence for murder. Through this relative he recovered some of his father's letters in which he spoke lovingly of his son, and his longing to see him. This story unfolded in the group over several months, during which time the group helped the man to work through his apprehension, his shock on discovering the news, his grief, and the repercussions of the newfound knowledge on him and his family.

Encounter with the law

Questions of injustice, unfairness, wrongdoing, culpability and false accusation frequently permeate the group and constitute an important dynamic which can spiral down into a group member's childhood antecedents. Sometimes this is given fresh relevance by a current or ongoing saga involving a brush with the law.

Vignette
A man in the group failed to come to a session without notification, which was unusual for him. When he appeared at the following session, he reported calmly that he had been arrested for suspected murder. The group members, including the conductor, froze in their seats. He went on to describe how two policemen had appeared outside his house and had asked him to accompany them to the police station, where they had questioned him about his whereabouts the previous day. It eventually transpired that his divorced wife, an alcoholic, had committed suicide, leaving a note accusing him of murder. The whole affair was speedily cleared up by the police, but when reporting it to the group, the group member himself had been unable to get in touch with the horror and fear that this episode evoked in him. He had unconsciously delegated to the group the function of feeling and expressing the appropriate reactions and holding them, as it were, till, in the subsequent sessions, he could own them and deal with them himself.

All this took place entirely within the group. In other instances, the reported brush with the law may beckon the conductor towards action outside the group. Some group analysts might question whether any kind of action is appropriate in an analytic group. The argument goes that group members are there to be helped to help themselves rather than receive actual help. It seems to us that it is an aspect of the art of group analysis to discern what is required at any given time. If action is needed, the important question is to determine the meaning of this action to the recipient. Actual, practical help can be a 'steering object' (*das Steuernde Objekt*) which the group member has missed out on in early childhood, arising from a defective mother–child relationship, and which has impaired the ability to interact appropriately with external reality (König, 1981).

Vignette
A woman in her late 50s was arrested for shoplifting. She told the group about the humiliation and taunting to which she had been subjected by the arresting police officers, which included racist jibes. At her behest the group analyst wrote a strong letter to the police authority and a supportive letter to the court. The group was deeply sympathetic to her predicament, but the action of the conductor had also cleared the way for an analysis of her behaviour in its dynamic context.

Trouble in the workplace

In an ongoing group that meets over some years it is likely that one or other group member will lose their job, or give it up voluntarily. In the former instance, the sense of anger, victimization by employer or society, and fear of financial collapse will be uppermost. Some of these preoccupations may also feature in the voluntary relinquishment of a job, but they are likely to be overshadowed by a crisis of self-doubt, fear about future employment or lifestyle, loss of the social network and dislocation of family life. In either case, the emotional impact on the group member will enter the discourse of the group.

When the job loss has been imposed, or when there has been an unsuccessful attempt to gain a new job or to be promoted, the group listens to and accepts the feelings of hurt and anger, the sense of failure and the fantasies of imminent destitution. These feelings may be fuelled by memories of early failures in the family, on the part of parents, at school, in friendships or in love. Once these emerge and are linked with the current job loss, the group members will be able to identify with the emotional state of the affected group member in any of these components. This will lessen his or her isolation and at the same time promote an active emotional participation by the group rather than the passive reception which is often confined to comforting remarks and advice-giving.

The report of a voluntary job loss is less likely to come as a surprise to the group. The intention and reason for it will probably have been voiced before and taken up, perhaps many times, by the group. When the group member eventually does take the final step, a wave of mixed feelings generally washes over the group: admiration tinged with envy, doubts about one's own ability to overcome habit, to forego security and venture into the unknown, or disapproval of an action deemed reckless or irresponsible. Apart from its practical implications, work has deep symbolic significance associated with status, gender, culture and life values. To walk out of the workplace is a fantasy which most of us harbour at one time or another; when it becomes a reality in the group, it offers a fertile ground for exploration.

Vignette
A woman had been struggling with career and employment problems for some time before starting group analysis. In fact, this was her main reason for going into therapy. This continued during her three years in the group. Her professional qualifications and practice had been appreciated by her various employers whom she had left, one after the other. With every change in employment she had explored a different aspect of her profession without finding satisfaction in any one of them.

The group had participated to a greater or lesser extent in her professional doubts and dissatisfaction, and some of the underlying origins had been laid bare, such as the influence of her parents on her choice of career. Eventually, she expressed the fear that she might be boring the group, or worse, that they might come to disapprove of her constant 'whinging'. Then one day she announced that she had come to a decision: she had gone through her finances and found that she could manage without a salary for one year. She was giving in her notice and would be free in three months. The group inundated her with questions: What was she going to do eventually? Was she not risking financial collapse? Was she sure she wouldn't regret it? What did it feel like taking such a step? Was she now happy?

The conductor felt that there was something missing with all these questions. Was the group simply asking for information, or were they expressing their own fears, doubts and hopes around the fantasies they may have had themselves? When she put this to the group, an animated discussion opened up, of work, careers, hopes for the future, and the wish to opt out of the rat-race. The woman herself remained quiet throughout this. At the end of the session she thanked the group and said that she had been helped by them in the expression of their own fears, hopes and aspirations. 'I know now that I did the right thing.'

In the handling of the individual life events of the group members, the analytic group does not act simply as a backcloth to the individual's crisis. Rather, it supplies a figure–ground constellation in which at one point the individual stands out as the figure, at one point the group, in an ever-changing dynamic. In a mature group, in which the language of group analysis has been absorbed, this happens without too much intervention by the group analyst. But at times the group may require sensitive steering away from the 'why don't you' and 'it will be all right' games, by eliciting associations from the realms of memory, experience and fantasy prevailing in the group.

CHAPTER ELEVEN

Bringing therapy to an end

'WELL DEAR, DID YOU TELL THE GROUP YOU WERE LEAVING?'

> The ultimate aim of the therapeutic process should be to strengthen the self so that the person is willing and able to actively plunge into the rough-and-tumble of everyday life, not without fear, but nevertheless undeterred
>
> Ernest Wolf

The ending of group-analytic therapy is an emotionally charged event. The process of analysis continues relentlessly to the concluding session, with the conductor constantly on the lookout for signs of avoidance of the pain, anger, sadness and anxiety attendant on the leaving process. Each group member will have a model of endings coloured by their life experience in relation to loss through illness, death or separation, and in the convergence of these experiences the group readily elides the symbolism of ending into the metaphor of death.

The ending of a group

The ending of a whole group is a very different affair to the ending of therapy for an individual. If the group has been run as a closed group, the ending will have been planned at its conceptualization and will be in each group members' mind from the beginning, a shared punctuation mark at a clearly defined point in the future. Regardless of the care with which this is addressed, it will be seen as an act of force, imposed by the conductor and under his or her control, like all dynamic administrative activities that belong to the setting. For this reason the conductor should return to it periodically during the life of the group, verbalizing the conflicts which it may evoke, bearing in mind that groups, as well as individual members, avoid the subject almost consciously.

As the group moves closer towards the moment of ending, the conductor becomes more active, highlighting the shared nature of the process by putting greater emphasis on group-as-a-whole observations. This tends to evoke a reflective mode in the group, in which the group members recollect their early group experiences and exchange reminiscences about themselves and one another. Some group analysts structure this phase quite actively, eliciting in sequence a recapitulation of the positive changes that have accrued followed by a recounting of the regrets and unfulfilled wishes associated with the therapeutic experience. This allows for important negative transferential material to emerge and also gives the conductor salutary feedback about the realistic limitations of the therapy.

The conductor takes care to achieve a balance between the creative fantasy that the ending of the group is a death and the constructive reality that it is a new beginning. In order to do this, the conductor may have to invite the group to project itself into the future, through the expressed wishes, hopes and fears of the individual members. This helps the processes of differentiation and separation which attach to the group ending.

The rituals of ending

Ending, in its biological sense, connotes a clearly demarcated process of change from one state to another. It is a process for which human society has evolved a range of organized activities designed to cope with the emotions stirred up by change. Janus-faced, we look back to the past and forward to the future at moments of change. The group behaviours surrounding change are designed to help us to manage the loss of the previous state, to prepare us for the future state and to ensure some form of continuity between the two. The rituals of mourning and celebration are the group activities which we have evolved for dealing with endings. Ceremony is the vehicle by which we convey these rituals, and rehearsal is the method by which we anticipate and prepare for them.

Therapeutic groups are not exempt from the rituals of ending. The penultimate session of a group is generally more productive than its last session, in terms of any final analytic working through. A dilemma nevertheless arises when the urge to express these rituals enters the analytic group in a very concrete fashion. It is not unusual for the ending of a group to be infused with a celebratory mood, marked by displays of affection or appreciation towards the conductor and one another. Typical ways in which groups tax the conductor's analytic propriety during the final session are to exchange cards, gifts or contact details, or to bring food and drink into the group room, often with only a hazy idea of when to perform these exchanges or partake of the offerings.

These acts beg for interpretation, especially when they are accompanied by interesting unconscious slips, such as bringing of a bottle of wine into the session, with not enough glasses to go round. The conflict between social convention and analytic austerity is further accentuated if the conductor, at odds with the spirit of the group, chooses to unloose a salvo of interpretations designed to quell the display. These drop into the group with some impact, but with no opportunity for working them through subsequently, and the conductor runs the risk of embarrassing gift bearers, triggering discomfort and being seen as churlish. It is best, therefore, to accommodate to such manifestations. If the group has orchestrated a farewell involving drinks or food, it is a good idea to encourage the ritual pleasantries to take place at the beginning of the session. This clears the way for the latter part of the session to address concluding issues in an analytic vein. In another contravention of the abstinent analytic culture, group members often hug one another and the conductor at the moment of parting. There is little to be gained from discouraging such spontaneous expressions of farewell.

Ending therapy in a slow-open group

Some people need to anticipate the ending by stipulating their own time limit at the time of joining the group. The conductor may have to accept this, knowing that this is likely to be discarded once the fear of group therapy is overcome. Further down the line, the fear of being abandoned often impels group members to try and retain mastery over the leaving process: 'to leave before one is left'. A person vulnerable in this respect might panic at the thought of the ending and engineer a premature departure, a row being a typical pretext for leaving.

Group members who have injected colour and energy into the group may well encounter a drag on their departure through reasoned arguments against their decision to leave. Partly to compensate for this, the group is likely to accord them a generous and grateful farewell when the time comes. Departing group members who have been more withholding and isolated during their time in the group are likely to be acknowledged with more token farewells. It is the less integrated members of the group who leave the group with less fanfare, supporting the adage that those who are best known are best grieved. For some, the emotionality of the ending is too much to face. It is easier to avoid this by absenting oneself from the group. This becomes labelled as 'dropping out', an unfortunate term with connotations of vagrancy, or, for those of us who have lived through the 1950s and 60s, the beat generation and the hippie culture.

The timing of departure from an ongoing group

A good ending needs plenty of time and preparation. A three-month period of working through a departure from a once-weekly group is probably optimal, although many group analysts settle for a contractual obligation to remain in the group for one month after making the decision to leave. The prospective group member will have been told before joining the group that the intention to leave should be voiced in the group when it first arises in one's mind, and that sudden departures are detrimental in that one can wish to leave for the wrong reasons – one of which is to avoid having to face frightening or unwanted feelings, thoughts or impulses.

Since every exit from the group constitutes loss and disturbance, the conductor must be on guard against pre-judging the announcement to leave as an avoidance of the emergence of painful conflict, or made under the influence of the repetition compulsion or any other anti-therapeutic impulse. But even when the conductor has avoided these pitfalls, he or she may still disagree with the patient's decision to leave. Here the group's judgement is helpful as ever, and often clarifies the multiple influences on the decision. Ultimately, the treatment aim of the conductor and the group member may not be the same, in which case the decision of the group member may well be the more realistic and must be the determining one. This has been pictured by Foulkes as being on a winding staircase with a number of exits. One may take any one of them, but if one chooses to continue the next one will be at a higher, or, if you like, deeper, level and will take more time to reach.

Defences against ending

One of the classic ways of avoiding an emotionally charged ending is to go away quietly and unexpectedly. Another way, frequently resorted to by group members for whom the fear of being abandoned is uppermost, is to provoke an angry confrontation, which, however difficult, is experienced as less painful than the passivity and terror associated with abandonment. Group members predisposed to this fear are often impelled to try and retain mastery over the leaving process.

The group member who storms out in the middle of a row and never returns is likely to be protecting himself or herself from the dreaded feeling of sadness and grief dating from an earlier time in life. Premonitory signs of this have to be swiftly picked up and analysed. Another characteristic way out of the sadness of ending is seen with the group member who takes refuge in jocularity and frivolity. This is a form of manic defence which denies the gravity of loss. Avoidance of the emotional impact of leaving also expresses itself at times through scattered absences or latecomings.

The return of the symptom

The stress of an impending end to therapy often reproduces the original symptom with which the person came into the group. This is especially the case with those group members whose presenting symptoms were obsessional, phobic or psychosomatic in character. The intensity of the symptom may well have weakened into an obsessional indecisiveness, phobic separation anxiety or milder forms of somatization, but even these diluted manifestations can alarm the conductor and the group into thinking of postponing the termination of therapy. It is probably a mistake to encourage group members who have regressed in this way on the eve of their departure to stay on in the group. What is required is an analysis of the meaning of the re-emergence of the symptom, so that the mourning process can be faced and worked through.

Attachment and separation in relation to endings

A good deal of the analytic work which takes place in a group is concentrated on issues of attachment and separation. The approach of an ending often heralds an intensification of separation anxiety, especially on the part of individuals who have experienced disruptive or traumatic separations in the past, and those who have not managed to negotiate the developmental separation which comes out of the mother–infant state of fusion and consequently fail to make anything other than an anxious attachment to the group.

Separation has the attribute of non-permanence. It can be undone, and the separated individuals can remain in a relationship with each other. Parting, on the other hand, constitutes a real ending. It is permanent, although we often like to deny that. The fantasy of reunion offers protection against the pain of loss. Some group members protect themselves from this pain by not identifying with the group at the outset. The conductor listens to rationalized explanations to the effect that the group has nothing to offer them, for example: 'I don't have anything in common with these people', 'No one here can understand my problems', 'Everyone here is too disturbed to help me'.

If no attachment has been made, or if the attachment is only to the conductor, it is easier to drop out of the group or leave painlessly when the time comes, but the therapeutic experience will have been threadbare. The group members who are most prone to this are those who enter a group reluctantly in order to please the therapist. It is the therapist to whom they are attached, and to whom they anxiously cling while in the group. This has to be acknowledged and worked through if a satisfactory ending to the therapy is to be achieved. A split transference between the therapist and the rest of the group can also manifest itself as anger towards the therapist, putting the therapy in jeopardy if it goes undetected.

Vignette
In a group which had been working for some time with nothing but a high degree of friendly candour and collegiate warmth, a woman who was the most recent entrant into the group began to show discomfort, and withdrew from the exchanges. This was noticed and remarked on by the group and repeated attempts were made to find a reason for her behaviour. Eventually she told the group that she had got a lot from the group and was most grateful for it, that everyone had been so nice to her and helpful, and that it was time to leave.

The conductor had noticed for some time how much this woman had been enjoying the sessions. At the same time she felt that something was missing and was being glossed over. She had noticed that in the woman's vote of thanks she, the group conductor, had been left out both verbally and visually. After staying with her uncomfortable feelings for a while, the conductor turned to the woman and said that she had been wondering whether, apart from the good feelings and gratitude, there were other feelings coming up in her which might be threatening the good ones. She added that these unwelcome feelings might be difficult to express at any time and place, but especially in this group, where all seemed to be lightness and warmth. Perhaps it was better to leave in time, the conductor observed, before they could become too bothersome and threatening.

There was a shocked silence in the group. The woman who had announced her intention to leave burst into tears and for the first time attacked the conductor: 'You destroy everything with your so-called understanding! All was well before.' Her rage with the conductor now broke out like a tropical storm. First one and then another in the group agreed with her, bringing up previous occasions when the conductor had intervened and 'sown discord' in the group.

From then on, aggressive feelings came up more often in the group. The range of feelings, some agreeable and civilized, others less so, widened and deepened. The sessions became less comfortable for the therapist, but more real and alive. The woman stayed on and was able to bring out the aggressive emotions which she had learnt to repress from early childhood onwards.

The group as a transitional object

Some group members show a pattern of sporadic attendance governed more by their emotional needs of the day than by a sense of altruism towards the group. They have only a dim awareness of the impact which their absence has on the group, and they express surprise when the group tells them that they were missed in their absence, and that their presence is valued. This mirroring response of the group in these cases provides a corrective emotional experience to what may well have been an unconfirming or rejecting childhood experience. Their to-ing and fro-ing from the group can be understood and analysed as a developmental phase in therapy analogous to the child's use of a transitional object, with the group taking on the aspect of a transitional object, to be picked up as a source of comfort at moments of anxious attachment and discarded when alternative sources of gratification present themselves in the outside world. This style of attendance may be resented by the group, and the therapist's objective is to pre-empt the group member's premature departure actuated by such resentment. By interpreting the group member's use of the group as a transitional object and at the same time addressing the altruistic obligation to attend, the conductor may succeed in transforming a pattern of acting-out behaviour into one of interaction which is contained entirely within the group.

Holiday breaks as a rehearsal for endings

Announcements to leave often come after long breaks, or after the absence of the conductor. This is another example of the wish to retain mastery over the leaving process, to leave before one is left. Group timetables should have carefully planned holiday breaks built into them to provide opportunities for experiencing separation, antic-ipating the ultimate leaving process and analysing the angry, powerless responses which accompany an imposed absence. The register of group attendances is an important diagnostic tool in identifying group members who are especially vulnerable in this respect. Attendance which fizzles out as a break approaches, and absence from the group on its resumption after a break, deserve analysis.

The conductor should also be prepared for blithe denial on the part of the group that there is about to be a break, angry reproach-es when the subject of the break is introduced, and the presentation by group members of vexing problems, recurring symptoms and gloomy prognostications on the eve of the break, as a parting reminder to the conductor that he or she is abandoning the group. The successful negotiation of a holiday break is often greeted with relief, although anger towards the conductor may show itself indi-rectly in accounts of bad experiences during the break.

Contact after the end of therapy

There is often a curious unwillingness on the part of therapists to anticipate the patient's future after the conclusion of therapy, or more specifically to contemplate the possibility of contact with the patient after a declared end point. This is in contrast to assiduous (and deserved) attention given to the relationship with the patient at the beginning of therapy. Yet therapy is a bell-shaped curve. Attachment and detachment, engagement and disengagement, hel-los and goodbyes, beginnings and endings, have a symmetry which is often injured at the departure pole. Disappearance into the world, the breaking off of contact with the patient, is often considered a healthy and therefore correct way of ending therapy. This may be so for many, but there are some who will need the possibility of spo-radic contact with the group analyst after they have left the group. At the very least, this is a possibility which should be offered, and left to the individual.

'Group analysis interminable'?

What about the problem of 'group analysis interminable', an echo of the criticism sometimes levelled at psychoanalysis? This thought can arise when a person has been in a group for a long time (usually a great many years). Psychodynamic therapists are increasingly self-conscious about the accusation of not letting go of their patients. The problem is more acute in a climate of economic pressure, but also in the light of successful advances in brief, short-term therapies. The long-term therapies are also being harried by a model of health-care which sees a state of health as a baseline from which the patient departs when ill and to which he or she returns when cured. By contrast, group analysis calls for a model of reconstruction and change which can sometimes be achieved in short-term therapy but more often requires a considerable time.

There is some validity to the charge of prolonging therapy indefinitely, and some responsibility to be owned for this by group analysts who come from an earlier tradition of psychoanalysis in which *chronos*, the objective monitoring of the passage of time, did not matter in the determination of treatment duration, and the only true marker for the process of analysis was *kairos*, time as experienced in the world of the unconscious. But the risk now is that the baby will be thrown out with the bath water, that premature endings will be engineered to satisfy managerial and societal attitudes, at the expense of therapeutically judged needs by patients themselves.

A timely ending

It is notoriously difficult to discern progress in therapy, and it is often only in retrospect, in a kind of looking over one's shoulder, that change is recognized. This is particularly so when thinking of bringing therapy to an end. Dreams can provide the internal evidence of deep-rooted change, a sign that the ending of therapy is timely. One woman expressed the imminent loss of the group by dreaming of a well-lit, warm room, full of friends, from which she walked out alone into a dark street, not knowing where it would lead. In another group dream, a man expressed his anxiety about his inadequacy by dreaming that he had arrived at an airport without a ticket or passport. He managed to get past the official at the gate (the conductor?), on to the plane, and wondered what would happen when he reached his destination.

Vignette

Early in her group analysis, a woman told the group that she had
been living with a fear, amounting to a conviction, that her house
was full of dry rot and was slowly disintegrating. At the same time
she knew that there was no evidence for this. She had had the house
looked over and pronounced free of dry rot. Later in the therapy
this dread disappeared from her daytime thinking but turned up in
recurring nightmares, in which the house was collapsing around her.

Three years into her therapy the group remarked on the drastic
change for the better in her life circumstances. She listened to this
assessment of her progress with an air of detachment. Soon after
this she told the group of a dream she had had the previous night:
'I dreamt that something in my house is collapsing ... I think it was
in the back wall and part of the roof. I'm not frightened, just curious. I go round to see. I can see that the roof is holding, and there
is a hole in the wall and I go through it. It leads out into a lovely
park where people are walking and laughing and enjoying themselves. The sun is shining and I join them.' She added with a smile
directed to the group: 'Perhaps it was you who were there.'

CHAPTER TWELVE

Therapeutic pitfalls

THE MAN WHO BROKE THE GROUP SILENCE

Pitfall: fig. a 'trap' for the unsuspecting or unwary; any hidden
danger or error into which a person may fall unawares   OED

Group analysis is sometimes described, tongue-in-cheek, as a broad
church. This implies that the analytic process can be furthered
through a wide range of styles and techniques of intervention, provided the therapist sticks to the boundaries which have been set up to
maintain the stability of the group. This is true up to a point, but it is
equally true that certain styles of intervention on the part of the conductor can put the group at risk or lead to unsatisfactory therapeutic
outcomes. Beginners and experienced therapists alike are prone to
counter-therapeutic tendencies, and the recognition of these is com-

plex, since many of them are governed by unconscious, counter-transferential dynamics. This is where supervision comes into its own. In this chapter we provide our own explorer's map, describing what we have come to recognize as some of the common pitfalls which await the unsuspecting therapist traipsing through the jungle of the group.

The reticent conductor

A conducting style which is predominantly non-interventionist and withholding may have the rationale behind it to offer the group members a blank screen which facilitates fantasies, projection and regression. All these are part and parcel of deep-reaching therapy. However, these depths can only be safely tapped if the conductor is first experienced as reliable, caring and holding. These attributes, and the conductor's empathic insights, are displayed by verbal interventions. The group therapist is, after all, the only one who owes the members professional attention and care. The others are under no such obligation; they come for their own welfare alone. The conductor's persistent silence can be experienced as uncaring and even unsafe. When the group is blocked, or when the anxiety level in the group is excessively high, the conductor's very voice can be reassuring and can help the group to return to its task.

The perils of active intervention

At the other end of the continuum is the over-zealous conductor who offers directive, controlling interventions in the form of a succession of interpretations. Ostensibly this is done to further insight, but the result may be to strengthen defences and bring about withdrawal and non-participation. The conductor may have been seduced into an all-knowing stance by the craving of the group for a strong, omniscient father figure who guides and relieves distress. In a crisis, or at a time of high anxiety, such a persona may have to be temporarily adopted. If so, it should be relinquished as speedily as possible, and a return made to a style of conducting which validates the importance of the group itself as the therapeutic agent. Overactive therapists tend to make their groups dependent on them for too long, and undermine the weaning process which is a prerequisite for achieving a secure, resilient, authentic self.

Tipping the scales towards problems and failures

An analytic group can at times develop a culture of immersion in problems and failures. This can be fuelled by a conductor who relates selectively to such material at the expense of narratives of success, achievement and pleasure. Group members who are going through a relatively fulfilled period in their lives may opt out of the discourse because they feel that their state of mind does not 'fit in', or because they fear the group's disbelief or destructive envy. This withdrawal is furthered by a conductor who consistently looks for an underlying denied conflict in all material offered and underestimates the importance of unqualified affirmation of good feelings and success.

Paddling in the shallows

The mere fact that group members are effortlessly communicating with one another in a spirit of mutual interest and acceptance, does not necessarily mean that the group is functioning therapeutically. Beginning groups especially, but also established groups, can fall back on a socially learnt repertoire of communication, such as a discussion of the issues of the day, exchanges of anecdotes, friendly banter, expressions of mutual appreciation and advice-giving. Any of these can form the starting point for an analytic journey, and it is unwise to interpret them as defensive too early. On the other hand, if this mode of communication goes on too long, or if it becomes a pattern in the group, the conductor has to look for an analytic talking point in the material and lead the group along this train of thought. In this way the conductor models the analytic attitude and the appropriate use of the group without crushing the spontaneity and sociability of the group members.

Trigger-happy interpretations

Group analysts can underestimate the perspicacity of the group, and its ability to reach insights in its own way and time. It is tempting at times to try and accelerate the therapeutic process by drawing attention to a connection which appears to be hidden from the group's collective gaze. The conductor unsure of his or her authority may also wish to impress the group with a virtuoso performance of insight and profundity, a temptation which might become especially strong if the conductor is nursing a suspicion that the group does not hold him or her in sufficiently high regard, especially if the group seems to be getting on very well on its own.

Every group therapist has experienced the silence which falls in the wake of an interpretation. At best, this is a reflective silence, experienced as food for thought. Less happily, however, it is a frustrated or bemused silence, implying that a process has been interrupted. A gratuitous interpretation sometimes has the effect of closing down a process which was already satisfactorily under way. If the interpretation is pronounced with a note of finality, it may sound as if the definitive verdict on the material has been delivered, giving the group the message that it should move on.

Preoccupation with individuals at the expense of the group

'Not seeing the wood for the trees'

Engagement with individuals in the group rather than with the group as a whole is a legitimate ideological position in some psychoanalytic group therapies in the tradition of Wolf and Schwartz, who consciously espoused an individualistic technique and eschewed group dynamics as a therapeutic agency. In Foulkesian group analysis, however, the conductor strives to achieve a balance between attention to individuals and attention to the group as a whole. Given this theoretical baseline, if there is a tendency to engage overactively with group members to the point where the rest of the group fades into the background and loses its effectiveness as a therapeutic agency, the trail is more likely to lead to the conductor's personal needs.

A conductor's over-identification with a particular group member, or with a particular sub-group (the men, or the women, for instance) is shadowed by over-identification with a larger archetypal symbolic representative of that person or sub-group, for example 'the helpless little boy' or 'the vulnerable mother'. Equally, the tendency to ignore some individuals and sub-groups may reveal a negative counter-transference to those group members.

Preoccupation with the group as a whole at the expense of the individual

'Not seeing the trees for the wood'

This can also be a legitimate style of intervention in certain experiential models of group dynamics, and in the psychoanalytic tradition of Bion and Ezriel, but it is not a style which accords with Foulkesian group analysis, and when it does emerge in a group-analytic setting, the origins are again likely to be found with the conductor rather than in the group situation.

The problem with predominantly group-as-a-whole interventions, as with excessive reticence, is that individual group members can be left feeling unheld or unrecognized. Anxiety and frustration are increased, and group members find it more difficult to interact freely with one another in a mutually therapeutic mould or tolerate one person holding the focus for very long. Such groups tend to be affected by an increased drop-out rate and function with an over-anxious, compliant culture.

It is often difficult to know when to focus on the individual and when to focus on the group. The concept of the group as a figure–ground constellation, offering ever changing configurations of dialogue, provides a useful working model and serves as an anchor to prevent the vessel from dragging too far in one or other direction.

Steering between the Scylla of the 'here-and-now' and the Charybdis of the 'there-and-then'

Group analysts vary in the extent to which they facilitate the exploration of interactions between the group members themselves, as opposed to exploration of material deriving from group members' relationships outside the group and past experiences. Excessive preoccupation with either mode can assume defensive proportions. Although the 'here-and-now' is an interactional field which holds much fascination, it is sometimes of more interest to the conductor than to the other group members, who may be longing to bring their life situations and outside relationships into the group but feel that they have to defer to the analysis of 'here-and-now' phenomena.

Conversely, the conductor, Ulysses-like, sometimes has to turn the rudder in the opposite direction, away from experiences outside the group and towards the 'here-and-now'. This is especially important when the group is going through a moment of change, such as a change in membership or an imminent holiday break, or when the group is struggling with an intra-group event, such as an unspoken tension between group members or a pattern of group destructive behaviour.

The way in which the group analyst conducts a group is determined to a large extent by the model that has been taken in during the training, but also by the conductor's personality. The group analyst's influence on the group must not be underestimated, and it is for this reason that he or she needs to monitor personal reactions and their expressions, an act of introspection which, in the rough-and-tumble of group life, is not at all easy to maintain without loss of authenticity and spontaneity.

CHAPTER THIRTEEN

Challenging scenarios

PROBLEMATIC SITUATIONS FOR THE GROUP ANALYST:
DUDLEY INSISTS ON BRINGING HIS OWN
PERSONAL SCAPEGOAT TO THE GROUP

The popular caricature of a therapeutic group, which serves us ill, depicts it as a place where highly disturbed individuals disport themselves uninhibitedly, presided over by an equally disturbed, but supremely controlled therapist. The reality is that analytic groups, protected by careful attention to the composition, setting and boundaries of the group, and by the conductor's awareness of what constitutes a therapeutic direction, seldom erupt into such extravagant or intrusive displays of behaviour. From time to time, however, the group presents the conductor with challenging scenarios which pose a threat to the therapeutic culture and put the stability of the group at risk.

Dropping out

A potential danger point in the group may arise when a group member suddenly announces his or her intention to leave the group. If this wish has an unconscious neurotic determinant, it is important to uncover it and help the patient to deal with it other than by flight. One such determinant can be the need to avoid painful and conflict-ridden departures in previous life situations, which are now being avoided or compulsively repeated. Announcements of the intention to leave often come after long breaks or the absence of the conductor for one reason or another. These may be in the nature of acting out the rage at having been left: 'If you can leave me, I can leave you.' More difficult to unearth and locate is the wish to terminate treatment due to an unconscious fear of having to face a conflict which has so far been avoided.

The premonitory signs of dropping out include latecoming, absenteeism, a pattern of stuttering attendance – sometimes clustering around holiday breaks – and withdrawal from group interaction. The last of these is not only manifested by silence on the part of the group member. The communication may take on a defensive, repetitious character, a shift from personal disclosure to a detached mode, and a distancing from the group as a whole. Potential dropouts often start to act like therapists, 'unjoining' themselves from the group. Other signs involve a change in the emotional coloration of the group member, such as a retreat into grim silence, or a dissociated internal preoccupation. Literally and figuratively, the patient stares out of the window.

Dropping out may be due to faulty selection in the first place. The patient may be unable, at that time at least, to bear a therapy which offers less protection than the one-to-one situation of individual therapy. Alternatively, the timing of entry may have been wrong for the group, which might then act out its rejection till it succeeds, and the newcomer drops out.

Vignette

A woman had had two years of psychoanalytic treatment with a male analyst, when he announced that he was leaving the country to return to his country of origin. He would therefore be terminating the therapy, he explained, but he recommended group therapy with Mrs X, a therapist whom he knew and valued highly. After due contact and preparation, the woman came into a suitable twice-weekly group, where she was well received. She seemed to have settled down, when she suddenly declared that she was leaving. Her reasons came tumbling out: How could she rely on anyone in the group? They might all be gone tomorrow. The group analyst, especially, could not be trusted. (The group conductor, like her departed analyst, was of foreign origin.) When asked by the group why she thought she could not rely on them, she said: 'After all, everyone looks only after himself.' In spite of efforts by the group conductor and the group to link her feelings to the sudden, painful desertion by her analyst, she left the group. From the initial interviews the group analyst knew that the desertion by her analyst constituted a repeat of an earlier, childhood one: her father had left the family, handing her over to the sole care of her mother, and she had not seen him again. The therapy situation brought up the seemingly unbearable pain of her childhood.

A patient dropping out leaves a sense of failure in the therapist, and often a sense of guilt in the group. In the case just mentioned, it is clear that it would have been of great benefit to this group member had she been able to face the re-awakened childhood trauma by working through it as she was experiencing it in the transference to the conductor and the group. But she was gone, and the opportunity was lost. However, there was still some possibility for therapeutic work: the emergence of feelings of inadequacy and powerlessness which her dropping out had evoked in the group could be investigated and analysed as having their origins in infantile omnipotence. And the group conductor, too, learnt from this painful experience. What had happened could have been foreseen and the transition from individual analysis and the loss of the old therapist better prepared for. Her entrance into the group should have been delayed. Drop-outs are failures in therapy, and though not always avoidable, well worth looking at in depth. Such failures, though not often discussed in the literature of therapy, are more instructive than success stories.

Attention to such phenomena as latecoming and irregular attendance is important in unearthing the transferential resistances which predispose to dropping out. Group members watch closely to see how the group analyst manages absence, and how he or she treats the returned member. A 'laissez faire' approach on the part of the conductor could imply an uncaring attitude. Equally unproductive is the opposite, a knee-jerk insistence on analysing as resistance all slippages in punctuality and attendance – an attitude on the part of the conductor which is often driven by a fear of losing group members or presiding over the disintegration of the group. The contextual trigger of dropping out may be around a specific, emotionally charged event in the group, such as the emergence and disclosure of a long-buried trauma, a conflictual exchange between members, a change in the group itself – the introduction of a new member, for example – or pressure from the group members' life situation outside the group.

Dropping out can also reflect a failure on the part of the group to recognize a healthy need to leave, in other words, to 'let go'. At some point a judgement has to be made about the wisdom of the person's intention to leave the group. Although this may mean acknowledging that the original decision to enter the group was ill-considered or ill-timed, it is best to end the therapy on a constructive, forward-looking note by converting a potential dropping out into a proper leaving.

A drop-out can sometimes be averted by one or more individual sessions during which the reasons can be more robustly explored and rehearsed for presentation to the group. It is not easy to decide when to make contact with a person who has left a group session early and unhappily, or is inexplicably absent from a session. Over-solicitous efforts at retrieval may have a counter-productive effect, and may be experienced as invasive or persecutory. But the opposite error of neglecting to act between sessions, more common in our experience, may equally jeopardize the therapy.

The scapegoat phenomenon

The ancient tendency for groups to appoint a carrier for their own badness, and then set about getting rid of that carrier, will probably always be part of the human condition, and therapeutic groups are by no means immune to the process. On the crest of an evolutionary wave between magical and symbolic thinking, the biblical scapegoat was chosen to act as the carrier for the sins of the community. At first the animal, duly crowned with a wreath of thorns, was driven out into the desert, but the wretched creature, unaware of its important communal function, tended to wander back, so a more thorough method of expulsion had to be devised, which entailed pushing the animal over a cliff. Exit the goat, never to return. Or did it? The problem with scapegoating is that it has a recurring dynamic. Sooner or later the goat does return, in the shape of a relative or ghost, and the cycle is repeated.

In therapy groups, an individual is more likely to become a scape-goat if he or she is experienced as conspicuously different from the other group members in ways which threaten the fantasied integrity of the group. This is important to bear in mind when composing the group and selecting new members. The conductor has to ensure the presence in the group of at least some members with the capacity for mutual identification with the new member, especially if cultural, ethnic or sexual orientation identity markers are likely to be a source of alienation and isolation. This does not imply a simplistic pairing up or matching exercise by the conductor. The personality attributes of the group members and their empathic and identificatory skills are more important than easily discernible traits, and are the chief safeguards against scapegoating.

Scapegoating is more likely to manifest itself in societies or groups which have been afflicted by a traumatic event which has threatened their integrity, or even their very existence. The fear or threat of recurrent adversity impels the group to seek out the source and origin of its affliction and take steps to get rid of it. These groups may develop a culture of conformity and an autocratic leadership, resulting in the progressive stigmatization and isolation of those considered a threat to the group's integrity.

In large groups, and in society at large, the scapegoat takes on a more representational role. Cultural myths and political slogans float to the surface from the depth of the social unconscious to feed the process. The actual behaviour of the scapegoat is less significant than the attributions of the group based on prejudiced and stereotyped thinking. In the small therapy group, these factors operate as well, but they are mitigated by the powerful communication processes available to the group. In the small group, the behaviour and personality of the group member plays more of a part than social or cultural attributes.

Monopolizing and victim behaviour are particularly deceptive manifestations which can lead to scapegoating, since they all too easily invite the self-justifying collusion of the group, including, at times, the conductor. The early warning signs can sometimes be seen in the exaggerated attention given to a potential scapegoat by the group, expressed as a mixture of concern and impatience. This spills over into frank hostility, expressed either by withdrawal from the scapegoat or blunt attack. This has to be effectively counteracted by the conductor in a series of interventions designed, first to arrest the process, ('Just a moment, let's pause and look at what's going on here') and then to draw the attention of the group to the projective mechanisms involved.

The disowning dynamic which is intrinsic to scapegoating works against the climate of mutual identification, reflective receptivity and empathy on which the group relies. To break the cycle, the conductor has to foster a spirit of empathy with the isolated group member. This means that group members, including the scapegoat, each have to be shown their part in the process and helped to re-own their projections. The attack on a potential scapegoat may revolve around disowned guilt, but it may also feature a host of other negative attributions such as disgust and shame. Underlying the process are blame, contempt and envy. On a manifest level, these can appear in many forms: over-solicitousness, avoidance of contact, verbal expressions of dislike or angry attacks.

The transferential fear or resentment towards the conductor often slips a cog and gets displaced from the conductor on to a vulnerable group member. A classic scenario is the unwelcome arrival of a new member, experienced unconsciously as a demanding new baby, delivered into the group by the conductor and gazed upon lovingly at the expense of the siblings. Only when these feelings have been acknowledged can the group confront the potential scapegoat with those aspects of his or her personality or behaviour which might have been colluding with the process. If the scapegoating is allowed to run its course unchecked, the group might at first feel a sense of relief and enhanced cohesion. But a deep sense of guilt predisposes to a recurrence, unless the underlying dynamic has been grasped and fully analysed.

Scapegoating can be an insidious process, but it can also occur with startling rapidity, and it may be vain to hope that the group will

arrest the process spontaneously. The conductor has to be the first
person to show an identification with the scapegoat. This can be perceived as the conductor 'siding with' the scapegoat, and the group
may then turn its guns on the conductor, a necessary and welcome
corrective to the dynamic of displacement which often lies at the
heart of the scapegoating process. This is work done with the group
as a whole, culminating in an understanding of the myths and
assumptions underlying the process.

Monopolizing behaviour

Often encountered and difficult to handle is the group member who
seems to need to hold the floor in the group's discourse. This is
done with detailed, lengthy descriptions of problems, states of
affairs or states of mind. Other group members' contributions are
used as hooks to hang this on, in a narrative which is then poured
into the group with disregard of its reception. The 'Group
Monopolizer' is the term coined for such an individual (Yalom,
1975).

Before considering an intervention, the conductor has to arrive at
an understanding of the cause of such behaviour, which differs from
person to person. The most likely cause is a high level of anxiety
which is self-perpetuating, and which increases as the monopolizer
becomes dimly aware of the growing resentment in the group.
Another reason for compulsively monopolizing a group originates in
an unconscious conviction that one is not heard or understood
unless one hammers home one's story. This conviction, likely to have
been acquired in childhood and perpetuated in adolescence, readily
surfaces in the group.

Whatever the cause, the group setting offers a good background
for reparation. This is not easy, since such group members evoke
impatience and irritation in the conductor as well as amongst the
group members. The conductor has to avoid showing irritation or
sounding forbidding or punitive when trying to bring the avalanche
of words to a halt. One reaction to such an attempt was: 'You told me
to say what's in my mind, and now you shut me up!'

As always, one has to observe the group's reactions. Is the group
using the monopolizer to hide behind? Is the monopolizer expressing the anger residing in the group and in this way allowing the

group to remain sensible and civilized while he or she is exposed? Is the group tolerating this behaviour without comment for fear of erupting into aggression which might get out of hand? If the underlying dynamic is picked up and voiced by the conductor, the monopolizing group member can be released from the role and encouraged to look at himself or herself with new eyes.

The conductor's task is made all the more difficult for having two seemingly contradictory aims: firstly, to protect the group's integrity in the face of a potentially group-destructive effect which might result in acting out behaviour such as absenteeism, sub-grouping or scapegoating, and then to help the monopolizing member to recognize their anti-social, isolating behaviour and wish to change it. Getting to the unconscious driving force of the behaviour will follow change. This is a prime example of Foulkes' dictum that insight follows change rather than causing it (Foulkes, 1990).

There is a distinction between monopolizing and attention-seeking behaviour. Monopolization of the group's time gets the attention of both the conductor and the group, but this is not usually the driving motive. Straightforward attention-seeking, on the other hand, is usually more accessible to consciousness and can therefore be more easily handled. It is readily detected by a mature group and usually treated with good-natured humour. This is not the case, though, when it expresses itself as an attack on the setting, such as persistent latecoming, or staying behind at the close of a session 'to have a word with you' (the conductor) with some apparently urgent information. When this happens, it is important to hold the line, and tactfully but firmly steer such an attempt at extra attention back into the group session, where it can be explored for its meaning.

Vignette

A young woman who had recently come into a group would invariably enter five minutes or so late and take her chair with a smile but no explanation or apology. After a while someone pointed out her latecoming and wondered whether her work or some other reason accounted for it. The woman was obviously pleased that her behaviour had been noticed but she still offered no reasons for it. The group analyst intervened with: 'Perhaps there are other ways of making oneself noticed here?' This intervention came dangerously close to being shame-inducing, but in the event it helped the woman to participate more, state her views forcefully, and discover that what she said was being heard and taken seriously. Much later in her group life she spoke of her family as boisterous and dominated by her two bright brothers, leaving little room for her.

Enactment of aggression in the group

There is a fine line between those angry exchanges in the group which are the lifeblood of open communication, and those which are coloured by aggression of a destructive nature, edged with sadism. As always, the conductor is poised to intervene if the group seems paralysed in spectator mode. The group member who discharges transferential anger or narcissistic rage impulsively has probably lost sight of the 'as if' clause necessary for analytic thought, but the group has to see this process through, eventually to restore a reflective climate. Perpetrators of verbal abuse sometimes assume that the group grants a licence to insult in the name of honesty, and tend to be oblivious to the impact of their aggression on others. This process has to be halted and named, and the abuser confronted with the effect of their utterances on the group. The same principle applies to more disguised forms of aggression which can masquerade as therapy: mockery, sarcasm and ridicule. These social devices have to be translated in the group, first into the aggressive motivation which underlies them, and then into ownership by the group member or members who have adopted them.

Vignette

Two women launched into a slanging match with each other over one of the woman's handling of her husband's violence, especially since it involved her child. The rest of the group looked on in stunned silence. The conductor, although aware of the transferential basis of this attack, was faced with a dilemma. Should he allow the interaction to escalate, or should he intervene, and if so, how? Each of the two protagonists was looking at the scenario from her own standpoint, governed by her own life experiences and the values distilled from them. The conductor turned first to the one woman, then the other, reformulating their angry outbursts in more moderate language. This freed the other group members to join in and identify with one or other element of the psychic substrate.

The therapist's ally

The unique strength of group analysis is that it mobilizes people's innate ability to act as therapists towards one another. Yet group members can sometimes hide behind this entitlement as a way of avoiding personal involvement in the group. The conductor has to judge whether the patient who wears this cloak of impersonality – which might, incidentally, be both insightful and helpful to others in the group – is doing so as a means of easing the way towards more personal involvement or as a means of avoiding self-disclosure and self-discovery. The language with which the problem is addressed is important. A typical intervention might run along the lines of: 'That's helpful, but where are you in all this?' Underlying this tendency to become the 'therapist's ally', there is sometimes a wish to remain in control.

The isolated group member

Isolation, in Foulkes' conception, is the antithesis of communication. All who join an analytic group bring with them areas of isolation, expressed in cryptic form as neurotic symptoms, which gradually get transformed into articulate language (Foulkes, 1948). This said, certain individuals are conspicuously isolated from their fellows and pose a distinctive challenge to the conductor and the group.

Some group isolates are locked into a position of silent and frozen watchfulness. Others struggle to maintain their psychic equilibrium by ladling out advice or indulging in wild generalizations and stereotyping behaviour, distorting the communications of the group as a means of retaining control. The therapist has to help the group to make links gradually with the isolated group member. This is achieved by encouraging the group to make transient identifications with the isolated person (Ormont, 2004).

Group members who are isolated may need a period in therapy which runs to many years, since what they require is a slow exposure to the nurturing processes inherent in the group. The integration of

isolated group members is helped if they can be brought into conflict with their own isolation. This is more likely to happen if the
isolated stance is keeping strong feelings at bay, which would otherwise erupt in unmanageable outbursts. Shame and poorly controlled
rage may be significant features of the self-presentation of such isolated group members (Behr, 2004).

Another manifestation of isolation is found in the group member
who has experienced earlier and more enduring traumatization than
the conflict-ridden isolate. It may well be that isolation in this case
protects against fantasied disintegration. Conversely, the defence
may serve the fear of being taken over by the group. The group is
usually sensitive to the latter form of isolation, and readily accom-
modates to the time-scale required by the group member to emerge
from the bunker of isolation.

The 'stuck' group

A certain amount of stability and predictability is necessary for the
analytic process. However, groups sometimes drift into the dol-
drums, entering a phase in which very little seems to change. The
question to ask is: 'What is missing from the group?' The group may
be in this state to avoid getting in touch with potentially excessive
pain or a fantasied dread. Having come to this conclusion, the conductor may decide to name the unconscious conspiracy, and the
reason for it; that is, to interpret it.

The experience of stuckness may take place in a context of relative
silence, or sporadic exchanges which appear to lead nowhere and fiz-
zle out, leading to an enhanced sense of futility. It is important,
however, not to mistake a fairly long prelude of silence for a stuck
position. Some groups have a culture of reverie which runs its course
before an utterance opens the discourse.

Sometimes the spell which entrances the 'stuck' group can be broken by an appeal to the group as a whole to identify the problem, but
it is probably more productive to appeal to one of the group members who seems more in touch with the group's collective
unconscious. This in turn releases the emotions, which, once they
begin to be put into words, break the barrier of resistance and lead
to a reinvigoration of the group.

Appeals, whether to the individual or the group-as-a-whole, are more likely to succeed if couched in the language of metaphor. This is because a metaphor is more in the nature of 'common property' and therefore more capable of producing resonances which lead in turn to imaginative thoughts and utterances. The choice of metaphor is a personal one. To lead the way with metaphor, the therapist must be prepared to venture into the realms of self-disclosure. To introduce a metaphor is to lay oneself open to efforts, whether jocular or serious, on the part of the group, to seize on the offering as an opportunity to view the therapist's inner world. The art of offering a metaphor or a dream is to know how and when to travel back into the self and then out again to the group.

Groups sometimes get stuck because the therapist is implicated in a dynamic to which the group dares not draw attention. Some examples of this are: an excessively emotional or partisan display on the part of the therapist towards or against a particular group member; a tendency on the part of the therapist to extinguish 'non-problem'-related conversations and light-hearted or discursive conversations, ostensibly in the name of therapy, or a recent incident which has been insufficiently explored.

Another effective method of challenging the stuck dynamic is to introduce a new member whose foremost motive for seeking therapy lies in the area which is being avoided by the group. This is an heroic step to take. The conductor is likely to experience a sense of trepidation, which has both realistic and counter-transferential aspects, for the group's equilibrium. However, in our experience, the introduction of a new member at this point can work like a charm. The new member immediately feels at home and understood, and the group undergoes a surge of energy. The new member is likely to act under the pressure of his or her problems by disclosing them quite soon after entry into the group, and this gives the group the impetus and permission to recognize the previously unacknowledged problem area and look it in the face. This applies especially to sexuality in all its forms, and to socially unacceptable fantasies or attitudes such as racism.

Malignant mirroring

> The real reason why Vronsky disliked the prince so much was that in
> him he could not help seeing himself. And what he saw in this mirror
> did not gratify his self-esteem.   Tolstoy, *Anna Karenina*

Mirroring is a therapeutic factor intrinsic to group analysis. It implies the opportunity to see oneself as others see one, as Robert Burns put it, in the thoughtful, caring environment of the group. But there is a down-side to it which can lead to the phenomenon known as 'malignant mirroring'. This occurs typically when two people sense in each other a disliked and often a hated attribute which they have in common. The similarity is unrecognized, dreaded and rejected. Louis Zinkin, in his seminal paper on the subject, sees the destructiveness in its 'controlling taking over' (Zinkin, 1983).

Malignant mirroring can become so intolerable for the pair engaged in the process that the only solution may be seen in one of the pair leaving the group. It can also endanger the group itself, who tend to react by observing the process in a state akin to paralysis. It is left to the conductor to act immediately and vigorously. He or she tries to take the unbearable burden off the shoulders of the embattled pair, with such words as 'I think I recognize the gnawing feelings you two are experiencing. I wonder whether the others do too.' If this does not have the desired result, and it must be said that it often does not, the therapist has to fall back on techniques normally reserved for working with individuals who are unable to own their part in a process. The intensity of the exchanges between the two protagonists in a malignant mirroring scenario is so great that for some time there is no room for reflective thought.

Vignette

A woman in a group attacked a man, accusing him of having no respect for women. He spiritedly defended himself, and counter-accused her of treating men as objects of contempt and ridicule. Both perceptions were to some extent accurate. The woman had been affected by a string of destructive relationships with men, who in one way or another had abused her or taken advantage of her. The man had similarly been affected by his relationship with a woman who had reduced him to a precarious financial state in the course of a destructive marital breakdown. What neither party was recognizing, since both saw themselves as victims in their respective partner relationships, was the attribute that they were harbouring in themselves of angry, potentially aggressive and abusive behaviour directed at men and women respectively. The therapist shadowed

> first one, then the other, allying himself with whomever he saw as immediately at risk of being further victimized, until he found the moment to draw attention to the similarities of their experiences. This detoxified the process and allowed time for the two protagonists to cope with the strength of their feelings and eventually modify them.

Malignant mirroring is a process which can flare up during the course of a single session, or it can simmer on and run a course of weeks or months, surfacing episodically, or burning away beneath the surface. It can tax the emotional and professional endurance of the conductor to its limits.

Enactment of erotic feelings in the group

Groups, despite their 'public' dimension, provide a safe forum for the exploration of symptoms and problems relating to physical sexuality. The group-analytic situation places these in their relational context, and the interactional and transference field of the group brings them alive for the group members. This presents its own specific set of difficulties. These relate, first of all, to the discussion of what is essentially a private function in what is technically a public arena. Sexuality has its own language, and is capable of evoking a strong sense of shame, guilt or arousal.

A group member may be tempted to act on their attraction to another group member. This undermines the group-analytic culture in that it creates a special relationship which works against the possibility of criss-crossing transferences. The secrecy surrounding the relationship results in isolation, with the result that the pairing couple often drops out. If the information comes back into the group in good time, the process has to be thoroughly analysed to divest it of its transferential component. If the couple insists on staying in the relationship, group-analytic work becomes untenable, and one or the other, or both, may be asked to leave the group.

CHAPTER FOURTEEN
The group analyst in trouble

THE DISSATISFIED GROUP PATIENT

Quis custodiet ipsos custodes?
Who will guard those self-same guardians?   Juvenal

Psychotherapists, let it be said, are prone to the same afflictions, ailments and vicissitudes of life which befall their clients. This has to be asserted in the face of a myth, cherished by not a few therapists, that the status of 'therapist' drapes a mantle of invulnerability around them. It is also fondly believed by both therapists and patients alike that the psychological state of health of the therapist, presumed to be the result of an arduous and thorough training which has included exposure to a deep analytic process, somehow confers immunity on therapists to the very conditions which they see unfolding before their benign and empathic gaze. In short, fantasies of omnipotence and invulnerability lurk within the therapist's mind, as they do amongst their clients. All who enter the healing professions have to develop defences for dealing with the constant barrage of illness, suffering and breakdown to which they are subjected.

This, coupled with a proclivity for 'workaholism' and a tendency to persevere doggedly in the face of messages reaching them from both their inner and outer worlds that all is not well, makes it difficult for psychotherapists to admit, let alone acknowledge to others, when they are beginning to experience difficulties which are starting to have repercussions on their work. Our lives are plagued by incidents which are either stress-related or visited upon us unexpectedly by environmental circumstances. As is often the case, a 'clinical' incident occurs when both converge. 'Death,' observed a wit, 'is nature's way of telling you to slow down.'

The group as a mirror to the therapist

The group analyst looks into a salutary mirror in the form of the group. However, there are good reasons why a group of patients cannot be relied on to act as the sole early warning detection system for the therapist's wellbeing. The first is that groups have a powerful incentive to protect the therapist from any forces which could bring the therapist down. As the provider of their therapy, the group analyst has to be kept healthy. His or her existence provides the *raison d'être* of the group, and any signs that the therapist is slipping into a less-than-good-enough mode of functioning are likely to be assiduously ignored. Psychological defences, notably denial, will be called into play, so that the illusion of safety and containment which the group offers can be maintained.

Although the group as a whole has a vested interest in preserving the therapist, individual group members express their anger towards the therapist in diverse ways, one of which is the attribution of illness to the healthy therapist. A scenario sometimes presents itself, spearheaded by one or two group members who watch the therapist like hawks and scan his or her features, expression and demeanour for any signs of change which could betoken physical or mental illness. Pallor, a cough, a lapse of memory or a stumble are among many innocent symptoms perceived as omens of a condition which could spell abandonment by the therapist through serious illness or death. Anxious vigilance of this nature usually has its origins in the particular group member's early history and this, when discovered, can be constructively worked on as a transference phenomenon. There are group members, for example, who have had to be alert to the needs of an ill parent. Their desire to harm or attack the therapist is disowned through projective mechanisms, converted into perceptions of illness and transferred onto the person of an otherwise healthy or slightly out of sorts therapist, who may in turn undergo a counter-transferential decline in a feeling of wellbeing. Ironically and paradoxically, when faced with real decompensation on the part of the therapist, the group as a whole tends to shut its collective eye and soldier on in an attitude of anxious avoidance.

Therapists cannot therefore rely on the reactions of the group to alert them to any concerns about their own wellbeing. The self-aware therapist will naturally reflect on small clues offered by the group and not dismiss the material which they proffer as belonging exclusively within the realm of the transference, but other, more reliable indicators of dysfunction are best sought and found, such as supervision and robust advice from friends, family and colleagues.

The absent therapist

The group dynamics of the therapist's unexpected absence are different from those which arise in the wake of an expected absence, for which the group will have been carefully prepared. Clearly the latter is desirable, but *force majeure* sometimes imposes itself, calling for an exercise in damage limitation. If the absence can be anticipated, the therapist has to consider how open he or she can be about the reasons for the absence. The development of an illness, undergoing surgery, a celebration, an unscheduled professional occasion, or a family bereavement, are some of the events which oblige therapists to absent themselves from the group, each presenting a different set of issues in terms of the predictable duration of absence and the emotional currency of the circumstances.

The imperative towards self-disclosure may be strong, but as always, the therapist treads a tightrope between exploration of the transference and the introduction of a reality that is impinging on the therapy. Carefully titrated information of a factual nature, to a level at which the therapist is comfortable, implies a respect for the group's maturity and generally does no harm to the process of transferential exploration. The transference asserts itself willy nilly and the therapist is likely to face strong, anxiety-driven expressions of anger in its various guises. The more time there is to prepare for the absence, the less the ensuing turbulence. Unexpected absence poses the problem, not only of what to tell the group, but how to let them know that the therapist will not be there. If the therapist is *hors de combat* an intermediary will have to communicate the information: a good reason why group records and contact details for group members should be easily accessible to colleagues and administrators.

Should the group meet in the absence of the therapist?

There are various views on the question of whether a group should meet in the event of the absence of the therapist. Some group analysts take a reading of the group's maturity and ask themselves whether there is an already established group-analytic culture and whether the setting will allow for it. The latter includes the availability of a responsible outsider to usher the group into and out of the premises. Others take the view that professional and clinical propriety demands that the session be cancelled, especially if there is a concern about some of the group members' ability to sustain a session without professional overview. Some group analysts would let the group meet on its own for more than one session, but this depends largely on the maturity of the group.

The dynamics involved in caretaking a group

The caretaking of a group on behalf of an absent therapist is an art which calls for a special set of skills. Like any other therapeutic manoeuvre involving dynamic administration, it is best thought about and planned in advance. Ideally, the handing over of a group from one therapist to another for a limited period of time should be a collaborative undertaking, planned with all the attention to detail accorded to the setting up of a completely new group. In reality, however, this is not always possible. Therapists sometimes have to step into the role of caretaker with very little notice, and the therapist's

absence through illness may render it impossible for the two therapists to make any contact with each other. This is a worst case
scenario, but it underlines the importance of having in place a system and structure which will facilitate a handover in the event of the
unexpected, or even expected, absence of the 'resident' therapist.

Caretaking responsibilities multiply when the group faces an
absence of long or uncertain duration. The caretaker should be
briefed about the history and composition of the group, and the
absent group analyst, if accessible, should tell the caretaker what
information he or she would like given about the circumstances and
duration of the absence.

So informed, the caretaker is braced for an anxious group, preoccupied with the impact of the therapist's absence on their own
therapy. He or she can expect to field questions about the therapist's
absence, how much the caretaker knows about the group members,
and the nature of the relationship between the caretaker and the
absent therapist. Group members whose life experience has sensitized them to abandonment, separation, family dislocation, illness or
unpredictability, will have strong reactions to the caretaking situation. Metaphors of fostering and step-parenting are likely to abound
and can be put to good use in transferential work.

A singular advantage of the caretaker is the 'outsider' status, rather
like that of a new group member. Being relatively ignorant of the
group's history and the history of the individual members, the caretaker is well placed to ask innocent questions which empower the
group to include him or her. This also provides an excellent opportunity for getting the group to retell its story and for individual
members to revisit their personal narratives. Far from being merely a
repetition, this is a therapeutic exercise that brings fresh perspectives
to bear on the past.

The caretaker should be on the alert for the group's tendency to
drive a wedge between him or her and the absent therapist.
Bewilderingly, the therapist might be embraced by the group, the
recipient of seductive overtures and omnipotent projections. Some
group members might form a strong attachment, welcoming, for
example, a 'sympathetic' woman as a replacement for an 'unsympathetic' man. Anger at the absent therapist expresses itself in a variety
of ways: the caretaker may be regaled with tales of the absent therapist's woefully inadequate insights or lack of understanding,

contrasted with the deep and helpful insights offered by the caretaker, in this way illuminating problems which have been vainly
struggled with for a long time. The caretaker's vanity and professional rivalry may be tested in this fashion.

Counter-transferential feelings of *schadenfreude* should be
addressed by exploring with the group the transferential origins of
their perceptions. Messianic fantasies about the caretaker have to be
challenged, as does the corresponding demonization of the absent
therapist. By contrast, there are those who silently identify with the
absent therapist, withdrawing from the caretaker, sniping from the
sidelines, absenting themselves, threatening to drop out or regress-
ing into more disturbed states of mind.

Administrative and therapeutic aspects of handing over a group

When a viable group is being handed over from one therapist to
another, the receiving therapist is greatly assisted by good clinical
records, including up-to-date clinical notes, a group attendance
sheet, and information about the group members' personal details
and professional contacts. A fresh link will have to be forged with
referrers of the group members and other professionals involved in
their care. If the venue will be changing as a result of the handover,
the receiving therapist has to perform the various dynamic administrative tasks associated with the establishment of the original setting
for the group, making sure that the clinical records follow the group
to the new venue.

In some respects the therapeutic issues associated with a permanent handover are similar to those involved in the caretaking of a
group. With a handover, however, there is the added feature of per-
manence. The group is saying goodbye to their former therapist, and
meeting a new therapist who is there to stay. Some outgoing therapists like to stage an introductory session at which both the
therapists are present as a demonstration of cooperation, an opportunity for the new therapist to meet the group under the benign gaze
of the old therapist. This seems to us the worst of both worlds: it
deprives the group of an uncomplicated anticipatory mourning
experience in relation to the outgoing therapist and it disallows an
equally uncomplicated fresh beginning with the incoming therapist.

As with a caretaking situation, the process of handover should be separated in time, enabling the 'old' and 'new' therapists to perform their respective tasks of leave-taking and getting to know the group separately.

The question arises whether the new therapist should meet each member individually before taking over the group, as a way of consolidating the professional contract between the patient and the therapist. In our view, it is better to experience the group members inside the group, where by now their unique personality is best expressed.

Family events in the therapist's life

The analytic process flows most smoothly when the therapist's private life remains in the background of the field and when he or she is able to maintain a professional equanimity. Sometimes, however, this is not easy. Relationship difficulties, the illness or death of a relative, or family problems, can push the therapist into a personal crisis. Group members resonate unconsciously to the therapist's predicament, and it takes a high order of professional control to retain a therapeutic stance, especially when the manifest material of the group bears directly on the specific issue with which the therapist is privately grappling. This is another point at which ad hoc supervision is useful, if ongoing supervision is not already in place.

Intrusions by patients into the therapist's personal and professional life

Intrusive behaviour, reflected in the various inappropriate demands and accusations which patients can make, is an occupational hazard of all who work in the caring professions. It is epitomized in the concept of stalking, a phenomenon which has come into prominence in recent years and which is somewhat belatedly being recognized as a disturbing issue in clinical and therapeutic practice, as well as in everyday relationships. Stalking is a pattern of behaviour arising out of an intense preoccupation with another person, often associated with delusions of merging, fusion and sameness. The person being stalked is experienced in some way as essential for the psychic integrity, survival and wellbeing of the stalker. The behaviour stemming from such a state of mind tends to be possessive and controlling towards the victim. In its extreme manifestations stalking can progress to a malignant stage of attempting to harm or even kill an elusive victim. More commonly, however, it is characterized by pestering behaviour, with the stalker persistently, resourcefully and tenaciously seeking contact with the victim. Protestations of love and identicality of spirit or purpose are often made in a context of grandiosity. Like all grandiose pathology, however, effusive positive declarations can easily convert into a hostile and persecutory stance if the object of the protestations evades the invitation to reciprocate and thwarts the stalker's attempts at intimacy.

Psychotherapy, which by its very nature allows and encourages the exploration of the relationship between therapist and patient, is a profession in which stalking is a distinct hazard. This is especially so because the issues of intimacy, dependence and identity are central to the psychotherapeutic relationship. The question of stalking in the context of group psychotherapy is twofold. First, does the fact that the therapy is taking place in a group context protect the therapist from this form of malignant attention? Second, is there a risk that one group member might become fixated on another group member and set about stalking that person?

Without being categorical, it is probably true to say that the stalking of a therapist by a patient is more likely to arise in a dyadic setting. However, the group setting is unlikely to dilute the intensity of the dyadic relationship, since the process tends to set imperviously into an encapsulated form. Stalking can transfer from one 'object' to another, if the stalker perceives an emotional connection between the 'primary' object of his or her attention and the other person.

The existence of stalking as a counter-therapeutic or even dangerous phenomenon is yet a further justification for the therapist to maintain an unremittingly impeccable professional distance from the patient, and to determine a clear boundary around the professional relationship. The quality of 'specialness' is intrinsic to the stalking phenomenon, and often takes root in an idealizing transference to the therapist. If this fails to yield to therapeutic interventions, the therapist may have to assert a strong stance and even end the therapeutic contact if a judgement is reached that the process has become intractable. The manner in which this is done is crucial to the successful termination of therapy. A kind but persistently firm formulation to the patient that the therapy has run its course, framing the decision as a limitation of therapy to bring about the desired change, may suffice. If the process is running a course towards a more malignant phase of aggressive, destructive, pestering or threatening behaviour, the therapist may have to have recourse to psychiatric interventions or legal sanctions.

Having 'favourites' and falling in love with a group member

Every conductor, if honest, will admit that from time to time there is one group member who is special to him or her, a favourite, as it were. The group is certain to notice this, and eventually expresses it with anger, jealousy or good-natured resignation. One group called such a favourite of their female conductor her 'Crown Prince'. The conductor might like to see this as a counter-transference phenomenon, and in this way divest it of its disturbing, unprofessional aspect. Yet deep inside, the conductor may own this special relationship to one group member. If so acknowledged, it can be contained, and if need be, actively counteracted in the conducting process. Honesty is always sensed by the group, and can be expressed, as it once was, with, 'she is human, after all'.

Falling in love with a group member is altogether more problematic, and none the easier to handle for its long history in psychoanalytic therapies. As early as 1907, Breuer handed over his patient Anna O. to Freud for treatment because he had fallen in love with her. And the other way round, there is a well-documented history of patients trying to seduce their therapists. This has happened, and continues to happen, in dyadic therapy. Is the group analyst equally exposed to these risks? It may be that the multiple relationships prevailing in groups offer a degree of protection. The group, when it represents the family, mobilizes the incest taboo. Also, the perceptions of the group, both on a reality level and a dynamic level, provide the conductor with early danger signs. These may take the shape of deep disappointment with him or her, angry jealousy, or at the very least, insistence on the group rules and the group ethics. Last but not least, there is the shield of the conductor's professional training, which should protect him from what might otherwise result in irredeemable professional and personal disaster. Here, once more, a supervisory consultation with a trusted colleague should be sought as early as possible.

Accusations of harm or failure to help

A phenomenon related to stalking, and one which can be incorporated into stalking behaviour, is found in patients who perceive the therapeutic relationship as being responsible for the perpetuation of their problems, or contributing to a deterioration in their health or wellbeing. However, not all such behaviour has sinister connotations, and an attitude of excessive therapeutic rigidity or inaccessibility does not necessarily protect the therapist from these sorts of incursions. On the contrary, it may weaken the empathic and identificatory bonds between therapist and patient.

Such accusations are more likely to occur in relatively long-term therapy with patients who start out in a state of ambivalent dependence, often with an admixture of free-floating anxiety and somatic symptoms. A premonitory sign of these mind-states lies in a gradual encroachment on the therapeutic boundaries, such as an attempt to make contact (professional or non-professional) outside the therapeutic sessions.

Accusations of the harmful effects of therapy are often stimulated by the negative reactions of family members, who feel left out by their inevitable exclusion from the therapy. They may coincide with a negative therapeutic reaction which comes in the wake of an unrealistic expectation of an immediate cure. It is important that this can be voiced in the group and accepted by the therapist without the slightest indication of hurt, let alone retaliation. There are likely to be group members who recognize the situation from their own beginnings and who will be able to help the complaining member over this discouraging obstacle on the therapeutic journey.

Disruption of the group setting

Every group analyst is likely to experience, at least once, a serious impingement on the setting of the group brought about by forces outside his or her jurisdiction. Examples of these are: the closure of a hospital or ward, sweeping changes by management in accommodation arrangements, or drastic depletion of secretarial staff. Worst of all, the very activity of group therapy may be truncated by a fiat from the powers that be. In such a situation, the entire group may regress to an infantile state of dependency, helplessness and anger, in which it holds the group analyst responsible for the damage inflicted on their therapy. The group must be helped to deal with the reality as it is, but before this can happen, the group analyst has to cope with the professional injury inflicted on himself or herself, and decide what sort of administrative action is appropriate, and how to present it to the group.

In all these situations and numerous other unmentioned hurdles of the private and professional life of the group analyst, the best insurance against their worst consequences is the availability of trusted colleagues. This is one reason for striving to work in close proximity with colleagues, as in a hospital team or group practice. Where this is not possible, good contact with fellow practitioners and access to supervision makes the life of a group analyst more secure and therefore more enjoyable.

CHAPTER FIFTEEN

The Large Group

The idea of using a group to enhance the analytic process inevitably gave rise to experiments with different sizes of group. There was excitement, but also caution at the potential of a larger group to lead to deeper individual insights. Added to this was a fear of its potential destructiveness should it break down into a mass. It was clear that communication in relatively unstructured larger groups tended to be more richly infused with a cultural and mythical flavour, and that more primitive collective processes were activated than was the case with small groups. Paradoxically, large groups also appeared to provide an atmosphere for heightened intellectual awareness and spiritual togetherness. This led to the hope that they could be used as a constructive medium for tackling the burning issues of the day. But it was also recognized that large groups provoked high levels of anxiety, and this gave rise to concerns about the fate of the individual in a large group, and whether such a group could be said to function as a therapeutic medium.

When is a group a 'Large Group'? On the face of it, this is a question of numbers. As a rule one thinks of a group of between 40 or 50 participants in the lower range, and up to several hundred participants in the higher range. More significant than the number of participants is the criterion identified by both Pierre Turquet and Lionel Kreeger: a Large Group is a group which cannot be encompassed by any one member at a single glance. Groups with fewer than 40 or 50 members have a different dynamic, and are referred to as 'Median Groups', a term coined by Pat de Maré. Large Groups give rise to interesting and frustrating complexities in the use of the therapeutic space. The diminished ability of group members to hear and see one another clearly, or to immediately identify speakers and locate their position in the group, makes some of the experiences in a Large Group disorientating, even capable of inducing psychotic-like perceptions.

The early development of the Large Group

The first experiments in large group formations took place in situations where there was, so to speak, a captive audience. Hospitalized patients provided the perfect population for such experiments. For these beleaguered souls, being in a large group offered a strange new experience in self-discovery as well as an attack on their isolation.

The model was soon extended to willing groups of participants. Enthusiastic organizers of courses, conferences and workshops for analytically minded people set up groups encompassing all the participants as an intrinsic part of their programmes. The 'Large Group', now dignified as a special entity by its capitals, was looked forward to with both anticipation and apprehension as an event in which to experience disturbing but hopefully productive insights into human communication. The Large Group took root in many psychiatric hospitals and became an established part of the culture in therapeutic communities, where it spoke for democratic participation in the life of institutions traditionally regarded as bastions of authoritarianism.

The Large Group was introduced as a concept for the first time at Northfield Military Hospital during the Second World War and came to form part of the culture there. The central ethos was that of 'the-hospital-as-a-whole-with-its-mission', an organic entity dedicated to the task of restoring psychologically disabled soldiers to normal function. S.H. Foulkes, one of the pioneers of small analytic groups, has acquired the reputation of sidelining the Large Group as a therapeutic tool in group analysis. Yet he played a major role in the second of the two great experiments in social therapy conducted at Northfield. His particular contribution was to link the 'Large Ward Groups' with the group-analytic treatment being offered in Small Groups (Foulkes, 1964).

Foulkes was also aware of the potential of the Large Group as an instrument to tackle wider social problems, 'the strained relationship between the individual and the community', as he put it. The range of the Large Group, he maintained, was as far and wide as the relationship between the individual and the community went, encompassing the treatment of neurosis and psychosis as well as addressing the issues of crime, rehabilitation, industrial management and education. 'In short,' he declared, 'every aspect of life in communities, large and small' could be addressed in the Large Group (Foulkes, 1975).

The contribution of Pat de Maré

One of Foulkes's colleagues, Pat de Maré, advanced a social and philosophical rationale for the establishment of large groups. He saw them as an expression of the democratic spirit and a tool for exploring the interface between psychotherapy and sociotherapy. De Maré started out with the view that the Large Group was the place in which the hatred which pervades society and generates societal conflict could be safely expressed, contained and transmuted into a form of communication which would bring society towards a more constructive state of existence. He took the concept of dialogue and restored it to the position it had once held in ancient Greece. Dialogue, he maintained, was the key instrument in the process of achieving peaceful resolution of conflict. The communication which takes place when a large body of people talks to one another in a carefully constructed group setting, he argued, is of a form which transcends the more intimate forms of communication which prevail in family and personal relationships. Such communication, according to de Maré, achieves a state of harmonious togetherness, which he likened to communion. Looking to ancient Greece again, he revived the word *koinonia*, meaning 'fellowship', to capture this concept.

In de Maré's vision, the Large Group would become a meeting place for minds, in which the collective intellect of the group would be mobilized and brought to bear on the problems of society. The intellect would be restored to its rightful place in the hierarchy of mental functions, leavened by the newly born state of communion.

The Large Group as therapy

There are different opinions as to whether the Large Group can offer analytic psychotherapy in its usual sense. Foulkes was unequivocally committed to the therapeutic potential of the Large Group, provided it could take place regularly and over an extended timescale. Pat de Maré, on the other hand, believes that the Large Group is not the place to elicit or work with transference issues which reflect family relationships and that it therefore cannot function as a truly analytic forum in the way that the Small Group does. Our own view, which has been shaped by our experiences in several psychotherapy training contexts, is that the Large Group, in addition to its social and cultural dimensions, is also a therapeutic group-analytic medium in its own right. The analytic function is more easily seen when Large and Small Groups exist in close temporal proximity to one another. In such settings, the Large Group produces rich material for therapy in the form of immediately accessible transference relationships which dovetail with the material of the Small Groups. However, even without the benefit of adjacent Small Groups, the Large Group in a containing setting such as a ward has a clearly discernible therapeutic effect.

Vignette

On a training course in which a number of small group sessions were followed by a daily Large Group, a young man had been especially attentive and caring to me in the Small Group, where I was his conductor. Then, in the Large Group, he asked me in mock innocence how my name (Liesel) was spelt. Was it 'Lethal'? His ambivalence and aggression had found its voice under the protection of the Large Group.

Others have seen and used the therapeutic potential of the Large Group in a clinical setting, among them the psychiatrist Rafael Springmann. He worked exclusively with large ward groups in the psychiatric department of Tel Hashomer General Hospital in Israel. In that setting, he found that patients who were otherwise reticent and withholding could reveal themselves. It seemed that in the presence of so many others they felt secure enough to express their aggressive, often murderous, feelings. The fantasy seemed to be that the Large Group protected them from getting 'out of hand' and warded off the expected retaliation. This was the case with disturbed and less disturbed group members alike (Springmann, 1975).

What happens to the individual in a Large Group?

In a Large Group, the individual is exposed to emotional experiences unique to such a situation, and these can be used to deepen insights into areas which are not easily reached in the small analytic group. The Large Group also furnishes insights into individual and group behaviour in the wider social setting in which we find ourselves throughout our lives.

In a Large Group set up specifically for experiential or therapeutic purposes, the individual may feel on the verge of being overwhelmed by a void where the sense of self is in danger of being lost. This is graphically illustrated in one account of a dream which followed a Large Group: the dreamer was a dot that was hurled into the blackness of the universe. But there can also be the opposite emotional experience, that of becoming one with a powerful body, in which the person feels free of personal responsibility for their views and actions. This is the case when the group is experienced as a mass. A group in this state appears to be longing for a powerful leader to take over responsibility and keep the group in order. In such a situation, the Large Group, more than the small therapy group, can be taken over by one member to whom the group seems to submit. It is as if the group has taken up this participant as its 'bad leader', who then takes charge.

Individuals defend themselves more or less successfully against the experience of becoming isolated, being taken over, losing their identity or being annihilated. This is achieved in a variety of ways: actions are proposed or displayed which are in effect an attack on the setting, such as inviting the group to sing, rearranging the chairs, shouting, declaiming, reading from a text, or proposing the signing of a political petition.

Large Groups lend themselves to exhibitionistic behaviour. They provide a ready-made audience for individuals whose anxiety makes it difficult to tolerate the reflective stance. Standing up, clapping hands, or doing a somersault in the centre of the room are some examples from our own experience. The impulse to startle or shock is often gratified by the range of emotional responses with which their actions are received. Such incidents generate associations of both an approving and condemnatory nature, highlighting the Large Group's proclivity for splitting. Less conspicuously, individuals may defend themselves by reading a paper, doing puzzles, turning away from their neighbours, or looking out of the window. Walking out is also not uncommon. The repertoire of defensive actions is limitless.

Some interventions startle by their content rather than their form. Highly personal disclosures or attacks on other group members can be made, which would be perceived as outrageous in a different social context but are somehow tolerated in a Large Group. If the conductor judges that an interaction is becoming counter-therapeutic, attention needs to be drawn to it if it is being denied in the general groundswell of group associations.

The therapeutic rewards of the Large Group come in the first instance when the individual discovers that the Large Group can tolerate and even positively connote a wide range of aberrant utterances, and secondly when it gives rise to new thoughts and insights of a personal and collective nature, accompanied by a range of emotional responses, variously experienced as uplifting, energizing or calming. The moment of finding a voice in the Large Group is also sometimes recalled as a therapeutic turning point. The subjective experience of being able to bring together disparate thoughts in a Large Group has led to the belief that the Large Group can provide a forum for creative and innovative thinking ('Nobel Prize Thinking') which could have application in other settings.

What happens to the Large Group itself?

The combination of a perceived lack of structure and heightened anxiety predisposes the Large Group to primitive defences. Of these, the most conspicuous is a splitting into polarized sub-groups, such as 'the men' against 'the women', 'the feeling ones' against 'the reasoning ones', those who feel safe against those who feel unsafe. This is achieved by wholesale projection by one sub-group onto the other, or at times by the Large Group as a whole onto some aspect of the outside world, such as the training course or hospital of which the Large Group is a part, or onto elements of society, such as political factions or cultural sub-groups.

The Large Group can also be creative. It provides a canvas for the mythology, cultural heritage and popular images of the society in which it exists. The past becomes present through the emergence of folk legends, myths, fairy tales, traditions and snapshots of history. At other moments the group becomes intellectually creative by touching on current social and political events and their moral evaluation. It is in the nature of free association in a Large Group that the content changes kaleidoscopically in mood and imagery. Probably the most impressive and moving moments in the Large Group occur when the group engages in what can be thought of as 'collective dreaming': one association follows another without apparent discord, leading to a thoughtful aftermath and a sense of new ideas having been formed.

Vignette

This is a Large Group which forms part of a group-analytic training course. There is a lot of chatter at the beginning, which takes a long time to die down. After a few minutes' silence one member says that she felt ill after the last Large Group – it is too much to have a Large Group straight after lunch. She gets indigestion if there is too much going on. A man says that at least it's warm inside the room [the weather outside is exceptionally cold], and he feels comfortable. Another man says he feels like a small particle in a microcosm with the cosmos out there. A few people associate to the warmth in the room and the cold outside. One man says the snowstorm outside comes from Iceland. It reminds him of guests at a wedding he once attended there, who all arrived frozen. A woman asks, 'Where's the bride in here?'[laughter]. After more associations contrasting the cosy interior of the group (a ski lodge, a spaceship floating above the earth) with the harsh outside (blizzards, space), one of the woman conductors returns to the woman who first spoke, saying, 'All this cosiness isn't nurturing for everybody'. She describes her impression of the snow-topped mountains from the aeroplane on the way to the course: they reminded her of breasts. 'And they were cold', she adds. [Laughter, followed by a spate of rapid associations.] The two female conductors are likened to two breasts. How can they be shared? Jokes are made about the male conductors having both. 'You have one breast and we'll have the other', says one man. Someone says two of the men in the group remind him of two little boys arguing about who'll have the top half and who'll have the bottom half. One of the male conductors says there seems to be a fear of what might happen if they get the whole woman. It seems that she has to be partitioned. More associations follow about the view from above. The earth is 'mother earth', but is the sun male or female? There is punning on the word 'sun'/'son'. Someone tells the story of Daedalus and Icarus, whose wings melted when he flew too near the sun. A woman conductor says he would have been better off flying in the middle regions. Someone observes that the women participants are very silent. It is the men who are talking loudly and clearly about their need for sex. What about the women? The other woman conductor quips: 'Why can't a man be more like a woman?' The group ends on time after one of the male conductors had mistakenly tried to end it 15 minutes too early, followed by laughter and jokes about his sexual anxiety.

Looking back on this session, one can see a certain sequence: the associations begin with a woman and a man telling of their feelings of discomfort and comfort respectively. Consciousness of the warm interior and the cold outside world turns into a multifaceted exploration of the contrasting needs of men and women. Several polarities ensue: nurturing and over-feeding; fear of the group-as-a-whole expressed in the metaphor of the woman's body; omnipotence as a refuge from this fear but with its own dangers (the Icarus image). Jokes, puns and myths are used as vehicles for the analytic process, providing a pool of associations redolent of dream-thinking, to be taken up and worked on at a personal level.

The leadership of the Large Group

The role of the leader of a Large Group is viewed differently by various group analysts. First and foremost is the question: should there be one conductor or a number of conductors? For example, should all the conductors of the small groups on a training course or workshop, or all the therapists and staff of a hospital ward, be present in the Large Group, and if they are, should they assume a leadership role? One view is that if all the conductors are present, a sense of completeness and unity is created which encompasses the whole training course, ward or workshop. On the other hand there is the view that the presence of more than one conductor is a complication which skews the transference away from the leader. A further objection is a puristic one, stemming from the analytic view that the transference relationship held within the small therapy group can be disturbed and disrupted through the encounters between group analyst and group analysand in the Large Group. Alternatively, the participation of everyone in a single Large Group is seen as essential for the coherence of the training course, workshop, or hospital ward in which those activities take place.

Some Large Group leaders prefer the term 'convenor' to 'conductor' or 'therapist', to highlight the primary task of gathering the assemblage into a venue within an orderly space and time setting. They may confine themselves to announcing the beginning and ending of the session. Lionel Kreeger, one of the pioneers of Large Groups in a psychiatric hospital setting, structures his interventions in this way. He is impressed by the Large Group's potential for engendering psychotic-like experiences, and sees the leader as the repository of powerful projections which have to be contained if the group is to achieve the rudiments of reflective thinking.

Gerhard Wilke is a group analyst who believes that it is possible to apply a Foulkesian Small Group approach to the Large Group. According to Wilke, the success of a Large Group depends first of all on meticulous dynamic administration (preparing the venue, consulting with the organizers, rehearsing one's position in the group room). Second, the conductor has to identify the location of disturbances in the communication network of the group and translate them for the group. This means being quite active. Third, the conductor does not put himself or herself consistently at the centre of the field. The group is allowed, in Foulkesian style, to interact in figure–ground constellations which move between the conductor, the group as a whole, and the protagonist of the moment (Wilke, 2003).

A contrasting approach to leadership is that of Josef Shaked, an Austrian psychoanalyst and group analyst with wide experience of Large Groups in different cultures. He sees the Large Group as an organic entity in dyadic relation to himself as the analyst. Shaked's interventions make use of Freudian formulations derived from oedipal and primal horde imagery to bring the group into relationship with him (Shaked, 2003). He offers himself for projection and transference, while also intervening in a personal manner with humour and jokes. Shaked sees joke-telling by the conductor not as an interpretation, but as a presentation of a situation which, if named, would be difficult to accept. But telling jokes can also be an expression of resistance. Shaked has observed that he sometimes finds himself using jokes when he feels tense or when avoiding facing a situation such as an attack on a group member or himself (personal communication, 2004). Other conductors who intervene actively to offer a structure to the group also make use of fairy tales and myths, or historical, popular and political allusions.

Styles of intervention differ widely. Some stay close to the group-analytic model of interventions, including full interpretations, given to individuals or the group as a whole. Others tend to offer interventions in the form of short 'Delphic' utterances. The balance between brevity and a lengthy exposition is difficult to gauge. One compromise could be to go for frequent but short interventions. Therapists who operate a dyadic model, seeing the relationship as one between them and the group-as-a-whole, confine their interventions to the interpretation of the transference between them and the group. For this reason they will not entertain other conductors in the group.

Vignette

During the course of a group-analytic block training programme one of the trainers had announced that she would be leaving the course after the next block. This is an excerpt from the Large Group which followed her farewell party the previous evening.

After some speculation about the reasons for her leaving, she tells the Large Group that in order to prevent the fantasies from getting out of hand, she is prepared to disclose her reason for leaving the course. She says that she has to take over a group at her practice in her home town because of the illness of one of her colleagues.

Everyone in the Large Group instantly takes this to mean that she has chosen her patients at home over and above them. Someone from her Small Group says that the real reason is that the other conductors have not taken good care of her. One man, addressing the staff, says that she is the best mother of all them.

The group becomes restless and excited. Someone says that the staff of the hotel [in which the course took place] have not been treated well by them [meaning the staff and students alike]. This was the reason why they 'threw us out' and we were unable to use the hotel again.

Someone else says he was told that the wine waiters were out of pocket after the previous night's farewell celebrations. People had not paid their bills and the waiters were the losers. Another asks angrily why the waiters had not asked for their money as soon as they had served them. Anyway, they [the waiters] had probably made a mistake. A woman says that she herself has been a waitress during her holidays. She tells the group how angry she used to get when customers did not pay. She felt that she had worked hard a whole evening for nothing. 'So I overcharged the next customer to get my own back,' she adds. Someone else puts in: 'Let's forget about the waiters. That's enough of them. I'm sick of talking about the poor victims.'

At this point one of the male conductors says something which includes a reference to the victims of starvation in a recent war in Africa [content not fully heard by me, ostensibly because I was sitting at the other end of the room, but probably because I did not want to hear what he said]. The remark is not taken up and seems to fall flat, probably for the same reason. The associations return to the departing conductor. 'We are going to be thrown out, and A [the conductor] is leaving.' 'The conductors are here because we [the students] pay them ... All is not well with the course ... The theory is bad ... B [another conductor] has told us that she doesn't prepare the theory. Why not, if she gets paid? She also said in the Application Group that she hadn't prepared anything.' Someone addresses me [as one of the conductors] and says that it is not only the students who are aggressive. We, the staff, are as well. I am told that I am aggressive. I say that I am aggressive, and that I feel it right now, but against the people in the room. [I reflect afterwards that the group is seeking another victim in addition to B, but that since I hit back I am dropped as a potential victim.] One of the male conductors says drily that we got the same fee six years ago as we do now. One of the local course organizers says, 'That's a lie.' This provokes laughter, and the session ends.

Comment
The farewell party had left everybody on a 'high'. This was the 'low' which had been denied the previous day in all the expressions of warmth and enthusiasm, and in the congratulations which had been directed to the course organizer. The group's rage at the conductor, who, in choosing to work with her patients at home rather than with them, is displaced onto another woman conductor, who is openly accused of 'failing' them. The rage is extended to all the conductors, but has to be hidden, for fear that they will all leave. In the group fantasy, everyone is expelled from the hotel because of their wickedness and delinquency. This is given further strength by my own expression of disapproval of them. (One of the woman conductors told me later that some of the 'most ferocious ones' had come up to her afterwards and said that they didn't know what had happened to them, and why they had attacked her so!)

When there is more than one conductor in the group, one problem that may occur is the emergence of strong competitive feelings amongst the therapists, which the Large Group tends to set up or play into. The Large Group then becomes an arena for power struggles amongst the conductors and their 'followers'. The unconscious components of this scenario have to be identified and energetically interpreted so as to maintain the therapeutic integrity of the group. One of the conductor's functions is to be on the lookout for distress signals and the possible emotional collapse of individuals in the group. In view of the large numbers, this is a demanding task which is easily lost sight of. One advantage of having more than one conductor is that this task can be shared. The conductor of the Large Group is always spotlighted as the individual who serves as a focal point in a sea of uncertainty. He or she carries a high symbolic charge at all times, whether vocal or silent, and attracts strong transferential emotions, whether taken up or not.

Our preferred style of leadership in a Large Group is one of controlled participation. This means that we retain the freedom to contribute personal thoughts, associations and expressions of affect. At other times we might call into play our analytic function in relation to individuals or the group as a whole. We are quick to draw attention to counter-therapeutic trends and defences such as attacks on the setting, sub-grouping, scapegoating and actions that threaten the integrity of the group.

The Median Group

De Maré's original conception of the Large Group as a vehicle for social change was an idealistic view. He himself later became disillusioned with the potential of Large Groups to reform and re-form society. Instead, he described a new type of group, easier to stage-manage and less prone to the vicissitudes of size, in which constructive dialogue would still be possible. This type of group, intermediate in size between a Large Group and a classic Small Group, he termed a 'Median Group'. Typically, this would consist of between 15 and 40 people, and its great virtue would rest in its applicability to a wide range of organizations and institutions prepared to look at their own dynamics without having to expose themselves to the anxieties, acoustic problems and disorientation occasioned by a Large Group.

Median Groups have flourished in diverse settings such as the army, the church, the prison service, commercial and industrial organizations, hospitals and training programmes for psychotherapists and counsellors. Median Groups are also used by psychotherapists to explore specific social and cultural issues, such as war and post-traumatic survival.

In practice most of the so-called Large Groups which are convened are, strictly speaking, Median Groups, if we accept Turquet's 'visual sweep' definition of a Large Group and de Maré's numerical stipulations for Large and Median groups. More important than the size of a group, however, is the setting in which it takes place. Large Groups consisting of several hundred participants are now generally held as an event at analytic workshops, symposia and conferences. The participants tend to be psychodynamically sophisticated and the group tends to take on social, cultural and political issues. Skilful leadership is needed to prevent the group from soaring into grandiose and polarized ways of thinking. Large Groups on group-analytic training programmes embrace the entire cohort of trainees. In addition to their therapeutic function, they provide an important forum for the exploration of course issues.

CHAPTER SIXTEEN

All in the same boat: the value of homogeneous groups

GROUP THERAPY FOR NARCISSISTIC PERSONALITIES

A therapeutic group which is put together to meet the needs of individuals who share a single, instantly identifiable problem or issue is sometimes referred to as a homogeneous group, by contrast with the more usual mixed group, referred to as a heterogeneous group, whose members are selected to encompass a wide span of problems, issues, personality traits and diagnoses. The strength of the latter group, whose shared issues only unfold with time, lies in its very diversity. The strength of a homogeneous group lies in the comfort and support generated by the early discovery of others like oneself, who have experienced, or are experiencing, life events or circumstances which by their nature are isolating. This might be a specific trauma, loss, illness or disability, or an issue relating to a particular stage in the life cycle, such as parenting or retirement. The homogeneity may also reside in a specific sex- or gender-related issue, such as being gay or lesbian, or being a woman or man who has been sexually abused.

Differences between homogeneous and heterogeneous groups

The differences between homogeneous and heterogeneous groups are evident from the first session of a homogeneous group. The instant recognition of fellow sufferers often brings a flash of relief. Strong bonds of identification are forged early in the process, uniting the group in a spirit of solidarity, and immediately reducing the sense of isolation imposed on them by the condition which has brought them into the group. This contrasts markedly with the beginnings of a heterogeneous group, where common features are not immediately apparent. The members of a heterogeneous group scan one another anxiously to discern common ground. Although they have an intellectual appreciation of commonality, they have yet to experience the emotional impact of it. Members of a homogeneous group, on the other hand, are aware, even before the group has met, that they will be coming together with others who are preoccupied with the same problems or issues.

The conductor of a homogeneous group may feel redundant or isolated since he or she is unlikely to share the attribute which unifies the group. It might therefore be necessary to draw attention to this difference if it exists, presenting it as both a strength and a limitation. The strength lies in the conductor's capacity to bring a professional perspective to bear on the group; the limitation lies in not having undergone the same experience, or not being in the same state or at the same stage as the rest of the group.

These limitations on the part of the therapist, however, are usually offset by the expertise residing in the collective experience of the group about its own issue. For example, there is often a pool of knowledge about the medical condition or disability around which the group has gathered, as well as a broad range of information about resources, strategies for managing the condition, support networks, agencies, and institutions linked with condition. This might also be a case for co-therapy, where one of the therapists has a more in-depth knowledge of the specific condition, perhaps through personal or professional experience, while the other therapist, though limited in that respect, brings to bear a psychological perspective and a grasp of group dynamics. Interventions are purposefully sparser than in a heterogeneous group, and the group culture is at times reminiscent of a self-help group.

Homogeneous groups founded on a shared illness or disability

A hundred years ago the physician Joseph Pratt captured the essential advantage of homogeneous groups with his observations on groups for patients with tuberculosis. 'They have a common bond in a common illness,' he wrote 'and a fine spirit of camaraderie prevails' (Pratt, 1907). We might think of this today as a form of empathy and mutual identification that springs from shared adversity.

This rapid cohesion is not an unmixed blessing in therapeutic terms. Although there is a reduction in the sense of isolation and a corresponding diminution in the feelings of shame or stigma which accompany isolating conditions, problems can arise at a later stage, if the solidarity which unites the group gets in the way of the individuation of its members. A defensive quality of togetherness can create a 'them−us' dynamic which can get in the way of group members' efforts at reintegrating into the world outside the group. Here the therapist has to become the voice of the outside world, speaking from a position of respectful ignorance in relation to the unifying predicament while at the same time drawing attention to similarities between the group members and others who do not share the problem. For example, the therapist may focus on family relationship difficulties which are manifestly unconnected with the presenting problem, enlisting the help of the group in much the same way as for a heterogeneous group. Discussion of these more widely existing problems universalizes and normalizes the group, and leads to a healthy awareness of differences between the group members as well as the obvious similarities. The therapist may also highlight the fact that there are different solutions for shared problems. In other words, the therapist moves the group towards a recognition of its innate heterogeneity, diminishing the pre-eminence of the presenting issue and encouraging individual expressions of difference.

A shared language is another unifying criterion in homogeneous groups, since it captures what is immediately familiar to everyone, for example technical descriptions of an illness and the procedures associated with it. This allows an opportunity to compare notes about treatment and leads to a more informed and questioning stance in relation to the professionals responsible for the management of their condition. In summary, a homogeneous group can provide a powerful impetus towards the emergence from isolation and the discovery of an intrinsic commonality based first on the condition in common and later on a more universal identity.

Homogeneous groups founded on psychological commonalities

There are patients whose emotional make-up, when first seen, points them towards a homogeneous group rather than a heterogeneous group. These are individuals who display a need to experience sameness rather than diversity. For long periods of their therapy they are inclined to express themselves through action rather than verbalization and they have difficulty in symbolizing and tolerating the frustration imposed on them by the more challenging environment of a classic, mixed analytic group. This applies to patients suffering from psychotic illnesses, severe psychosomatic disorders and severe narcissistic disturbances. In a heterogeneous group, such members are experienced as overwhelming and putting a brake on the progress of the group as a whole. However, the limitation of a homogeneous group for such patients is the absence of a rich matrix. By this is meant a resource for the recovery of seminal psychic events in earlier phases of life, the experience in the group of projections onto one's children or grandchildren, which may be afforded by, say, a younger member in a group for 'retired people' or any group member who falls outside a 'common band'.

Homogeneous groups may also develop common defence mechanisms. This happened in a group of young women with eating disorders: as soon as any one of them seemed to be well on the way to a 'cure', she was shunned by the group as if she no longer belonged. The eating disorder seemed to have the function of a membership card for the club, as it were. For this reason and others, psychologically homogeneous groups require more interventions and an increased conducting activity on the part of the group analyst, who cannot expect the group to supply these as is the case in a well-functioning heterogeneous group put together and maintained on the Foulkesian principle of the widest possible span of sex, age, ethnicity, social background and personality, without isolating any one member (Foulkes, 1948).

Groups in a psychiatric inpatient setting

These groups are homogeneous in the sense that all the members share the same residential setting, and all are likely to carry a diagnosis of severe psychiatric illness. Groups flourish in this environment. Community meetings are often part of the culture, as are activity groups, including occupational therapy, art therapy and music therapy groups and groups held in various psychological treatment modes (small and large group-analytic groups, psychodrama, cognitive behaviour therapy, cognitive analytic therapy). Groups are also used to address specific neurotic or behavioural issues, such as phobias, obsessive compulsive disorders, anger management and assertiveness training.

It is often difficult to sustain a culture of continuity because of a rapidly changing patient population, capricious changes in staffing arrangements, and the relatively low priority accorded to psychodynamic methods of treatment in many hospitals. Techniques may therefore have to be modified in the direction of psycho-educational interventions, short-term programmes, and a focus on the here-and-now, as represented by the dynamics of the ward and the vicissitudes of institutional life. Inpatient groups are sometimes regarded by patients as the prime opportunity to capture the attention of elusive staff in order to discuss the practicalities of their hospitalization, such as their medication, discharge and diagnosis. Ward groups and community meetings are lent weight by the presence of senior professionals, not just as visiting dignitaries, but as regular, active participants.

Homogeneous groups founded on a shared trauma

There are many examples of groups for people who have undergone a shared trauma, either through having been together at the same time and place, such as being caught up in a robbery, terrorist attack or natural disaster, or through having experienced the same trauma in kind, such as sexual abuse, massive social trauma on the scale of war or persecution.

The principles of conducting such groups may be stated as follows: equipping the participants with strategies for coping with the symptoms of post-traumatic stress disorder, allowing them to relive the traumatic experience within a containing framework, steering them from a position of passive victimhood towards active mastery of their lives, and helping them to re-connect with the so-called normal world. The group culture enables them to describe what they may feel to be shameful, humiliating experiences, and to express their feelings of grief, blame, revenge and rage. Individuals who have constructed a new identity for themselves around the traumatic experience may need to follow up their therapy in a homogeneous group with long-term group-analytic therapy in a heterogeneous group, in order to help them to re-establish connections with non-traumatized people.

Two examples of homogeneous groups

From the multitude of groups for people with shared concerns or characteristics, we have chosen to describe two groups from our own experience: one, a group for parents whose children have a shared illness, the other a group for people going through a common stage in life.

Group for parents of epileptic children

The shared illness in this case was epilepsy, a condition which, more than many, symbolizes the uncertain ground between mind and body, between wilful behaviour and loss of control. Despite the advances of modern medicine, many questions remain unanswered about this complex and multi-faceted condition, and the person with epilepsy has to cope with a stigma dating back to antiquity. Parents of children with epilepsy face many concerns about their child's lifestyle and relationships, both in the present and in the longer term. This six-session group for parents with epileptic children illustrates many of the features of a homogeneous group set up for those having to cope with the same illness. The group was run by a paediatrican and a child psychiatrist in a hospital setting. It was intended for parents, but in the event only the mothers attended.

The letter of invitation

Dear (parents)

We are writing to you as one of the families whose child attends the Epilepsy Clinic. Some of the parents whose children come to the clinic regularly were interested in having the opportunity to meet with each other and some of the doctors. This would give everyone a chance to discuss some of the difficulties and worries that arise from having a child who has fits.

We are proposing to arrange a series of meetings which will begin after the summer holidays. We hope that if you are interested you will commit yourself to attending the whole series. The meetings will take place on Wednesday mornings from 11am to 12 noon on the following six dates ...

If both (or either) of you are interested, please would you let us know by completing the enclosed stamped letter. If you are interested but cannot come at this time, please also return the letter.

We look forward to hearing from you.
(signed by both therapists)

Comments written on the completed forms, asking parents to mention 'Important things to talk about'.

Parent A: 1. 'How best to cope when the child has a fit.'
2. Has modern medicine made any progress towards a permanent cure or even prevent it?'

Parent B: 'Behaviour of child.' 'Education.' 'My child Darren has had no attacks for nearly two years but is afraid to go on a lower amount of drugs because of anxiety.'
'Unfortunately my husband cannot attend because the time is unsuitable. Even if an evening time were suitable I would have to coax him to come as he doesn't believe in the efficacy of talk.'

Parent C: 'Reason for fits.' 'How to avoid them in future.' 'How to make people aware of a child's problem without making the child feel "different".' 'The future for the child.' 'Current developments in research and medicine.'

Parent D: 'Parents' difficulties and experiences with children with epilepsy – how do they cope? – how does the epileptic child fare in school? – how active (sports) a life can the child lead? – have their children had learning difficulties? – is it possible to tell, to discover the area of brain damage and therefore tell what difficulties the child will have in learning – whether it will be in language, or in processing math information? etc. – there are really so many questions – as I find the whole subject overwhelming, mysterious. Look forward to joining you at these meetings.'

PS Was the first blood test Laura had since taking medication OK?'

Parent E: 'School Days.' 'Swimming.'

Excerpts from the group sessions:

Session 1

The mothers were already engaged in animated conversation as the therapists entered the room. One mother said jokingly that they had already said all that needed to be said. After the introductions, one mother began by saying that she felt that people didn't want to listen to her talking about her child's problems, and that she had to 'bottle up' all her feelings. Another mother said that she made a point of talking to people about her child's condition, imposing a positive view on it and refusing to listen to negative views. All agreed that schools should do more to educate pupils and teachers into being open and sharing their problems. One mother added that the 'Americans' were 'far in advance of us' in this respect.

The conversation moved to an exchange of information about their children. The group, including the therapists, responded sympathetically to one mother whose son is very self-conscious and desperately wants his mother never to refer to his epilepsy, or even mention that he has a hospital appointment or has to take tablets. He talks across her and makes up stories about having to visit relatives when she tries to tell someone that he has to attend the hospital. Another mother described her nine-year-old daughter as having frequent temper outbursts, during which she seems like a changed person. She found it difficult to set limits for her daughter. The group encouraged her to be firmer, but she seemed reluctant to consider this, saying that she saw that as countering violence with violence. There was an exchange of stories of how their children were teased at school, one being called a 'spastic wally', another being provoked into hitting a child who had mocked him by drilling his finger into his temple.

The conversation moved to the issue of how parents should form a united front, both in relation to the child and the school. There were various suggestions about how the children could improve the quality of their lives and enhance their self-esteem. Genuine talents and preferences needed encouraging, it was agreed. There was talk about the siblings who are not epileptic. Towards the end of the session the talk drifted to the topic of the husbands and other men in the family, with jokes about their inability to communicate.

Session 2

The atmosphere was more subdued this time. One mother said she had gone away feeling despondent and frustrated by her inability to deal with her child's behaviour problems. The group talked about their fears of their children suffering brain damage through seizures. One mother recalled her panic when her child had suffered the first fit and her conviction that her child was going to die. There was an attempt to draw consolation from the fact that there were other children with epilepsy who were worse off than theirs. One mother recalled a visit to an inpatient unit where she had encountered a child who was severely impaired through brain disease and had undergone surgery. It had taken a long time for the doctors to diagnose her own child's epilepsy, and she wryly recalled how the doctor had exclaimed in delight when the diagnosis was finally made. Discussion turned to how husbands are less inclined to panic and disapprove of their wives' tendencies to panic. The parents listened closely to one another describing various aspects of their children's illnesses and behaviour. The question of the risk involved in swimming came up. One mother asked if it was better for her child to suffer frequent petit mal seizures or have the occasional grand mal seizure about once a month. Towards the end of the session the conversation again turned to their other children. One described her other child as very supportive; another confessed that she frequently sent her other child to his grandmother so that she could concentrate on her epileptic child. Apart from asking a few questions requiring professional knowledge about lifestyle, medication and the different manifestations of epilepsy, no demands were made of the therapists. The parents seemed content to talk amongst themselves.

Session 3

This time the atmosphere was light-hearted and cheerful. There was talk about taking up their familiar seats and choosing a comfortable chair. One mother said that when she had first seen the male therapist in the room she had wondered whether he was the only father who had dared to come to group. This provoked laughter.

One mother in particular talked at length about her child's unhappiness and difficult behaviour. He was being teased and insulted, wanting to change schools but not wanting to go to a special school. She began to cry while talking, saying that she felt herself to be in a different position to the other mothers. The group demurred, responding with suggestions as to how she could be more effective in setting limits for her child's difficult behaviour and at the same time boosting his self-esteem.

A discussion arose as to whether her son's behaviour was a function of his epilepsy or a reflection of difficult family relationships. Here the mothers turned to the therapists. How protective should one be? Is it advisable to stir up concern on the part of the school? One mother voiced the opinion that she did not want to be too much of a 'crutch' to her child and that he should be allowed to struggle to achieve independence on his own. The therapists were more active in this discussion about managing relationships, drawing attention to mixed messages and the implications of colluding with a child's plea for secrecy and playing down the difficulties.

As in the previous session, conversation drifted towards the role played by fathers. This time criticism was more outspoken, except for one mother, who had become something of an authority figure in the group and tended to adopt a caring and counselling role towards the other mothers. She described her husband as 'perfect'. The therapists drew attention to the strikingly different perspectives which were emerging in the group. Afterwards they reflected that a hierarchy of vulnerability and neediness was developing, with an outwardly competent and coping sub-group and a depressed, needy sub-group.

Session 4

The session began with one mother asking whether it was appropriate to talk about problems other than their children's epilepsy. Given support to do so, she described a traumatic incident in which her older child had been involved in a skirmish at a local pub which had culminated in violence and assault resulting in injury to another boy. There were threats and legal consequences which had plunged the family into a crisis. This took up most of the session. The therapists linked the incident with a flare-up of difficult behaviour on the part of her epileptic child. The group resonated to the theme of violence, everyone talking of having been affected by violence at some point in their lives.

Session 5

The group was eager to follow up the saga of the previous week. The mother concerned said that she felt much better, but was now very worried about her epileptic child, whose behaviour was getting increasingly out of control. The group revisited old ground about setting limits, praising her child when things were going well and not blaming herself for her child's condition. Another mother said she was not so worried about her child now but was thinking ahead to when he would be 14, 15 or 16, and what problems he might face in a relationship with a girl. This triggered a conversation about the fear which someone with epilepsy might have about sexual relationships, how much to tell a prospective partner and the question of the inheritance of epilepsy.

Towards the end of the session the therapists asked about the usefulness of the group. There was a consensus that it had been very helpful. One mother asked if it was possible to arrange a group for the children; another said she felt guilty that she had taken up so much of the group's time.

Final session

The therapists were surprised to see that one of the mothers had brought her 11-year-old son with her to the group, explaining that it was half-term. He sat next to his mother and joined in happily with the conversation, drawn into it by the other mothers. To his mother's surprise he said that he did not mind when his mother got angry with him, which led the other mothers to remark that their children also did not seem to mind when they got angry with them. One mother observed that her daughter seemed quite relieved and even pleased when she was told off about something, as if it was preferable to be seen as naughty rather than fragile. The youngster present said emphatically that he did not want to come to a children's group or be seen on his own. However he was very much in favour of attending again with his mother at any future groups for parents and children.

Towards the end, the parents talked again about the group, all saying that they had found it beneficial. One mother said that she had been able to take in a lot although she said apologetically that she had not been able to express herself very well. She was assured by the other mothers that she had been fully understood and that she underestimated her ability to express herself. One mother was strongly in favour of an evening group at which fathers could be present, but the other mothers were not enthusiastic about this. One said that the morning time was suitable and that she could not see her husband participating as he tended to trivialize everything. There was more talk about how men tend to keep their emotions well hidden. The group ended with expressions of gratitude and good-humoured farewells.

Retirement group

The second example concerns a group for people facing retirement. The prospect of imminent retirement, and the year or so following it, constitutes a radical change in the individual's life. One's place of work offers the pursuit of a familiar daily routine, a network of human contacts, and a status in the wider society. It also implies a stable position in the family. The exchange of all these for the unstructured freedom that retirement brings can be longed for and welcomed, but it can also be experienced as a near-traumatic change in the course of one's life. In the family setting, too, retirement may require the re-negotiating of relationships. (This is well expressed by the wife who complains to her friend: 'I married him for better or worse, but not for lunch!')

The negotiation of the shared experience of retirement lends itself particularly well to a homogeneous group, and it is to be regretted that this facility is not more readily available under the provisions made by society for its citizens, other than when they become casualties.

The group

In the setting of a private centre for group therapy, a group of people who had recently retired or were about to retire, met weekly in a time-limited group of 18 months. The group consisted of four men and two women. Two of the men had recently retired, and two were about to retire. The women were in full-time professional jobs and were about to retire. The group members found common ground almost immediately, and the talk flowed easily: mostly, but not exclusively, around their work and retirement. The conductor noticed that the emphasis of the exchanges was on similarity and consensus, and that differences were avoided, although these clearly existed. It was as if the common fate of the imminent loss of normalcy, routine and certainty in the workplace had to be recreated in the group. To the conductor, it seemed important to allow time for this process to develop, to hold it, and to refrain from any interpretive interventions, while registering in her mind the defences which were being employed against the task of negotiating individually the minefield of imminent changed life situations.

The first to acknowledge insecurity and fear of the future was a woman still at work. She had been in a position of authority and power for the best part of her professional life, and retirement was, on the face it, with her full agreement. 'It is time to go,' she said. A man added, with a forced smile: 'Or so they say'. Not much more of this was said in this session, but it seemed that the wall of denial had been broken through, and that feelings of loss, doubts, and fear of the unknown could be voiced and faced.

There followed a period of reminiscing, recalling of triumphs and disasters, success and failure at work, with friends and in the family. The conductor was seen as part of the audience rather than as a therapist. However, one of the participants revealed a troubled past which, she feared, made the present, and the prospect of retirement, more frightening and problematic. The group sensed this and treated her with sensitivity and caution in their responses to her. The level of trust and intimacy prevailing in the group made it possible for the conductor to suggest to the woman that she might want to explore her fears and problems in a different therapeutic setting, a suggestion which was received with relief by her and the group.

In the last phase of the group, a member left before the designated end, ostensibly for practical reasons, but almost certainly because he could not face the ending imposed on him by the group's timetable, which mirrored the retirement imposed on him by his firm. The conductor did not interpret this late dropping out. This would not have fitted the culture prevailing in this group. Instead, she addressed the sense of loss in the group, which was acknowledged by everyone. The group was eager and ready to get on with their farewells to one another and to the whole 'group event', as they called it. It seemed that the group members were well on their separate ways into the next phase of their lives.

CHAPTER SEVENTEEN

Groups for children and adolescents

MARVIN, THRILLED TO BE TOLD BY HIS THERAPIST THAT
HE WILL BE JOINING A GROUP, RUSHES OFF TO BUY A NEW GUITAR

A group is an effective way to provide therapy for children and adolescents with a wide range of problems. However, the fear of being humiliated or isolated by their peers is particularly strong, especially in youngsters whose difficulties in peer relationships constitute part of the presenting problem. Active intervention is needed throughout, to maintain a climate of safety and ensure that no youngster becomes marginalized or scapegoated. A well-functioning children's group raises self-esteem, offers new interpersonal solutions to family and social problems, and helps the youngsters to cope with the experience of illness, loss and trauma.

As with other forms of therapy in child and adolescent services, group therapy has to be actively supported by parents or carers if it is to be effective. Parental reservations typically hinge on the assumption that psychological problems are contagious, the fear that the child will be influenced to behave anti-socially, or the anxiety that family secrets will be disclosed and intrusive enquiries made into family life. Parents who are reluctant to accept the notion that family relationships might have played a part in the genesis of their child's problems are unlikely to allow the child to enter a form of therapy which rests on such a premise.

Which children benefit from group therapy?

Groups provide a therapeutic setting in which the child is expected to interact simultaneously with an adult and other children. On the face of it, this suggests the best of both worlds. But groups make demands which are not felt in individual therapy. They impose an obligation on the child to help others with their problems, to tolerate not always being the focus of attention, and to deal with a host of challenging interpersonal situations.

In considering a youngster's suitability for group therapy, it is as well to think about their ability to empathize and identify with others. Children and adolescents with a poorly developed sense of self, such as those with a psychotic or autistic disorder, are likely to experience disorganizing anxiety and become isolated in an analytic group, although they may benefit from a group structured towards their particular needs, for example one with a focus on the development of social skills. If the presenting disorder has taken over the child's sense of self, as may be the case with abuse, post-traumatic stress disorder, severe or chronic physical or mental illness, and some forms of disability, the first port of call in terms of group therapy might be a group which is homogeneous for that particular condition. For example, a child who has been sexually abused may need to have the experience of being together with other sexually abused children in a group before joining a group of children with a mixed range of problems.

The youngster's ability to manage interpersonal stress is another factor to be taken into consideration. Hyperactive children and those with a tendency to resort to physical aggression in the face of slight provocation are likely to reproduce such behaviours in a group. Moderate levels of these behavioural disorders can be contained, but with more than one such child in the group the therapist may find it difficult to sustain a reflective culture. On the other hand, children who deal with interpersonal stress by being excessively emotionally controlled, such as those with phobic and obsessional disorders, eating disorders, psychosomatic disorders, anxiety states and depression, are likely to use a psychodynamic group well, provided their initial anxiety about the relative lack of structure can be overcome. Such children tend to rely heavily on intellectualizing defences and controlling manoeuvres at first, but they can usually be helped into more relaxed patterns of relating which pave the way for symptom relief and behavioural change.

Independently of diagnostic considerations, the child's attitude to the idea of group therapy is in itself a useful indicator of likely success. The child who is curious about the workings and membership of the group is more likely to engage than a child who balks at the idea and only succumbs to parental or professional pressure to join the group. It is, however, possible to engage a reluctant child through preparatory individual sessions in which apprehensions can be fully explored.

Planning and composing the group

If the therapist prefers to create a setting which pulls children 'upwards' towards more developmentally mature modes of communicating, all that is needed in the room is a circle of identical chairs. A more versatile setting involves some play or drawing materials, even for older children and adolescents. Whichever model is chosen should be adhered to throughout the group.

But before working out the practical arrangements, several key questions about the group have to be asked: From which population of children will the members be drawn? Will there be a specific focus or theme, and if so, what will it be? For how long will the group run, bearing in mind that the time-scale for children is different from that of adults? Who will lead the group? How will the sessions be structured? It is also worth thinking about what other support systems might be needed while the group is running (family therapy, for example), and what liaison will be maintained with professionals and agencies involved with the child. Parents will need regular contact so that therapeutic change can be integrated into the family dynamic. A parallel parents' group is a good forum for this purpose.

Potential group members can be thought of in terms of their similarities and differences. Which characteristics will the children obviously have in common and in which respect will they be obviously different from one another? Groups which emphasize similarity might be made up of children with similar disorders (e.g. eating disorder, post-traumatic stress disorder), children who have experienced similar life events (e.g. adoption, refugee status), or children who share an institutional context (e.g. a hospital ward, residential care unit). The shared characteristics unite the group in its early stages, rapidly diminishing the child's sense of isolation. Later in the course of the group, individual strengths are recognized and different solutions to the same problem are discovered. Most groups achieve a mix of complementary personality traits and shared characteristics. If possible, articulate and emotionally expressive children should be balanced by inhibited and less verbal children. In practice, however, children undergo surprising metamorphoses in groups, and it is never easy to predict how a particular child will behave in the group.

Some therapists favour the model of a closed group, others prefer an open or slow-open group. An intermediate model, which we have found useful for school-age children, allows a group to meet as a closed group for ten to twelve sessions, usually on a termly basis, with the option for some children to continue for another block of sessions if further therapy is indicated.

What is the optimal number of members for a children's group? Our experience is that five or six make up a good working group. Effective therapy can take place in a group with four, or even three children, but the element of social challenge and feedback is weakened. Groups of seven or eight are also possible, but are more difficult to contain. With regard to age groupings, 5 to 7 years, 8 to 11 years, 12 to 15 years and 16 to 21 years seem to lend themselves well to shared therapy, but the developmental level and social maturity of the child is more important than actual age in terms of group placement. The question also arises as to whether a child should be placed in a same-sex or mixed-sex group. Each type of group has its advantages and limitations. Mixed groups tend to promote the development of self-presentation, while same-sex groups permit a fuller expression of self-doubt and the exploration of more intimate, potentially shameful issues.

Vignette

A mother complained that the therapist was too permissive with her 12-year-old daughter, and that the group was inciting her to acts of defiance at home by encouraging her to 'stand up for herself'. This was dealt with in a parallel session with the mother, but the message also had to be brought into the group, where the child's tendency to play off the group against her mother could be addressed.

Vignette

Several children in a group wanted to visit one of the members who was in hospital. The therapist discouraged this, framing it positively as a caring impulse but also seeing it as an intrusion into the child's privacy and an infringement of the confidentiality boundary surrounding the group. At an administrative level the therapist carried the responsibility for conveying the good wishes of the group to the hospitalized child.

Preparing the child for a group

Group therapy is best discussed first in a family interview. Afterwards, individual sessions with the child may be needed to prepare the child further for the group, especially if the child has had a bad experience of peer group life inside or outside school To allay their fears, it is important to describe the group in some detail, telling the ages and sexes of the other children and even sketching out a few of the typical problems which they bring. This 'trailer' to the group reduces anxiety about encountering extreme levels of disturbance. Parents are sometimes relieved to see that care has been taken in putting together a group of children who are likely to help one another.

To many children, therapy means being made to talk only about the painful and problematic areas of their lives. It helps to tell the child that this is not the case, and that there is no expectation to talk about anything until they feel ready to do so. The idea of helping other children often appeals, and enables some children to retain a sense of control in what is potentially an overwhelming situation. The confidential nature of the group is underlined, making the concept meaningful with words like: 'What we talk about in the group is only for us'. In similar vein, social contact outside the group is discouraged. It is also made clear that no physically aggressive behaviour is allowed. This is an issue on which the group therapist, unlike his or her counterpart in an adult group, represents societal norms and the law. The spelling out of these 'rules' generally reassures parents and children alike.

Therapeutic factors in children's groups

The discovery that one is not alone

Probably the single most therapeutic element in any group is the discovery that one is not alone in one's plight. This discovery leads to others: that there is more than one way of coping with a problem; that one can have difficulty in a certain area of one's life and yet have the strength and skill to be of help to others; and that professionals are not the only source of useful information and psychological support. For children, whose very status implies dependence and vulnerability, a group can mark the beginnings of empowerment and mastery of feelings experienced as overwhelming or out of control.

The group as a place to tell one's story

For many children, the act of telling one's story, whether through play, in pictures or in words, is therapeutic in itself. Groups have a powerful way of casting light on the shadows of the past. Children who have been harbouring memories of sad, painful or traumatic events may find, perhaps for the first time, that these memories can be expressed in the presence of others who are trying to make sense of them. Children are good at supplying one another with words and trading experiences. The therapist is there to ask the right questions, to make links which underline the shared nature of the experience, and to model respectful attention to what is being said.

The group as a playground

The group uses and extends the art of play, both verbally and with the help of play materials, and enables the child to experiment with newly learned interpersonal skills. Self-defeating patterns of behaviour, such as tendencies to monopolize, disrupt, control others, resort to aggressive or placating manoeuvres, seek an intense attachment to one person, and withdraw from collaborative interaction, tend to be extinguished when spoken about understandingly. New possibilities of relating in a social context are offered, either implicitly through the availability of alternative models presented by the other children, or explicitly, through the therapeutic conversations.

The group as a mirror

A group enables the children to see themselves in others. This can be affirming, but it can also be anxiety provoking, as when a child recognizes his or her own unwanted traits in others and sets about attacking them. Interventions by the therapist help the children to recognize their own attributes and accept others for who they are. The collective response of the group towards a child also functions like a mirror, reflecting back to the child a self-image less distorted than one which might have arisen in the family context.

The group as a container

Containment is achieved through a balance of acceptance and limit-setting. The stability and predictability of the group reduces anxiety. Children for whom excessive control is a problem discover that they can afford to relax and express their thoughts and feelings more adventurously. Children in whom control is too easily lost find that the combined firmness of the therapist and the collective reactions of the group as a whole provide a powerful incentive to regain control and develop alternative coping mechanisms. The group boundary, protected by the therapist from the frequent assaults to which it is subjected in children's groups, reinforces the experience of containment.

Interpretation

Interpretation, in the sense of linking seemingly unconnected phenomena in order to bring about a greater awareness of the origins of a particular problem, has a place in children's groups. The therapist interprets, but so too do the children to one another, bluntly and incisively at times, and in ways which the therapist may have to soften by rephrasing in more moderate language.

The group as a transitional space

A group reduces the intensity of interactions which are driven by high levels of anxiety, such as hyperactive behaviour, anxious attachment, phobic avoidance and impulsive aggression. The combination of a consistent structure and an external space within the group creates a climate within which it is possible for the child to find new, imaginative ways of expression. Playful interactions, discussion of dreams and pictorial self-representation are all techniques which help the children to develop more reflective ways of experiencing themselves in relation to others.

The altruistic factor

Expression of the innate urge to be there for other people, even in adversity, is perhaps what makes a group unique as a therapeutic medium. The youngsters in a group know that they are expected to help one another as well as themselves, and this confers on them a sense of importance, duty and skill not evoked in other therapies. The self-esteem of the children is boosted by the discovery that they are capable of supporting and advising others despite their own predicament and relative dependence, and that the solutions which they have developed to their own problems are copied and appreciated by the other children.

The technique of conducting a children's group

The start of the group

The first group session imprints itself strongly on the children and sets the tone for the rest of the group. The therapist should be active from the outset, leading the process and taking responsibility for determining where the focus of attention should be. A withholding stance heightens anxiety, and one cannot rely on the spontaneity of the children to knit themselves together as a group.

Long silences should not be allowed to develop. The therapist can facilitate exchanges by means of open-ended questions to individual children, such as: 'How have you been since we last met?' This prompts personal stories, and opens the way for other children to come in with their own questions and comments. If this does not happen, the therapist can draw them in. Going round in turn is a useful technique for helping all the children to find their voice. Observations about the group as a whole are generally unproductive except towards the end of the session, by way of a question, for example: 'How do you all feel now that the session is ending?' The therapist engages readily in conversation. Later, when the children are confident enough to sustain the interaction themselves, the therapist can afford to be more contemplative, but never for too long.

The established group

It is not easy to discern a progression from 'superficial' to 'deep' in a children's group. These concepts in themselves have a different meaning for children, and the language which they use to express their states of mind has to be understood accordingly. Important personal issues can be broached in the first session, and powerful therapeutic shifts can occur at any time in the life of the group. By the same token, a group can become superficial or stuck at any time. Ultimately it is up to the therapist to judge when the group needs to be steered towards issues which are being evaded. An established group has a momentum of its own. Children understand that they are there to talk personally, and they generally report eagerly on the vicissitudes of their daily lives. They exchange information about their families, school experiences and leisure-time pursuits. They offer solace and advice together with kernels of childish wisdom and insight. The therapist should be prepared to engage promptly with any child who seems to be becoming distressed or isolated, or whose behaviour is threatening to disturb the therapeutic culture.

The following is the third session of an outpatient group for young people aged 12 to 15 taken by two co-therapists, a man and a woman.

Julie:	(*to therapists*) Why don't you give us a subject to talk about?
Other group members:	(*chorus*) Yes, give us a subject!
Male therapist:	All right then. How about: 'What I did at the weekend'.
Stephen:	Practically nothing.
Julie:	This is like primary school. We had to write things like that in books. I used to tell a pack of lies.

Andrew:	Well I did nothing really.
Julie:	Well then, that's the end of that subject.
Roger:	Anyway, that wasn't a subject – it's a question or a statement.
Female therapist:	Maybe everyone needs to take responsibility for what we talk about.
Roger:	We'll have to vote on that, then.
Male therapist:	OK, in that case I propose the motion.
Stephen:	I second it.

(*They vote. The two therapists vote for it*)

Julie:	(*to male therapist*) You can't vote for it. People who propose a motion can't vote.
Male therapist:	I'm sorry, you're wrong. It happens like that in Parliament.
Julie:	I don't care what happens in Parliament, I'm going to abstain.
Roger:	I'm going to abstain. What about the people who aren't here? (*two group members are absent*)
Stephen:	It doesn't affect them. They're not here.
Roger:	Does this mean we all have responsibility for the group?
Stephen:	Yes, we're all the bosses and none of us is the boss.
Roger:	(*to male therapist*) Are you the boss?
Julie:	(*to male therapist*) Neither you nor Mrs S (the female therapist) is the boss.
Roger:	Yes they are. It's like the Queen and the Prime Minister. The Queen has more power than the Prime Minister.
Andrew:	I'm against the monarchy.
Stephen:	So am I. I'm against the Queen. (they get up, walk over to each other and shake hands)
Julie:	I think you're all wrong. The Queen knows everything that's going on because she was born into it.
Stephen:	Would you know if you were born into it?
Female therapist:	Maybe it's to do with the fact that the Queen is a woman and the Prime Minister is a man, and when you're thinking about them you're thinking about your own parents.

Roger:	(*to Julie*) Does your dad help with the housework?
Julie:	My dad's divorced – but he was a lazy sod. He used to come home and just sit in front of the television and send us out to get his cigarettes even though he had just passed the shop a few minutes earlier. Women do all the work. Women have to have babies and carry them around.
Stephen:	Men carry babies around on their backs in China.
Julie:	This isn't China.
Stephen:	Women can't do men's jobs...
Female therapist:	(*interrupting*) Just a moment, Julie was starting to talk about something really important and you've taken us over to China, Stephen.
Louise:	(*to Julie*) What happened if you refused to go? (for the cigarettes)
Julie:	You must be joking. He'd go crazy. He once chucked my food in my face and broke the plate over my head ... he punched through a wall once.
Louise:	What did your mum do?
Julie:	Nothing. She's got a temper, too. She beats me with a spoon if I don't finish my food.
Louise:	My dad's coming for a visit ... I don't want to be there. I'm going out.
Julie:	(*to therapists*) You won't tell my parents what I've just told you?
Male therapist:	You know that what's said in the group is confidential.
Roger:	(*to Stephen*) What if your parents ask you what happened in the group?
Stephen:	I just tell them to mind their own business. I couldn't tell my parents what I'm up to anyway.
Julie:	I went up to the flat of a 30-year-old man once ... If my mother knew, I wouldn't be here to tell the tale. I was lucky he was too drunk for anything to happen.
Louise:	My friend's mother's drunk all the time. Her father gets a strap to her if she doesn't go out and buy the booze.

Julie:	My friend's mother's also drunk.
Roger:	(*to Julie*) Does she go out and get the drink?
Julie:	She has to ... he beats her if she doesn't. I want to have a little girl. She wouldn't swear or do anything horrible.
Male therapist:	(*to Julie*) Males are not very popular with you.
Julie:	Well what would you feel if you were brought up with six women? I've been with women all my life ... My mum's been very good to me – I've got nothing to complain of. My brother's got a problem – he's with women all the time.

Comment

The boys express solidarity with each other and with the male therapist. The girls form a parallel identification with the female therapist. The reader will no doubt be able to discern several other themes which could have been developed for their therapeutic potential. The two therapists chose to play along with the 'rebellion' against authority at the start of the session, then they intervened more directively to reinforce personal disclosures about family life. The excerpt shows a typical development from collective banter to individual narratives of a painful and disturbing nature. Finally, one of the therapists ventures an interpretation which might prompt the group to think reflectively.

Ending the group

In a slow-open group, holiday breaks provide the opportunity for the children to think about their feelings of attachment and dependency and to rehearse the ultimate ending of their therapy. At the start of the group, it is a good idea to give each child a timetable containing the dates on which the group is due to meet, and when the breaks will be.

If the group has been a good experience, the prospect of ending is appropriately tinged with sadness. Children need help to separate from one another by thoughtful discussion well in advance of the ending. It is important for them to talk about whom and what they will miss, what they might have gained from the experience and how the group could have been better. Sometimes the prospect of ending brings out earlier anxieties, and the therapist may be dismayed to see some children becoming more demanding at the last minute and slipping back into more immature ways of self-expression, but generally these are short-lived and give way to mature farewells.

Critical moments in group therapy with children

Certain critical moments in groups have the potential to be turned to therapeutic advantage or to develop into bad experiences which set back progress.

The emergence of distressing life events

A group is replete with stories of distressing life events which have a bearing on the very problems which bring the children into therapy. Children talk with candour of family breakdown, abuse, physical or mental illness, and premature or traumatic deaths. Feelings of shame, guilt, fear, sadness and anger surround these narratives.

When a child begins to tell such a story, the others relate what they hear to their own inner world, privately trying to match it with their own experience. Some may offer supportive comments or share their own stories, while others may try to distance themselves and resort to diversionary tactics. The therapist has to be particularly active at this point, facilitating the process with empathic listening, questioning and commenting, but also recognizing the need to maintain protective barriers until a greater sense of safety can be achieved.

Aggressive behaviour

Children become acutely aware of their differences as well as their similarities. One child may see in another traits which provoke dislike or disapproval, perhaps mirroring their own concealed traits. This can express itself in overt criticism and in any of the repertoire of aggressive behaviours learned in the playground, such as teasing, mimicking, accusing, challenging, refusing to cooperate, or even physically attacking. The therapist has to intervene quickly, physically if need be, to prevent harm. Such a response carries its own risk in today's litigious society, and calls for careful documenting and discussion in supervision. It is best to engage first with the initiator, and work with this child until a calmer frame of mind is reached. It is not helpful to allow an argument or conflict to escalate. This can result in one or more of the protagonists dropping out of the group. Nor can a group be trusted to police itself. That is the lonely task of the therapist. Once a more reflective mode has been achieved, the group can be asked to think about the source of the aggression.

Scapegoating

Children readily resort to scapegoating. Those children whose view of the world is already resentful and persecuted, and whose solutions to life's problems involve blaming others, are more likely to cast a vulnerable group member in the role of the scapegoat. This applies particularly to children who come from a background of deprivation and abuse, and whose self-esteem is precarious and rests on the disparagement of others.

Scapegoating can be insidious, or it can flare up and run its course in moments, before the bewildered therapist can intervene. It takes many forms, such as persistently ignoring someone, labelling them as ill or alien ('not one of us'), or attributing dangerous or malign intentions to them. To stop the process the therapist has to align himself or herself with the scapegoat. The ringleader of the scapegoating process has to be confronted, and the group has to be confronted with their projections onto the scapegoat. The therapist then focuses on similarities between the scapegoat and the others. Eventually the scapegoat is helped to look at his or her own contribution to the process. If scapegoating prevails and the child drops out, there may be a feeling of relief, but the template remains and the cycle is likely to recur unless confronted.

Peer group phenomena which appear in therapy groups

Teasing

Teasing is an ambiguous communication which treads a fine line between affection and aggression, and its impact can last well into adult life. It has a useful social function, teaching children the art of playful give-and-take, and helping those on the edge of the group to conform to the group mores. Often, however, teasing assumes a sadistic quality and takes the form of scapegoating and bullying. The effect may be to drive a sensitive child out of the group. As with scapegoating, intervention must be prompt, first interrupting it, then helping the group to think about its meaning.

> **Vignette**
> A 13-year-old boy arrived in the group smelling of aftershave lotion. This prompted another boy to call him 'Pongo', which the other children echoed with hilarity. Another child ridiculed the boy as effeminate. The therapist stepped in, asking the leader of the attack to tell about his own personal experiences of being called names. The therapist then invited others to do the same. This led to a group discussion of teasing and being teased in their families, in which all participated.

Joking

Joking, like teasing, is a useful social device. Children's groups are frequently assailed by joke-telling and wisecracks which can be turned to therapeutic advantage. Jokes provide an opportunity to open up taboo topics such as illness, disability, sexuality and ethnicity. The therapist has to be quick to challenge jokes which act as a vehicle for prejudice. As with teasing, the therapist has to explore the joker's hidden assumptions and spread the exercise to the group as a whole.

In-talk

The language of children and adolescents is peppered with expletives, repetitive 'fillers', and everyday words given a radically different meaning in the adolescent demi-monde. Slang serves to protect the group culture from outside incursions. The element of secret understanding confers power by keeping out uncomprehending adults. When such expressions come to the surface in adolescent therapy groups, the therapist should ask for translations. This serves as a way of looking at differences between the therapist and the group, and relates to issues of inclusion and exclusion.

The specific nature of adolescent groups

Adolescence is an age of extreme attitudes and posturings. The adolescent mentality is particularly prone to idealization and devaluation, which becomes more pronounced when there is marked stress. This is reflected in strong identifications with 'good' or 'bad' subcultures, popular heroes or anti-heroes, and a set of values which often stand in opposition to the prevailing establishment culture.

These positions are replicated in adolescent therapy groups, where the therapist has to contend constantly with an array of extreme happenings, many of which occur at the group boundary, or even right outside the group. Intrusions into group members' physical and psychological space, and disruptive or distracting actions inside and outside the group room are some of the ways in which the therapist's authority and bona fides can be challenged. The adolescent's preoccupation with sexuality and sexual identity often emerges aggressively and provocatively, by way of denying the underlying insecurity and anxiety. The therapist has to take a central role in translating these defensive manoeuvres into their true meaning and opening up a realistic and reflective group discussion.

The guiding philosophy is to put an immediate stop to events that could be destructive for the group and steer the process towards a search for the origins and meaning of the event. The therapist moves deftly between confrontation and support, amplifying the constructive forces in the group and moving it away from acting out towards self-reflection.

Co-therapy for children's groups

A children's group can be led effectively by one person. However, there are advantages in having two people leading the group, especially if the group is focused on a particular disorder or disability, when it helps to have one therapist with specialized knowledge of the condition (a paediatrician or health visitor for example) working alongside another who has the training to keep an eye on the psychodynamic aspects of the group. In certain groups the gender of the group leaders can be an issue. For example, a group of girls who have been sexually abused by men should have at least one woman therapist.

A further advantage of co-therapy is that it offers a model to the children of how two adults can cooperate. When differences or disagreements arise between the therapists, the group can witness these and join in the attempt to resolve them. This provides a corrective emotional experience for those children who associate disagreement with escalation into conflict, violence or family dislocation. Children also like hearing their issues discussed thoughtfully by two adults.

CHAPTER EIGHTEEN

Family therapy: a group-analytic perspective

Don't tell my mother I'm living in sin,
Don't let the old folks know:
Don't tell my twin that I breakfast on gin,
He'd never survive the blow.

A.P. Herbert, 'Don't tell my mother'

The family is unquestionably a group, subject to group dynamics in much the same way as a typical analytic group composed of people who are strangers to one another at the start of the therapy. By the same token, family therapy is literally a form of small-group therapy. But in many ways the differences between the two types of group are so great that, not surprisingly, the two forms of therapy have developed entirely different techniques and separate trainings.

The contribution of group-analytic theory to family therapy

Is it possible to speak of a group-analytic model of family therapy? S.H. Foulkes remarked only briefly on family therapy in his writings. He recognized the family as a 'life group', a naturally occurring network, or 'plexus', as he called it, in which the members were 'vitally interrelated' and interdependent. Although speaking positively of family therapy, Foulkes acknowledged that his own experience in the field was limited.

'I myself have treated families only off and on,' he wrote, 'sometimes with considerable success and in a very short time, relatively speaking' (Foulkes, 1975, p.13).

But he leaves us in the dark about his technique. He makes the point, however, that although the family is a group, it does not follow that we should address and treat it all the time as a whole. 'On the contrary,' he states, 'here as at any time we treat the individuals composing this group in the context of the group' (Foulkes, 1975, p.14).

He was more enthusiastic about the 'psycho-diagnostic' value of family interviews. The nuclear family, 'with its intimate, inter-linked system of interaction and transactions', provided a special opportunity to study transpersonal processes and to discover patterns of interaction in their chronological sequence, passed down from one generation to the next. But such study, Foulkes believed, had to await the individual's emergence from childhood. 'As far as I can see,' he wrote,

> this primary family is best studied at a later stage when the children are more or less adolescent, or even adult. One can then get a clear picture as to the way in which they have been moulded and forced into shape by the conditions prevailing in the family into which they were born, and of which they form a part.   (Foulkes, 1975, p.16)

This curiously adult-centred approach to family therapy has little appeal to family therapists, the vast majority of whom work with children, and for whom the techniques of communicating simultaneously with children and parents are the very lifeblood of family therapy. Having given family therapy his blessing, Foulkes retired from the fray, and it was left to one of his colleagues, Robin Skynner, to develop a specific group-analytic approach to family therapy. However, Foulkes did make one important point which has profound implications for the technique of family therapy: the family as a group contradicts every criterion set out as ideal for the composition and treatment of a group made up of individuals who have never previously met, the so-called 'stranger-group'.

To develop this point: the family is an established group before it meets the therapist, unlike the stranger group, whose composition has been masterminded by the therapist and whose members have been carefully prepared for the analytic task, having never set eyes on one other before the start of the therapy. The family group has grown together organically and comes into therapy bristling with a ready-made set of defences against change. The roles into which family members have been cast, and the myths which every family elaborates about itself, carry the authority of generations, even centuries of tradition. In therapeutic terms, the family usually presents itself to the therapist with one member clearly nominated as the 'problem'. The stranger group, on the other hand, has no single member who carries the symptom for the group. All are carriers of their own symptoms, and all are seen as having equal potential strength in the group.

These differences help to explain the divergent techniques which have developed for the two forms of therapy. The crisis atmosphere of many families presenting for therapy, and the complex spread of different developmental and motivational attitudes, means the family therapist faces a race against time to effect change. The stranger group, having been carefully assembled by a therapist and unencumbered by a shared past, is an immediately well-functioning group. Such disturbance as there is, is initially contained within the individual members and is only later shared within the group-as-a-whole. The pace of engagement can therefore be much slower, governed in the early stages by all group members' mutual lack of knowledge of one another, and the need, first of all, to reduce the anxiety of unfamiliarity (literally the anxiety of not being in one's own family).

The integration of psychoanalytic and systems theory

In Foulkes we can discern the faint beginnings of a systemic approach to groups. Skynner elaborated on this and based his group-analytic model of family therapy on the integration of systemic and developmental psychoanalytic theory. Systems thinking, a relatively undeveloped strand of thought in group analysis, has had a profound influence on the family therapy world, leading to the development of highly specialized interventions, techniques, and schools of practice built around the notion of the family as the prototype of an open system.

In the 1970s and 1980s mainstream family therapists embraced systemic thinking as the core approach to family therapy. The systemic and structural approaches to family therapy regard the interpersonal structure of the family and its interaction in the here-and-now as the main theatre of operations (Minuchin and Fishman, 1981; Hoffman, 1981; Haley, 1976; Palazzoli et al., 1978). Richly developed models of structural, systemic and strategic family therapy hold sway. A range of techniques has evolved, based on active, carefully orchestrated interventions calculated to influence family systems which have become dysfunctional. These schools of family therapy place the therapist firmly in the driving seat, and issue a licence to use directive, 'head-on' or, if need be, subtle techniques to pit against the family's formidable and versatile opposition to change.

Psychoanalytically orientated family therapists tend to focus more on historical aspects of the family such as unresolved mourning, obsolete inter-generational attitudes based on family myths, and failure to negotiate crucial transitions in the family life cycle. Skynner wove into the systems framework a psychodynamic way of thinking which retained the emphasis on the here-and-now, but respected the importance of individual development, and the value of transference and counter-transference as therapeutic tools.

The family therapist as an outsider in the family group

The Foulkesian tenet that the conductor can, for the most part, entrust the task of therapy to the group as a whole, does not apply to families. With the stranger group providing its own social microcosm, the therapist can afford to be relatively unobtrusive. In the case of family therapy, however, the therapist is faced with a monolithic, dysfunctional group, and shoulders the responsibility of

becoming the sole agent of social reality. Single-handedly, the therapist holds up a mirror to the family, turning it this way and that, to
reveal to the family their patterns of dysfunctional communication.
It is the family therapist, alone and unaided, who has to perform the
numerous tasks designed to achieve therapeutic change which in the
stranger group are happily distributed amongst the group members.

Not only is the family therapist alone in these tasks, he or she is
also vulnerable to rejection by the family. If we consider the dynamics of the group which is formed when the therapist 'joins' the family
group, we see a group which provides a striking contrast with the
stranger group. The stranger group is also, strictly speaking, a group
of individuals who have been 'joined' by a therapist. With this tilt of
the lens it can be seen that the therapist who 'joins' the family is
more conspicuously the outsider than the therapist who 'joins' the
stranger group. The family therapist therefore has to mobilize techniques designed to counteract the group dynamic by which the
group rejects an outsider, who is first and foremost the therapist.

The risk of the family therapist being excluded is all the greater
because the therapist 'joins' the group at a bad time, namely at a
point of great stress or crisis in its life, and this is always an omen for
potential scapegoating. On top of that, this new member, the therapist, assumes a leadership role in the group, purporting to tell the
family how to change, attempting to challenge the group's
entrenched mode of functioning, and imposing a new set of rules on
the family. The therapist becomes not only the 'new' member of this
group but its leader, a precarious position at the best of times. This
new member/leader will be challenging the group's entrenched
mode of functioning and facing the group members with their cherished defences. Then, at the end of the session, the therapist goes
one way and the family goes another, leaving them to continue their
interaction as a group, with plenty of time to reassert their longstanding patterns of communication and decide whether or not to
accept this most recent and troublesome member. The family therapist is only too well placed to become the group scapegoat and suffer
expulsion from the group. If this happens, it means in effect that the
family will fail to engage in therapy.

The alternative hazard to scapegoating is idealization, an equally
precarious position, since it can slip into scapegoating if the group's
unrealistic expectations are frustrated. The family may invest the

outsider-therapist with disproportionate power and adopt a correspondingly helpless and compliant position. In counter-transference terms, the therapist may feel tempted to offer dramatic solutions to the family's problems, only to be defeated by their unconscious intransigence. Success in family therapy often depends on the therapist's capacity to divest himself or herself of projected power and imbue the family with its own power to change.

Creative use of the scapegoat role

Robin Skynner drew attention to the therapeutic advantage of intentionally taking on the role of the scapegoat, borrowing it, for a while, as it were, and thereby relieving the scapegoat nominated by the family of that role. Skynner argued that the therapist, by virtue of his or her articulate, detached and authoritative position, is in a strong position to take on the role and use it to fight back and confront the family with its projections. For the operation to succeed, the therapist first has to speak for the designated scapegoat, draw the fire, and then use the authority intrinsic to the professional role to return and redistribute the family's projections. This involves furnishing the parents with an understanding of their child's difficult behaviour as a communication, a technique which may at first seem as if the therapist is 'siding' unconditionally with the child, but which, if there is a modicum of understanding within the family, can lead to other members of the family owning their own part in the process (Skynner, 1979).

Identifying what is missing in the family

The therapist who listens to the family with an analytic attitude begins to sense that some element is missing which is rendering them dysfunctional and symptomatic, and which the family is trying inarticulately to get the therapist to provide. This might be something as elusive as 'authority', 'containment', 'fathering' or 'mothering'. Within the counter-transference, the therapist experiences the emotions which attach to these elements and becomes aware of a pressure to compensate for what the family is lacking. As with scapegoating, the therapist temporarily 'adopts' the symptom as a prelude to returning it by way of exchange to the family as a whole.

Communicating with children and adults together

The family therapist is faced with the complication posed by the co-existence of children and adults in the same therapeutic setting. It is necessary, therefore, to have in mind a model of communication which takes account of the different developmental stages of children, adolescents and adults communicating within a fraught, often crisis-ridden context. This introduces a dimension of specialized practice involving an understanding of childhood language and logic, play and activity, and the ability to interpret and translate developmentally governed modes of communication into meaningful signals both within the family and between the family and the therapist. The group analyst's capacity for using metaphoric and symbolic language finds extensive application in family therapy, where small children interact through the media of drawing and play, and with the obligatory logic of childhood cognition.

Mirroring and resonance in family therapy

An important therapeutic element in stranger groups is the mirroring function provided by the group. Individuals become aware of hidden aspects of themselves which they see reflected in other members. The group as a whole may reflect back to individual aspects of themselves of which they were previously unaware. A sense of shared identity and commonality emerges with the passage of time. The dysfunctional family can be a grotesquely distorting mirror, reflecting ugly images, freezing images in time, imposing the features of the dead on those of the living, turning the young into the old, the old into the young, or, like a vampire, failing to reflect any image at all. The family may be collectively blind to many aspects of its own identity.

The therapist is, in a manner of speaking, a mirror to the family. For some families, particularly isolated, emotionally blind families, the mirroring role of the therapist is especially important. The therapist may at first simply describe what he or she sees, deepening the communication later to reflect the hidden layers of meaning within the family communication network.

Resonance calls for the therapist to fall in with prevailing patterns of communication within the family in order to become accepted by the family. In stranger groups, each communication resonates at some level with the group matrix, opening up further opportunities to communicate at any of the levels. In families, resonance occurs when the therapist mingles with the family in its style of language and expression, making it easier for any member of the family to express a hitherto unexpressed thought or feeling. The therapist sounds a note, as it were, which echoes through the family and triggers off other notes. Mirroring and resonance may have to be introduced quickly into the family as techniques of engagement, while in stranger groups they evolve slowly over many weeks and months, affecting all group members simultaneously.

Enabling the family to tell its story

For many families, the collective exercise involved in telling their story to a stranger is in itself therapeutic. Families often confess that this would not have been possible without the enabling presence of an outsider. They remark with gratitude on the unexpected benefits of talking for the first time about issues which were being harboured silently, distorted into acrimony, or displaced into symptom formation. The authority of the stranger who assembles the family and, in a manner of speaking, compels them to talk openly, provides a significant impetus for change. But this calls for the careful sequencing of questions to include all members of the family, especially children and adolescents, who can all too easily be sidelined in a parley between the adults. In order to bring in the less articulate members of the family, the therapist may have to present them with a tentative form of words, couched as speculations or suppositions, which can be accepted, repudiated or elaborated on.

Families present their stories in many guises. For some families, the story begins with a current relationship difficulty. For others, the first chapter of the story lies in the past, located in a loss, perhaps, or a traumatic event. The therapeutic situation forces family members to listen to one another, perhaps for the first time. Parents often listen with astonishment to a child announcing fears, wishes and perceptions about family life, or revealing memories of family events thought to have been unnoticed or forgotten. Conversely, children listen with ears flapping, as parents tell stories about the family previously shrouded in mystery and secrecy.

For some families, the act of telling the family story is enough. These are generally families with relatively low levels of intrafamilial conflict who are attempting to come to terms with traumatic events in the past. Families who are working towards the integration of new family members, for example a step-parent, or a new partner's children, need more than the story-telling forum. They need strategies for coping with the inevitable intrafamilial tensions and conflicts which accompany reconstituted families.

Intervening in the conflict-ridden family

In a stranger group, conflict occasionally flares up between group members. This can be constructively addressed through an analysis of the transferential relationships which lie behind them. But this may seem like a luxury in the hothouse of family therapy. In many families, conflict at home is generally managed, albeit ineffectually and inconclusively, by such devices as storming out or resorting to displays of verbal or physical aggression. The therapeutic situation militates against this, but the therapist still has to introduce strategies, such as prescribing a course of action or setting a task designed to alter the interpersonal chemistry of the family. Only then can the family begin to explore the psychodynamic origins or transference implications of their behaviour.

The separation of close ties

Families which have been sensitized to loss frequently develop an over-close pattern of relating, perceived by outsiders as overprotective and excluding of others. This may occur within a dyad, for example mother and child, or within the family as a whole, in relation to the outside world. Cohesiveness within such families results in oppressively close, mutually dependent relationships in which healthy expressions of anger are feared and avoided. By the same token individuality is stifled, the inner self is intruded upon, and family members remain bound to each other through strong affects which limit their capacity for secondary process thinking. In systemic terms, the boundary around these families or dyads becomes relatively impermeable, so that the flow of communication between the family and the outside world is reduced. In dynamic terms, projection and splitting readily occur, creating a strong 'insider–outsider' dynamic which makes it difficult for the therapist to engage with the family. Such families tend to produce symptoms associated with conflict avoidance, such as phobic anxiety states and psychosomatic problems. To join with these families the therapist has to help them to verbalize negative emotions and experience the aftermath in a supportive context.

The symptomatic nature of family secrets

The deliberate withholding of information within a group, for fear of the destructive consequences of its disclosure, creates an area of isolation which disturbs the network of communication. The isolated and therefore symptomatic area becomes walled off by a barrier of tension across which thoughts and fantasies are projected. Individuals in a stranger group harbour secrets until the levels of tension accompanying them have dropped to a point where they feel safe enough to disclose their secrets. This can take months or years, or it may never happen. Feelings of shame and guilt, and fear of punishment may prevail, but the therapist has to persevere in the effort to render the symptom redundant. In the case of secrecy, this involves a careful analysis of the fears surrounding it and the creation of a climate in which the emotions of shame and guilt are universalized.

In families, the dangers of disclosure are experienced more profoundly, with fantasies, which may be close to the reality, of deep rifts opening up in family relationships, or the break-up of the family unit. Secrets involving the safety or wellbeing of a family member, such as abuse, are held on to with conscious tenacity, and the therapist may have to search for unconscious clues, not only to the nature of the secret, but to the key for unlocking it.

Multiple family therapy

Multiple family therapy, the gathering together of several families for therapy, is a powerful instrument of change calling for techniques borrowed from both stranger group therapy and family therapy. In practice, three or four families provide an optimally sized group, with anywhere between 12 and 20 participants. A model that works satisfactorily in our experience is based on the traditional group-analytic workshop design, with several sessions planned on a single day. This could include separate sessions for the parents and children as well as 'plenary' sessions for all the families together.

Multiple family therapy is an exercise which demands a strongly leader-centred style of intervention. Families have to be introduced to each other, and each of the children present has to find a voice. To start with, the therapist might collect, using a turn-taking technique, 'safe' information, such as a list of proposed topics for discussion and wishes for change. Writing these up on a flip-chart or board helps everyone to focus on their own and others' points of view. The group discussion generally takes off from this platform, and leads quickly into parent–child relationship issues, with members of different families comparing notes and offering support, ideas and suggestions, after the fashion of a beginning stranger group. Separate parents' and children's groups complement the material worked on in the plenary groups. Multiple family therapy can be staged as a 'one off' event, constructed, for example around a specific parenting theme, or it can be offered as a short-term programme staged over several weeks or months. It is a model which can be applied equally to inpatient, day-patient and outpatient settings, and to adult and child patient populations alike.

CHAPTER NINETEEN

The application of group analysis to non-clinical settings

The advent of systemic thinking and practice raised a fundamental question that had been taken for granted in the individualistic outlook of the first half of the twentieth century: who exactly is 'the patient' or 'client' when the therapist addresses a system such as a family, or an articulating entity such as an organization? The nature of the contract between the professional and the client came under scrutiny. In clinical practice this first came to the fore in the field of family therapy, where the conventional notion that an individual harbours the problem and therefore deserves the treatment was challenged. A related issue arises in non-clinical settings. Group analysis has made its own distinctive contribution to this field, and there is now a specialized training in organizational group analysis established by Ralph Stacey at the University of Hertfordshire. Stacey is a group analyst who has developed a theory of relating which challenges both systems thinking and psychoanalytic determinism. He speaks of complex responsive processes which stipulates that our communications are shaped by conscious and unconscious gestures and responses to one another (Stacey, 2001).

Group analysts are increasingly called upon by organizations and institutions as diverse as the Fire Service, the Civil Service, schools, religious institutions and voluntary organizations, to apply their expertise to maintain the well-functioning of the organization. The present climate of innovation and rapid change tends to increase stress, and this in turn can result in absenteeism, excessive sick-leave, latecoming, or a rapid turnover of personnel; all of which endanger the organization's efficiency or profitability, or both.

The group-analytic perspective, with its centrality of communication and relationships, seems well suited to the investigation and possible resolution of such aspects of organizational malfunctioning. Most group analysts engaged in organizational group-work and consultation find that the focus and technique acquired in their clinical work requires considerable modification. Others see little difference in their interventions, and in the ultimate aim: 'In both cases, the task is to allow true novelty to emerge in a way that is useful to its members, their role in the group and the tasks of the group' (Rance, 2003). Yet others point to the need to keep in view power relations, politics and cultural backgrounds, and pay less attention to interpersonal and intrapersonal phenomena (Wilke and Freeman, 2001). Be this as it may, it seems to us that the aspects that are specific to group analysis in organizations will be influenced in procedure and content by questions such as: 'Who is the client?' 'With whom is my professional contract?' It is not simply that 'he who pays the piper calls the tune'. Few group analysts would agree to play a tune that runs counter to their professional integrity and ethics, or indeed any tune prescribed them for purposes other than the needs of the group members of the organization in question. Rather, it is the pressure points that could result in outright conflict which the group analyst will feel called upon to discern and resolve.

Pressure points and areas of potential dysfunction can come about through a variety of occurrences: reorganization, change of management, planned or sudden redundancies, financial stress or threatened collapse. In the public services, new legislation, relocation and changed working conditions or demands figure large in the potential dissatisfaction and stress experienced by the employees. In all such situations, it is essential to have a clear and unambiguous under-standing of the terms of engagement before meeting the designated groups. These include such questions as: Who decides the composi-tion of the groups? What roles and functions do the participants fulfil within the organization? Is attendance obligatory or optional? Will representatives of the organizational hierarchy participate?

Then there are the objectives of one's engagement to consider, some manifest, others latent. Amongst the manifest objectives could be the welfare of the personnel, the reduction of stress, sick-leave and absenteeism, an increase in productivity, and conflict resolution between sub-groupings. The latent objectives may have to be teased out by subtler means, since they are unlikely to be stated openly in the contract: Is the group analyst being called in to take trouble and responsibility off management's hands? Or to get rid of troublesome personnel? Or to boost the organization's public image as one that takes care of its workforce?

These questions and their answers provide the basis for the group-work to be undertaken. However, even when the group analyst has informed himself or herself about all these matters to the best of his ability, the intrinsic issues of loyalty and confidentiality will persist throughout the engagement. The organization's needs, and those of the individuals in it, will emerge in an ever-changing figure–ground constellation. The group analyst's aim is to bring the two aspects – the requirements of the organization and the optimal welfare and fulfilment of the group members – into a pattern of communication which is innovative and creative for all concerned.

In the group's dialogue, one or other of the participants may pres-ent personal needs or problems that manifest in the workplace but are not created by it. This presents a temptation to the group analyst to become the therapist, and for the group to veer towards a therapy group. If this were to succeed, it would undermine the group's task-centred orientation without being able to give the appropriate help. Better to name the conflict or problem and direct the individual to an appropriate source of help, such as a counselling service. Perhaps the central activity of the group analyst is to facilitate a free-floating exchange of ideas, feelings, hopes, fears and disappointments centred on the workplace. This should enable the participants to see themselves more clearly in the structure of the organization, recognize potential power struggles and conflict areas, and in exchange with others, increase their potential for constructive, creative resolutions. The ultimate aim is to steer the organization towards the language of relationships. In any conflict between management and group members, the group analyst should be receptive but neutral. The aim remains that of all organizational group work: to engender communication and creative dialogue, and to establish participatory relationships in the context of the organization.

Information-gathering at the outset

How much detailed information about the organization should the group analyst gather beforehand? Unlike a clinical or therapeutic encounter, where the client at the first meeting is likely to remain the client for the duration of the therapy, the person who makes first contact with the consultant is by no means necessarily the one who will participate in the exercise to come. Work with an organization can therefore be considered as a preliminary information-gathering exercise followed by the operation itself, the two being dynamically interrelated. The group analyst entering this particular arena may be offered a picture of the existing structure and objectives of the organization, its history, the way in which staff relate to each other hierarchically and informally, and the current concerns. It is these questions that provide the clues for composing the groups around which the consultation is to be built. There has to be a match between the organization's wishes in this regard, and the consultant's judgement of what will constitute the setting for an effective intervention. Which personnel should be in and out of the group? And will a final judgement be expected of the consultant at the end of the day? To whom should this be delivered, and in what form and setting? These basic questions can determine the success or failure of the enterprise.

Consultations to the helping professions

Groups conducted for the personnel of the helping professions or voluntary or religious organizations have a character all of their own. Their members are usually acquainted with the language of therapy and they display personal needs that arise from their work and in their workplaces. Their personnel often meet with needy or deprived clients in their daily work, and easily get invaded by their depression or anger. Groups for such personnel provide a space in which the emotional burdens which the workers carry day in and day out can be shared. This may require the group to be conducted more closely along the lines of an experiential group. However, the group analyst keeps the group from tipping over into a therapy group by the nature of his or her interventions, steering clear of interpretations and directing attention to the context in which the narrative of the group takes place – that is, the workplace.

A detail which assumes significance in these consultations is the venue for the consultation. Realistic and neurotic wishes have to be reconciled when decisions are taken about where to meet. For example, some organizations are keen to invite the group-work consultant to their place because their personnel are 'too busy' to find the time to get away. Alternatively, they may want the visitor to see the difficult conditions under which they have to function. Staff can feel understood and supported by a consultation in situ. However, a consultation on the organization's home territory is more likely to be unconsciously sabotaged by interruptions. Conversely, some staff welcome the opportunity of leaving their workplace to visit the consultant. The respite from their own work setting helps them to stand back, reflect, and engage in innovative thinking. However, visits to the consultant's environment can engender a sense of envy provoked by the contrast of the calm, lack of interruptions and space of the consulting room compared with their own working environment. This will have to be addressed to enable the group to engage in the work set it.

Working with hierarchy and leadership

Managers and senior personnel may have particular problems using a group. The calling in of an outside person to examine the interior of an organization triggers fears similar to those experienced by a patient about to be examined by a doctor. Fear, suspicion and determination to retain mastery of the situation may point to the need for a step-wise method of engaging the organization. The type of leadership within an organization deserves attention. The original Lewinian categories of autocratic, democratic, and *laissez-faire* styles of leadership still have a certain psychological validity. None of these is either 'good' or 'bad' in itself. Rather, each one of them may be appropriate to the task the leadership is to perform. The consulting group analyst may have to lay aside preconceived ideas acquired in clinical training and practice, and allow the needs and aims of the organization to define the type of leadership as constructive or potentially destructive. This aspect of group-analytic consultancy has been explored since 1995 by 'Working Conferences' convened by Marlene Spero at the Institute of Group Analysis in London. Questions of leadership, authority and interdependence are experienced, rather than talked about, in small and large groups, and evaluated as to their efficacy to deliver the tasks set to the conference (Spero, 2003).

A useful indicator of leadership style is the system of channels through which information flows between senior and junior levels in the hierarchy, and the degree to which group settings are used to promote communication within the organization. A much laboured concept in organizations is that of the team, and the related virtues of 'team spirit' and 'team building.' The latter, in particular, is vaunted by healthcare and business organizations alike, and may draw on the services of a group analyst to facilitate the process. As an exercise, it is often seen as an indication of organizational health.

Power issues in organizations

Power issues are likely to emerge in a variety of ways amongst both management and personnel in their various groupings. It is therefore advantageous for the consulting group analyst to become acquainted himself with the power structure of the organization. This will influence the composition of the consultation group, especially in the extent to which management and personnel can usefully share the same group. The discrepancy between invested power and latent power may be a significant source of tension in the organization, and therefore in the consultation group.

CHAPTER TWENTY

The supervision of group therapy

I KNOW YOU'RE HAVING PROBLEMS WITH YOUR GROUP, DR SMITH, BUT I'M AFRAID THE MENTAL HEALTH ACT DOES NOT ALLOW YOU TO SECTION THE WHOLE GROUP

Supervision has become an essential part of the group analyst's professional development. It is an intrinsic part of the training experience and an adjunct to good practice throughout the therapist's professional lifetime. The supervisor, destined in most cases never to meet the patients in the group whose progress he or she influences, functions as a catalyst in the interaction between the therapist and the group.

The primary purpose of supervision is to throw light on the therapeutic relationship; its secondary purpose is to enhance the supervisee's skills as a therapist. In group supervision, it is not only the experience and 'know-how' of the supervisor which makes a difference, but the dialogue between colleagues of the supervision group, each of whom has a different perspective on the therapeutic situation. In this group, only the presenter has first-hand knowledge of the group, but along with that come the counter-transferential distortions which the supervising group, with its greater distance and objectivity, is able to discern, or at times unconsciously re-enact, and in this way make relevant to the narrative. The supervisee, like a journalist reporting from the scene, retains the power and freshness of first-hand knowledge, immediacy and empathy. The other members of the supervision group provide the editorial comment.

The supervision group can be conceptualized as a figure–ground constellation, the foreground of which is usually occupied by the relationship between the therapist and the patient group, while the background constitutes a kaleidoscopic pattern of configurations that connect a variety of other relationships. These include the relationships between therapist and supervisor, between therapist and supervision group, between the therapist and the superior system in which the therapist functions, and occasionally the relationships around the therapist's personal life events, should these impinge on the group work. Any one of these may emerge into the foreground and become a focus of the supervision.

The interface between supervision and teaching

Supervisors vary in the extent to which they inject theory teaching into what is essentially a clinical and therapeutic exercise. Some argue that supervision should address itself exclusively to the supervisee's intuitive resonance with the group, and that any didactic input interferes with this process. If, however, it is accepted that supervision is a collegiate dialogue, it would seem a wasted opportunity if the conversation did not occasionally stray into theoretical waters. Supervision has, amongst its many functions, the transmission of a model of therapy, and clinical interventions have to be justified in theoretical terms. In our experience, reference to theoretical concepts informs and enriches the supervisory dialogue, and gives therapists a stronger foundation on which to build their technique and practice of group analysis. There are, however, group analysts who report on how they benefited in their supervision from being given no explanations or directions of any kind, but were encouraged with 'and what happened next?'

The interface between supervision and therapy

There is often a temptation to use supervision as if it were therapy, especially when counter-transference phenomena are impeding the work. The urge is felt to be more pressing if the supervisee is not in personal therapy, and there is occasionally a tendency, in which the supervisor should avoid complicity, to smuggle therapy into the supervision group. If it turns out, however, that supervision provides the only forum for the mention of personal issues which are affecting the supervisee's work, it is legitimate to go a little way down the therapeutic road, with the objective of providing containment and support, and if need be, to counsel the supervisee towards personal therapy. It has to be remembered that the supervisor has no therapeutic contract with the supervisee, and the licence is not there to make analytic or interpretive interventions.

The institutional context of supervision

Institutions are, by and large, formidable and impersonal bodies that make demands on both the supervisor and the supervisee. In the case of a hospital, there may be an expectation that patients should be in the group for a limited period of time, or that the group itself should be time-limited. This sort of demand should be clarified at the outset. Trainee therapists, in particular, have to be alert to possible contradictions between training and institutional requirements. Even if the therapist is working in an honorary capacity, or is a visitor to the hospital, there will be an obligation to conform to its procedures and mores, and this may enter the domain of supervision, for example on the question of how and by whom patients are assessed for group therapy, and who carries the ultimate responsibility for deciding on the suitability of a given patient for the group.

The trainee therapist may have to submit to both 'internal' and 'external' supervision. The two supervisions may be of a very different character, but as long as the needs of both the hospital and the training institute are met, the experience can be complementary and enriching. Alternatively, the triangular interaction between the supervisee and the two 'parental' bodies can be fertile ground for splitting, confusion and conflict, especially if the ground rules have not been set out in advance. Some form of preliminary communication between the hospital and the training institute, or between the internal and external supervisors, spelling out mutual expectations and obligations, sets the stage for a harmonious working relationship between all three parties.

Whenever supervision is offered within an institutional context, regardless of the nature of the institution, the supervisor has a separate set of obligations to the two interested parties with whom he or she is in a relationship: the employing institution, and the supervisee. There should not, in theory, be a conflict of loyalties here, and if the employment contract is carefully considered, any such conflict can be avoided. The areas to be on the lookout for are questions over who has the authority to include and exclude members of the supervision group, a possible request to report on the supervisees' progress, the need to maintain confidentiality, and the procedures to follow in the event of difficulties arising between the supervisor and the supervisees.

Composition of the supervision group

The supervision group, with its emphasis on performance and professional scrutiny, puts the supervisor in the position, when composing the supervision group, of having to take account of such factors as the hierarchical relationship of the supervisees to one another, their core professional identities, and, in a training setting, their seniority within the course. The supervisees may also know one another in other professional contexts, especially when they happen to work in the same hospital or training institute. Such familiarity may make for cohesion and intimacy in the group, but it can also result in excessive competitiveness, jealousy or prejudice, which may be displaced from previous encounters on to the supervision group or the supervisor. These are disruptive and potentially destructive relationships, which can throw a spanner in the works. They should be detected as soon as they arise, opened up to discussion, and, hopefully, resolved.

The supervisees' experience in group analysis, or the lack of it, also comes into the equation. Difference can be enriching, or it can act as a constraint on openness and learning. Generally, however, the model of diversity provided by the composition of a group-analytic therapy group serves as a useful default position when composing a supervision group. That is to say, a mix of professions, levels of experience, and familiarity with group analysis generally provides a creative amalgam, leavened, it is hoped, by the maturity of the participants.

Structuring the supervision session

Some sort of turn-taking is necessary in a supervision group, to ensure that all the members have an opportunity to present their groups, and the supervisor is best placed to structure this and monitor the time boundaries. In this way, reticent supervisees, and those who may not yet be running a group, can discover the wealth of material to be derived from discussion about such apparently marginal phenomena as the setting, the process of preparing for a group, or the psychopathology of an individual at the assessment stage. An equal allotment of time allows all the participants to reflect fully on their work, at whatever stage it may be. Supervision groups that meet weekly might have a rhythm that allows for an abbreviated slot to discuss pressing, anxiety provoking or urgent issues, and it may not be necessary for all the supervisees to present every week, as long as the principle of turn-taking is adhered to over consecutive weeks.

Styles of conducting sessions also vary widely. Some supervisors invite the circulation of profiles of group members. Others prefer to rely on purely verbal accounts of sessions, illustrated perhaps by a diagram showing the names of group members and their disposition in the group room. Painstaking reference to written notes, other than as an *aide-memoire*, can fail to bring the material to life. The supervisor should be flexible enough to allow the reporting of the material to run uninterruptedly, so long as the reporting has emotional currency, but prepared also to intervene early, and frequently if necessary, if the reporting is becoming lost in a fog of obsessional detail, or if a point in the presentation deserves challenging before it gets lost.

There is an element of containment to supervision, which calls for a degree of structuring by the supervisor, especially at the beginning

and end of a presentation. In the middle, full use is made of the associations of the supervision group as a whole. The views of the other
members of the supervision group may have to be actively canvassed
and their contributions woven together by the supervisor. If there is
disagreement, or in cases where, in the supervisor's view, the nettle
has not been grasped, it falls to the supervisor to disclose his or her
own preferred course of action, while at the same time encouraging
the group to think about a parallel process, in which a dynamic from
the group being presented is replicating itself in the supervision
group. Apart from achieving a better understanding of the dynamic
of the group being presented, the supervisee needs to leave the
supervision session armed with some instruments with which to
remedy an ailing situation. A prescription from the supervision
group often helps the supervisee towards a solution, whether or not
the supervisee agrees with the prescription. It is also the supervisor's
brief to shift the focus to where the emotional energy lies. For
example, a supervisee who is clearly distressed is in no position to
dwell on the dynamic of the group, and may need containment or
exploration of the counter-transference before proceeding to a
dispassionate analysis of the group itself.

Supervision in psychotherapy and psychiatric units

In some psychotherapy departments and psychiatric units there is an
unspoken assumption that group psychotherapy is second-rate in
comparison with individual therapy, or that analytic modes of therapy are less effective than other psychological treatments. The
unassertive and unsupported supervisee may have to be coached in
the art of 'selling' the group and proclaiming the virtues of group-
analytic psychotherapy. This may involve participating in case
conferences and clinical discussions and being a visible presence in
the unit rather than a disconnected outsider.

Supervision in a training context

Supervision is one point in the triangle that constitutes the training in group analysis. It connects the trainee's therapeutic
experience, the theory as taught in seminars, and the practice of

group analysis. This is the model of supervision which we have found to be applicable and efficient, but there are others: some training institutes keep the three components well apart, and insist that the personal therapy of the trainee should be kept separate from the theory and supervision. Where the triangular training model is observed, the supervisor keeps in mind that the supervisee can use the therapy group if and when the group being conducted touches on present or latent emotional problems or residual neuroses. These are likely to emerge in the narrative of the presentation in supervision, where they should be named and referred to where they belong, namely the therapy group. Such a procedure is usually received with relief by the trainee, but if it is not, or if the blockage is unrecognized or denied, the question arises whether the supervisor should consult with the training therapist. If so, how much information should be provided? This is a tricky problem, to which there may be no definitive answer. Training group analysts and supervisors have different views on this. If they are part of the same training scheme and institute, some contact will be accepted, and will have been discussed with the trainee from the outset. That said, feedback between supervisor and training group analyst should be reserved for exceptional circumstances only, and should at all times take place with the knowledge and agreement of the trainee. Where the therapy occurs outside the training institute, it is usual for both parties to want no contact, other than on the rare occasions when one or the other considers that the training should be temporarily or permanently discontinued. Training institutes generally have clearly defined procedures for negotiating the boundaries between the different components of the training.

This brings us to the question of the area and degree of responsibility resting with the supervisor. In a training programme, responsibility for all aspects of the training which concern the trainee is shared amongst the trainers. The responsibility concerning the patients in the trainee's group, however, can be considered to come within the scope of supervision. It is conceivable, for example, that a supervisor will be presented with groups encompassing 30 or more individual patients from, say, four supervisees. Even with the most careful note-taking, the supervisor cannot be expected to keep each patient's situation sufficiently in mind to be able to foresee danger points or looming crises. He or she will have to rely on the super-visee to evaluate such situations and bring them into the supervision in good time. This said, we know of no supervisor who does not feel involved and responsible when a crisis arises, the more so where rel-atively inexperienced supervisees are concerned. But potential or actual casualties occur at all levels of experience and are brought to supervision. Our own view is that the ultimate responsibility for the patient must rest with the senior clinician responsible for the patient's care, or if therapy is being held in a private setting, with the patient's general practitioner or the medical referrer, and that in an emergency, or when one threatens – severe cases of anorexia, a psy-chotic breakdown, or a potential suicide come to mind – the supervisee should be encouraged to consult with and refer back to these professionals.

Supervision after training

Discussion of one's therapeutic work is the lifeblood of professional practice. The notion of 'Continuing Professional Development' has become incorporated into professional life. This includes some form of supervision. Some therapists apply the term loosely. They simply get together informally, or on an ad hoc basis, to discuss interesting or problematic issues over a cup of coffee. However, if we practise what we preach, communication between professionals is essential to achieve the breakdown of the professional isolation which predis-poses to erroneous judgements, blind spots and lack of awareness of current issues.

Clinical meetings at which groups, individual patients and thera-peutic issues are presented, form an important part of professional development. As with patients who benefit in groups from the dis-covery that they are able to help others, so too do therapists learn best in dialogue with others. Once the training has been completed and the trainee emerges into the hurly-burly of professional life, the loss of regular supervision is felt with a pang of uncertainty, even a feeling of deprivation. That said, however, there is also a view, rather surprisingly espoused by Foulkes, that neophyte group ana-lysts might benefit from the experience of standing on their own two feet for a while after qualification (Foulkes, personal communi-cation). In practice, not all group analysts are able to build into their professional activity a slot for supervision. It remains an open question whether supervision should be construed as an essential element of the work routine, or a luxury for which few can afford either the time or the money and which belongs indispensably to the student role.

For more experienced therapists the term 'supervision' itself feels uncomfortable. The notion of being looked at from above is less appropriate amongst trained peers than it is within a training context, and it would be preferable for a term other than 'supervision' to gain currency. Terminology aside, the benefits of discussing one's work with colleagues, in whatever setting, are considerable. Group analysis rests on the assumption that interpersonal disturbance comes about through isolation. The corollary of this is that a group which fosters open communication provides an antidote to isolation. If this is true of therapeutic groups, it should be true of groups in which fellow therapists contemplate their work together.

Technique and pitfalls

The supervisor aims to be receptive and respectful of the supervisee's presentation, while holding on to the task of facilitating, clarifying and occasionally directing. This requires an alertness to what is being overlooked, misunderstood, or given too much emphasis by the supervisee. The supervisor should explore these in a non-confrontational, non-authoritarian manner, which avoids the danger of conveying a lack of skill, or worse, shaming the supervisee.

The manner in which supervisees present the unfolding material of a session offers a valuable insight into their strengths and weaknesses. Is the focus placed on the individuals in the group at the expense of the group as a whole? Is process neglected in favour of content? Does the presenter intervene frequently or stay in the background? Are the conductor's emotional reactions and responses reported or left out of the presentation? Is room left for reflection and observation, or is the supervisor and the supervision group being flooded with detail, all pre-packaged and summed up? In the answers to all these questions, the supervisor uses the supervision group's reactions as a guide to his or her own, so as to detect, evaluate and remedy weaknesses, blind spots or omissions.

Transcultural issues in supervision

Supervision with supervisees of an ethnic background different from that of the supervisor and the rest of the supervision group can be rewarding for all concerned. It offers a rich learning experience of the unspoken, usually unconscious, historically and culturally conditioned assumptions and attitudes which we all bring into our professional lives. Such attitudes and prejudices are hidden in similarity and surface in diversity. The home-grown language and idiom of the supervision group may not match that of the ethnically different group members, thereby opening up an area of incomprehension or misinterpretation. Also, body language and mannerisms can differ widely. All these require space to surface in the supervision, and time to be accepted and understood for their meaning by all concerned. Different habits, attitudes to gender issues and social structures need to be taken into consideration when evaluating content and presentation of case material. When supervisor or supervisee find themselves working in a culture whose healthcare and therapeutic services are alien to theirs, it behoves them to acquire a working familiarity with them. These look like a daunting tasks when enumerated in this way, but it really boils down to what is expected of the supervisor: an all-pervasive, tolerant, ever-receptive outlook and attitude that shuns uniformity and cherishes diversity in the personalities and professional expertise of the supervisees.

CHAPTER TWENTY-ONE

The group analyst as a professional

The early twenty-first century finds the practising psychotherapist hedged in by a thicket of constraints and obligations brought on by society's growing awareness of its needs, demands, privileges and rights. The cavalier days of early twentieth-century practice in which omniscient professionals were unassailable in their judgement have been consigned to history, although frustrated expressions of that mentality still surface from time to time, to the distress of patients and the vexation of professional bodies.

A professional attitude on the part of the psychotherapist implies a quality of empathy combined with abstemiousness. This is often encoded in the rules, regulations and protocols issued by training institutes, registering bodies and accrediting organizations. Most of these rules are designed to protect the patient, so even before emerging from the cocoon of training therapists have to look to themselves and ensure that there is a protective carapace overhead, of insurance, familiarity with institutional codes of ethics, and professional back-up or 'cover'. Supervision is also nowadays an integral plate in this carapace. Today's climate has created an awareness of bad practice and the right to complain, salutary at best, hypervigilant and litigious at worst. This makes psychotherapy a perilous journey. The very nature of our work calls for the probing of sensitive areas, encroachment on private and intimate aspects of the self, and the stirring up of painful or undesired feelings. Many of the people who attend for psychotherapy have been affected by life events that have damaged their sense of trust in others. Activation of old or forgotten traumas in therapy may have unexpected repercussions on the therapeutic relationship, whether or not mediated through the transference.

Groups, no less than the dyadic situation, are fertile ground for these booby traps. In dyadic psychotherapy there is the complication that there is no witness to the propriety of the professional encounter. In group psychotherapy, the therapist is watched by the whole group, but there is still ample opportunity for being ambushed by oneself in a careless or unguarded moment, into making a crass intervention, letting slip confidential information, losing one's temper, or giving inappropriate advice which then backfires. Group analysts, as indeed all psychotherapists, have a dimension to their profession which is absent in other professions. They deal with an area which they share with their patients – the expression of psychic processes, at times conscious, more often unconscious. This is the rationale for undergoing personal therapy, a process which should lead to an understanding of one's own emotional reactions to the patient. It is important to distinguish between the real and neurotic attitudes governing the therapist's interventions. Concepts such as transference and countertransference lend themselves to the denial of real negative reactions on the part of the therapist. S.H. Foulkes cautioned his students: 'Don't hide behind transference. Transference needs a hook to hang on, and this may be in you' (Foulkes, personal communication).

Not hiding behind the transference may at times amount to the realization that one has developed more than the usual interest in a group member, or even that one has fallen in love. This can be a devastating realization, not because it is in itself 'wrong', but because it runs counter to the exercise of one's stated and contractual aim, which is that of therapy. There can be no hard and fast rules as to how to deal with such a situation, other than that there must be no acting out of these feelings. Self-scrutiny and a professional training which demands abstemiousness should help, as should a frank discussion of the emotional dilemma with a trusted colleague or supervisor. The sensitive perceptions of the group can make the situation more perilous by weakening trust in the therapist, but they can also help the therapist back to the required professional stance.

Ethical aspects

By their very nature, ethics are not absolutes. They change as the cultural and scientific evidence demands. Some ethical dicta are specific to group analysis. The group analyst subscribes to the ethic of recognizing and dealing with his or her own personal conflict outside the group, especially a conflict that has been revitalized by events in the group. If this is not done, the unresolved problem will be introduced into the group matrix, as well as distorting the therapist's perception of group content. This is particularly important in view of the influence and power which the therapist wields in the group.

Therapy groups, by contrast with dyadic therapies, have a public dimension which can introduce specific ethical issues around confidentiality. These can range from the apparently insignificant and innocent, such as the inadvertent disclosure of a group member's address, to the introduction into the group of material elicited in a dyadic setting without having obtained permission. The most taxing dilemma arises when a group member tells the group about an actual criminal offence committed, or an offence being contemplated, such as violence against a child or partner, stalking, or possession of an illicit weapon. The group analyst has to decide where, at the interface of public duty and professional confidentiality, his or her responsibility lies. This is inevitably a personal and therefore arbitrary decision which cannot be institutionally prescribed.

The group analyst in private practice

Private practice can be a lonely undertaking, not only when things go wrong, but when the work is in full swing. A practice in which more than one therapist operates offers a wider choice to patients wanting to join a group. When groups are full or need filling, a system of cross-referral is important, and this is more easily achieved within the same practice. For these reasons, many group analysts prefer to set up in practice with other colleagues, or at least one other colleague. Practice meetings and informal discussions help the practitioner to keep abreast of professional trends and thinking in the field.

Psychotherapy can be seen as a business, calling for efficient management, planning and marketing. Cynthia Rogers, a group analyst in private practice in London, has written in detail about these aspects of professional practice, as well as the various precautionary and self-protective measures which the psychotherapist needs to think about in parallel with the therapeutic work itself (Rogers, 2004).

Public relations and advertising

Psychotherapists, including group analysts, find public relations a difficult exercise to contemplate. Reluctant therapists, who wish to have no truck with the techniques and paraphernalia of modern promotion and public relations, may find themselves marginalized, struggling to attract referrals and working with a shrinking population of patients. Many group analysts, though performing excellently in the therapist's chair, have difficulty in promoting themselves in the wider network. This skill was once seen as immodest and disdained by psychotherapists as out of keeping with their professional status, at best an unnecessary exercise, at worst a cheap ploy smacking of charlatanry. Now, if anything, it has become an indicator of good practice, since it raises the profile of the profession and encourages the kind of transparency demanded by the public of a calling once shrouded in mystery and obscurity.

All professionals have a desire to make their work known. But how and where to achieve this? The group analyst relates to a public confronted by a bewildering array of therapeutic options. A veritable army of professionals including psychologists, psychiatrists, psychotherapists and counsellors of many persuasions, has set up camp in modern society. The field of mental health has become a conference hall foyer in which therapists display their methods and approaches to the public and professional gaze, eyeing one another warily and critically from their stalls. 'The Psychiatrist is In', says the billboard of Lucy Van Pelt. The modern therapist is not only 'In', but 'Out There' in the marketplace, distributing informative literature and materializing colourfully on websites. It is not always easy to distinguish the tried-and-tested from the experimental, the new from the newfangled.

Twenty or thirty years ago the only way in which professionals made themselves known was through the publication of papers in learned journals, exclusively the preserve of a small, often closed group of colleagues, or from the lectern at scientific meetings, again to a closed group of similarly qualified, if not like-minded, academics, clinicians and practitioners. The increased sophistication of the public and the spread of knowledge through the media has presented psychotherapists with a fresh opportunity, but also a fresh ethical dilemma. Is the proclamation of one's skills in the media at odds with professional propriety? Does presentation in the media colour the therapeutic relationship? The more entrepreneurial amongst professionals have seen a way forward in offering a range of public activities, an appeal to the intellect through lectures, newspapers, radio and television appearances designed to broaden the appeal of a particular method and attract an audience of interested lay people as well as professionals. The current spirit of professional transparency, and the fact that information is easily available to the public at large, through the internet for example, poses less of a dilemma to today's psychotherapists than to their predecessors. However, there is still a boundary where ethically acceptable advertising crosses over into self-serving advertising.

The group analyst in the public sector

The great advantage of the public sector is that it buzzes with collegiate life. There is a confirming resonance with fellow practitioners, the opportunity to compare notes, exchange views, share the anxieties of daily work and spark off one another with ideas and challenges. The public sector also provides opportunities for training and educational enhancement. Like group therapy itself, the public sector provides a dynamic matrix of interactive processes through which therapists can avoid isolation. On the negative side, therapists may have to do battle with bureaucratic stipulations, prescriptions and procedures; they may find themselves stuck in a quagmire of administrative organization and reorganization; and they may have to submit their practice to the critical and at times ill-informed scrutiny of managers and clinicians. All these hazards require a set of skills apart from therapeutic ones: the ability to argue a case based on research and experience, to teach and learn in a professional setting, and to maintain good communication with the clinical network which supports the group-analytic therapy.

The education and support of other professionals

Education and support are two sides of the same coin. Group analysts are well placed to contribute to the professional development of adjacent professionals like general practitioners, health visitors, paediatricians and psychiatrists, whose knowledge of psychotherapy may be peripheral to their work, but whose work intrinsically involves a working relationship with clients and patients about emotionally charged issues. Educational events can easily be structured to meet the needs of specific groups of professionals. The 'Balint groups' for general practitioners have seeded in many parts of the United Kingdom. A more recent model of group-analytic input is to be found in the work of Gerhard Wilke and Simon Freeman, who worked with groups of general practitioners, helping them to play a constructive part in the major re-organization of primary healthcare in the United Kingdom (Wilke and Freeman, 2001).

We have found that meetings with healthcare professionals can usefully be structured along didactic lines. Topics covering a range of psychotherapeutic, group therapeutic and clinical issues can form the subject of 'one off' meetings, workshops or symposia. At the same time, professionals are interested in discovering ways of reducing their 'stress level', but are wary of doing so in an unstructured setting. Workshops offering an outlet for the feelings and frustrations generated by clinical work, and an escape from the accelerating treadmill of clinical practice, hold an appeal for some, although the very people who would be the greatest beneficiaries of these workshops are often the least inclined to depart from their busy schedules in order to participate. Of course, traffic flows two ways in meetings between group analysts and other professionals. The group analyst becomes aware of a body of knowledge and practice, and a language and technique acquired in settings different from the world of psychotherapy.

Communication with the professional network

Each patient is linked to a network of professionals whom it is important to identify at the outset. These may be, in a typical example, a general practitioner, a previous or current therapist, a social worker, a psychiatrist, another medical specialist, a counsellor, a lawyer, an employer or a teacher. It is useful to get the names of these 'dramatis personae', details of how to contact them if necessary, and most importantly, permission to contact them or a clarification of the patient's reasons for not wanting this.

Letters and reports written to professionals in a language which eschews jargon, and in the prevailing culture of transparency and accessibility of notes by patients, should be couched in terms which will be understood and appreciated by the patient. A junior, psychotherapeutically minded colleague who wrote to his patient's general practitioner informing him that the patient had an 'anal personality', rightly incurred the opprobrium of his consultant when the letter was discovered in the case notes, and no doubt provoked derision and incomprehension from the recipient. What the patient might have said had he read the letter can only be a matter for amused speculation.

The cultivation of professional life

Training is too often experienced as onerous and stressful, and its successful ending is usually greeted with a sigh of relief. This can eclipse the pleasure and excitement of new learning. However, professional life has to be cultivated and extended throughout the group analyst's working lifetime if a fully rounded practice is to be achieved. Life experience grows alongside clinical and therapeutic experience. Connections are made over years of seeing many people and running many different groups. The physician Sir William Osler observed that seeing patients without reading books was like going to sea without a map, but that only reading books without seeing patients was like never going to sea at all. Attendance at lectures, symposia, workshops and congresses, and involvement in the professional life of one's training organization, such as committee work and teaching, keeps one in touch with colleagues and enables one to absorb and influence new developments. Along with this goes the pleasure of keeping up with the professional literature, time-consuming though it is for the busy group analyst. It is a common experience that teaching and writing are not only effective ways of learning, but also a means of discovering one's own creative professional identity.

CHAPTER TWENTY-TWO

The changing landscape of group analysis

THE MARVELS OF TECHNOLOGY IN GROUP ANALYSIS: THE MOBILE PHONE

S.H. Foulkes died while conducting an analytic group composed of devoted senior colleagues. Somehow it was fitting that the man who had pronounced that 'we are born into a group' had died in one. The year was 1976. He had hewn his theoretical stance out of the building blocks that were in place in the 1930s, and the first of his four classic texts on group analysis was published more than half a century ago. It would therefore be a mistake to read his writings like a sacred text. If anything, Foulkes the writer is difficult to read, at times obscure and very much a reflection of the times, perpetuating the dogmas of conservative postwar psychiatry along with the rich seam of original thought which characterizes his approach.

255

Group analysis since Foulkes

What changes have occurred in group analysis since Foulkes's day? To answer this question we have to look at the way in which group analysis is now taught, practised and researched, and what new theoretical ideas have emerged, both within and outside the group-analytic movement, which are making us overhaul some of the original Foulkesian tenets. Above all, we have to look at the way in which society has changed and the impact which this has had on the practice of group analysis. Psychotherapy advances along a broad front, but in our eagerness to be in the vanguard, we must be careful not to lose touch with the body of knowledge which has stood the test of time in everyday clinical practice. A professor once remarked sadly to one of his students: 'What you have written is both good and new. Unfortunately, that which is good is not new, and that which is new is not good.' This verdict could also reflect the traditionalist's reluctance to accept deviations from the sacred text, which represents the opposite sin.

Training in group analysis

Professional training in psychotherapy has become more rigorous, in tandem with the increasing demands of an ever-watchful society. In keeping with this, the process of group-analytic training has become inflationary. Although it still retains its tripartite structure of personal therapy, supervision and theory, each of these elements is undergoing its own separate evolution, putting more strain on a system which places a high value on the integration of the three elements. Courses have become longer, entrance and qualifying requirements are more carefully stipulated, and more demands are made of trainees in terms of clinical and academic tasks. The trend seems to be towards greater complexity, closer scrutiny and an expectation of enhanced performance. However, the unintentional consequences of this might be the curtailment of emotional spontaneity in one's clinical work and a fear of imaginative innovation in the theory and practice of group analysis.

This metamorphosis in training derives partly from the exigencies of professional life. In response to this there has been a radical diversity of training formats. Block training, the intensive packaging of training events into blocks of time separated by wide intervals, has attained a parity with the traditional weekly or twice-weekly model of training. The original rationale for the block method, to bring in trainers from far afield in order to impart group-analytic skills to local professionals, has led to the discovery of its intrinsic merit – closer integration between different elements of the training, a greater sense of being part of a training community, and the incidental benefit of freeing up most of the working week in order to achieve a greater continuity of working life.

Training programmes have also become increasingly tiered and specialized, in recognition of different professional needs. 'In-house' training takes account of the needs of mental health professionals in the public sector to acquire a working familiarity with group analysis without having to undergo an extensive course leading to qualification as a group analyst. In the same spirit, there has been a growth in the number of introductory and applied courses, workshops and teaching events designed to interest a broad spectrum of the professional and lay community in the principles and practice of group analysis.

The role of personal therapy in training is also undergoing a re-evaluation. How integral is it to the training process? And how can the trainee's need for confidentiality and privacy be reconciled with the training body's need to monitor professional capability? The tradition derived from psychoanalysis holds that the relationship between analyst and analysand is sacrosanct, and should be impervious to scrutiny by the training body. The contrasting position in this dialectic arises from the assumption that the overriding function of personal therapy in a training context is to equip the trainee with the insight and interpersonal resources needed to practise, and that all the training activities of the student, including personal therapy, should, in some measure, be open to evaluation and the subject of communication within the training body, so that the professional competence of the trainee can be established.

The question of what is taught is similarly undergoing constant reappraisal. Foulkes's philosophy and basic tenets continue to form the backbone of the training, but there has been a steady infusion into group-analytic curricula of ideas and themes derived from research into psychotherapy, experience of other methods of practice and different social and psychological theories of group behaviour and human development, together with an emphasis on the cultural, societal, ethical and political influences on group analysis. Training institutes are no longer confining themselves to the transmission of a syllabus developed within themselves, but are drawing on the resources of academic institutions and the wider professional community to inform their training.

Changes in the practice of group analysis

With the difficulty that psychoanalysis is having in convincing most of the professional community and the public at large that it is an effective therapy, there has been a general movement towards the search for psychotherapeutic techniques which would shorten the duration of the treatment and bring about more immediately discernible beneficial therapeutic outcomes. Other changes have come about through the confluence of ideas derived from different psychological treatment modalities. Cognitive, analytic and behavioural group methods, once held in carefully guarded compartments, are combining in a variety of forms to provide the consumer with a bewildering array of choices. The distinction between counselling and psychotherapy is by no means clear, nor is the distinction between the various analytically orientated therapies. And that is not to mention therapies such as psychodrama which draw on activity techniques as well as group techniques. The waters are further muddied by the increasing specialization within applied group therapy. Techniques have developed for the treatment of certain categories of patients and for the treatment of groups in different environments. This diversity, despite its confusing aspect, offers a richer choice for patients and a greater opportunity for constructive dialogue between practitioners, teachers and researchers.

Holistic thinking in mental health

Apart from the greater diversity and confluence of psychological treatments, the teaching and practice of medicine itself has become more holistic. The term 'holism', coined by Jan Smuts, a Boer general who studied philosophy at Cambridge and went on to become Prime Minister of South Africa during the Second World War, was a prominent concept of the gestalt school of psychology. Nowadays holism as a philosophy of patient care has entered the mainstream of medicine. Interrelatedness, which holism embodies, is now a construct which permeates every branch of scientific knowledge. Boundaries between disciplines, bodies of knowledge and methods of practice have become more permeable in a creative way, and it is difficult to recognize the entrenched positions which previously separated the medical, social and psychological realms of discourse.

Research into group analysis

Research has tended to lag behind the growth in popularity of group psychotherapy. The gap between clinical experience and demonstrable proof of the efficacy of group therapy has acted as a spur to the development of research methods which could match clinical impressions with scientific evidence. Group psychotherapy's acceptance, at times sporadic and reluctant, by the public and private health services, makes new demands on its practitioners. They have to demonstrate not only its effectiveness as a means of treatment but also its cost-effectiveness. Such proof is recognized by the profession as being politically essential, when scarce public resources are being allocated, as well as for insurance companies that underwrite private treatment. The patients themselves increasingly 'shop around' for proof that what they undergo will actually deliver the goods.

Research into group psychotherapy has been going on since the days of Kurt Lewin in the 1930s. Group-analytic psychotherapy has recently been found to be effective for a wide range of diagnoses and personality disorders, in a variety of population groups (Lorentzen, 2000). However, there is still a dearth of solid research studies, and a continuing reluctance on the part of its practitioners to subject their patients and groups to rigorous research methods, because they consider that these interfere with the therapeutic contract between them and their patients and with the transference relationship. There is also a view that the imposition of research methodology tends to discourage imaginative departures from accepted practice.

Peter Fonagy puts another angle on the conflict between practice and research. He calls psychoanalysis an 'embattled discipline'. 'What hope is there,' he asks, 'in the era of empirically validated treatments, which prizes brief structured interventions, for a therapeutic approach which defines itself by freedom from constraint and preconception, and counts treatment length not in terms of number of sessions but in terms of years?' The trouble is that both psychoanalysis and group analysis engage with the very elements that provide the most difficult and intractable problems in psychological life: our emotions and the maelstrom which is generated by their unconscious interaction with the more rational facets of our minds. Fonagy calls for the systematization of our knowledge, which he admits is difficult, since our 'frame of reference depends on ambiguity and polymorphy'. As he succinctly puts it, 'data is not the plural of anecdote' (Fonagy, 2003). The world of empirical validation is intertwined with the world of the bizarre, the irrational, the intuitive, the imaginative: in short, the world of the unconscious mind.

The problem would seem to be insoluble were it not for a third element, the world of communication with language as its vehicle, which bridges these two seemingly unassailable fortresses, each with its own defences. This is where training institutes come in. They can reduce group analysts' reluctance to cooperate with research, and can encourage them to use their own work to conduct rigorous research, by opening up the procedures of their ethics committees to a scrutiny of research projects submitted to them and bolstering their curricula with research-oriented teaching.

The social unconscious

The social unconscious is a concept that is increasingly exercising group analysts. Earl Hopper is a group analyst, psychoanalyst and sociologist who has brought these three disciplines together in a formulation which views the social unconscious as both a constraint on human behaviour and an expression of the unconscious fantasies, thoughts, feelings and actions on the social system itself.

Hopper sees the constraining element of the social unconscious not merely as a restriction but as a formative influence on society. The group-analytic space is there not only for patients to unravel their tangled relationships but also to imagine how their identities have been formed at particular historical and political junctures, and how this continues to affect them throughout their lives (Hopper, 1997, 2001). This requires the therapist to be fully aware of the effects of social forces and to acknowledge them when they surface in the course of group analysis.

Our own work with therapy groups in various countries in Europe supports Hopper's theoretical conception of the social unconscious and its clinical application, even in a historical milieu which has survived massive trauma, like Germany. Vamik Volkan's work on trans-generational transmission, which he developed over 20 years in a psycho-political context with large enemy groups such as Arabs and Israelis, and Croats and Serbs, is also applicable, in our experience, to groups that are not in a state of enmity, such as generations affected by radical economic change (Volkan, 2001). In a setting with a relatively trauma-free history, like Norway, the economic changes from a poor fishing economy to the well distributed riches of a flourishing oil economy surfaced in a variety of emotional attitudes towards powerful male and female figures, which had clear trans-generational echoes in both small and large therapy groups.

The social unconscious is also the repository of the particular cultural and linguistic roots of the group members. This is the emphasis given by Dennis Brown, a group analyst who worked extensively with intercultural groups. Brown postulates a link between this aspect of the social unconscious and the deepest of the four levels of group relationships and communication delineated by Foulkes, the primordial level of shared myths and archetypes – the elements of the foundation matrix. Brown does not see these elements as universal, however, in the sense of the Jungian collective unconscious, but as varying according to the particular family, culture or language in which the individual has been steeped, and which he or she considers to be natural. Confrontation of differences with others can either be experienced as enriching or threatening, says Brown, according to how secure the individual feels, and this is an important theme for group analysts to hold in mind in the therapeutic setting (Brown, 2001).

A radical view of group analysis

Critics of Foulkes have identified a contradiction in his thinking between, on the one hand, his rootedness in psychoanalytic and systems thinking, and on the other, his adoption of the process sociology of Norbert Elias. Farhad Dalal is one such critic, a group analyst who has undertaken a radical re-appraisal of Foulkes's contribution to group psychotherapy. Dalal's book *Taking the Group*

Seriously is a persuasive assertion of the primacy of the group in our daily lives and in therapeutic practice. He refers to Foulkes's two strains of thought as 'orthodox' and 'radical'. The former is seen as Foulkes's identification with Freudian individualism, the latter as his unfinished attempt to resolve the dichotomy between the individual and the group by invoking Elias's central tenet of social relatedness as the basis of group functioning.

According to Dalal, Foulkes was unable to relinquish his attachment to the dyadic model of relationships, and did not go far enough into the implications of Elias's sociology to reformulate group-analytic thinking. Dalal tackles the conundrum of individual and group by discarding the instinctual, family-hierarchy driven model of human relationships and putting in its place a model of group functioning based on our need to belong and create our own groups. In Dalal's conception 'function' and 'self-esteem' are of primary importance in shaping our group identity, more so than genetic and kinship connections, although the two may coincide.

Dalal takes his readers into the territory of power and racism in groups. He sees racism broadly as the hatred of one group for another, based on an assumption of immutable difference. The social unconscious, he maintains, feeds these assumptions of difference, and groups make use of their power, the existence of which is often denied, to attain or reinforce their supremacy over other groups. This, Dalal believes, is where the challenge of group analysis lies (Dalal, 1998, 2001).

Complexity theory

Ralph Stacey is another group analyst in the forefront of the debate on the evolution of group analysis. Like Dalal, Stacey has drawn attention to a perceived contradiction in Foulkes's thinking. Unlike Dalal, however, he advances an entirely new theory of groups and group therapy based on complexity theory, which, according to Stacey, replaces both psychoanalytic and systems theory as a basis for understanding and explaining the therapeutic process.

Complexity theory, like its predecessors systems theory and chaos theory, purports to provide an explanation for all natural phenomena, including human behaviour. Stacey points out, however, that the complexity sciences can never simply be applied to human action.

They can only serve as what he calls a 'source domain' for analogies with it. He supports Elias's view that there is no 'whole' or 'system' as such, only a process of interaction producing further interaction. Like Foulkes, Stacey emphasizes the importance of communication in this interaction. He takes this further, however, by examining the nature of the interactive process in terms of evolving patterns of language and gesture which create social acts and new symbols which have meaning. The self emerges, says Stacey, through a 'conversation of gestures'.

Stacey rejects the notion of 'an unconscious' which shapes our lives. He prefers, instead, to recast it either as unformulated communication, not yet consciously grasped, or as habitual, easily repeated communication which is taken for granted, and therefore, in that sense, outside of conscious awareness. The mind is not, he believes, an internal world of representations, with the unconscious as its agency. The so-called unconscious is a social construct relying on a spatial metaphor – the internal world. Equally, there is no room for concepts such as projection and projective identification in his theory of complex responsive processes. Transference and countertransference simply become repetitive themes with little scope for amplification into some new pattern of relating.

By the same token, Stacey rejects what he sees as a reification of the group matrix. Rather, he reformulates it as a process which deals with the intersubjective narrative themes that organize the experience of being together in a given place at a given time. There is no room here for the linear causality contained in the psychoanalytic interpretation. Instead, he stipulates a model of self-reference and self-organization in therapy groups. This leads to the idea of non-linear, circular causality, in which patterns are continually replicating themselves, producing stability and non-stability, invariance and novelty. This is the process in therapy, which makes possible small differences which amplify into major changes (Stacey, 2000, 2003).

It is possible to hear echoes of Foulkes in Stacey's radical transformation of psychoanalytic theory into the language of a new theory of complex responsive processes. We can recognize and relate to the importance of communication, evolving patterns of interaction, and the breaking down of the Berlin Wall which divided the psychic world into internal and external. But in our view this does not mean that 'internal' and 'external' are no longer valid concepts, or that the unconscious, whether social, cultural or individual, no longer has a place as a theoretical construct to imply a constellation of mental processes governing human behaviour outside of conscious awareness. Terms like 'projection' and 'projective identification' serve a useful shorthand purpose to convey aspects of a relationship which complexity theory might have to translate into more elaborate language and perhaps diminish in so doing. It seems to us that the group analyst working with patients, whether individually or in groups, has to hold in mind a model of therapy which draws on more than one theory.

Sigmund Karterud, a Norwegian psychiatrist and group analyst, rejects Stacey's view. He too sees the need to rethink the perception of group dynamics, but considers the appropriate model to be sought in text interpretation. The text genres best suited to group analysis, he maintains, are the text of fiction and the text of drama. In order to perceive the prevailing text, the group conductor requires distance and objectivity, the opposite of Stacey's intuitive participation in the matrix. Karterud defines the matrix as a depth structure of the group's narrative (Karterud, 2000).

Is there an anti-group?

Foulkes was unequivocal in his espousal of the virtues of group analysis. He referred to disruptive events in groups, but there is little in his writings about destructive processes in the group and he gave no indication that his method might be subject to hazards intrinsic to the group itself. The case for a contrary view was waiting to be made, and the moment came in 1996 with the publication of Morris Nitsun's book *The Anti-Group*, an eloquently argued case for the existence of a dynamic within groups which, if left unchecked, could result in the destruction of the group. Nitsun views the anti-group as a natural part of the group's development. Its rampant expression and the ensuing destructive outcome will only occur if the container function of the group breaks down. Nitsun is therefore by no means a therapeutic nihilist. He believes that the anti-group can be harnessed for its creative potential, provided that group members are able to recognize their part in its formation and take responsibility for the wellbeing and development of the group. Nitsun's point of view has provided a salutary corrective to the idealization of the group which

Foulkes instigated. It has led to a more balanced evaluation of the strengths and limitations of group psychotherapy and a search for methods and techniques which can be used to transform the anti-group into a therapeutic force. Whether the anti-group can be conceptualized as a 'thing-in-itself' – an entity capable of manifesting itself in identical form wherever it appears – or whether the term is better used to refer to an anti-group dynamic, of which scapegoating and malignant mirroring might be seen as typical examples, its therapeutic implications deserve greater prominence than they have been given until now. Nitsun has performed a signal service to group analysis by identifying and naming the phenomenon (Nitsun, 1996).

Group analysis and politics

From the social and cultural domains it is but a short step into the political. Post-Foulkesian group-analytic thinking has been marked by an emphasis on the political, historical and economic contexts in which psychological processes are formed. There is a tendency amongst some innovators to give these forces precedence over the psychoanalytic model of intra-psychic drives and object relations dynamics (Blackwell, 2003). This can be seen as an extended formulation of the earliest influence to which Foulkes was exposed and which he absorbed and utilized – the political ideology and inter-disciplinary investigative work of the Frankfurt Institute of Social Research in the 1920s. The informal 'sessions' of an assembly of academics such as Horkheimer, Adorno, Fromm, Landauer and Elias, in what was aptly called the Café Marx, can be seen as the prototype of the analytic group. It was there that Foulkes took in the spirit of free expression, the liberation of repressed modes of thinking, and the appreciation of the 'Outsider's' views. This is the essence of group analysis, and the basis of all group-analytic therapeutic interventions. However, a word of caution is needed: if the perception of the 'context' is itself based on a political ideology, this should be acknowledged, so that the clinical practice of group analysis is not in danger of being distorted by it.

Mark Ettin, a clinical psychologist and group psychotherapist in New Jersey, draws attention to the differences between the group therapist and the political leader. Both are 'faced with constituency problems relating to inequality (of opportunity or skill), different levels of development (whether of ego-structure or socioeconomic status), and discrepant assessments of personal worth that result in uneven participation and power differentials' (Ettin, 2001). Both types of leader realize their position of power. However, the group therapist 'does not lead by dictating communal mores or by legislating behaviours. Rather than imposing an institutional will on members, the group therapist acknowledges common dilemmas and challenges members to face them more adaptively' (Ettin, 2001).

An even more inclusive perspective brings the political dimension of group analysis into harmony with art, aesthetics and ethics. Felix de Mendelssohn, a psychoanalyst and group analyst in Vienna, sees group analysis as 'a prism through which the aesthetic dimensions of political life can be differentiated and appreciated as forming a complex creative human activity akin to art, science and psychoanalysis itself'. De Mendelssohn maintains that this all-encompassing perspective on unconscious processes provides a creative extension of politics as a network of relationships (de Mendelssohn, 2000). Blackwell, Ettin and de Mendelssohn are among a growing number of group psychotherapists who see groups as a means of moderating political climates and integrating the political and personal dimensions of life.

Groups as a medium for conflict resolution

A photograph on the cover of Patrick de Maré's book *Perspectives in Group Psychotherapy* (1972) depicts a meeting between North Korean and United States delegates at an Armistice Commission in Panmunjom, in the wake of the Korean war. Stony-faced, the two sets of adversaries face each other across the conference table in a silence which, we are told, lasted without interruption for four hours. Perhaps even group analysts might be daunted by such a protracted encounter. Yet these are situations with the potential for intervention by dispassionate and insightful third parties who are accepted by both sides.

'Conflict resolution' is one of those phrases which has a ring of optimism that is positively uplifting. Bringing together the opposing sides in an entrenched conflict has never been easy, as any couple therapist or mediation worker will testify. The hope in family disputes is that mediation will reduce the need for legal battles. The political counterpart of this has been diplomacy, once regarded as the continuation of war by other means, but now aided by a category of disinterested third parties who see scope for the application of models of conciliation making use of such concepts as the social unconscious.

Group psychotherapists working in this field recognize that the conflict is not between individuals but between groups. Maurice Apprey, a psychiatrist at the University of Virginia, points out that it is important to see the two areas of 'Self' and 'Other' as fluid and changing. It is the notions of fixity and absoluteness, says Apprey, which lead to the tendency to dehumanize the 'Other'. On the other hand it is equally important to resist the impulse to merge into one big unity, which can be seen as a denial of diversity (Apprey, 2001). Earl Hopper refers to the process of 'massification/ aggregation', the group members giving up their individual identities and embracing a monolithic group identity in the face of a threat to the group. He regards this phenomenon as a primitive group response to danger of the same order as Bion's three basic assumptions, operating unconsciously, and incongruent with the group's manifest behaviour (Hopper, 2003). This gets in the way of self-stability and differentiation. A group's identity needs to be preserved, and this can be threatened by too great a readiness to change people's ideas about themselves.

When groups in conflict get together under the intermediacy of a third party, an exchange of images is called for, according to Apprey. He maps out four stages in this process. First, each side needs to define itself while being allowed to demonize the other. Then, each side needs to differentiate within itself while recognizing the multiplicity of positions on the other side. Third, the mental border separating the two sides can then be crossed using metaphor and dialogue. And finally, the culmination of the process occurs when both sides are capable of creating concrete and mutually beneficial projects together. In this exercise it is important to recognize the influence of history, and how it recurs in different guises (Apprey, 2001). Vamik Volkan uses the metaphor of 'vaccination', in which groups recognize their conflicts but are still able to engage each other, so that the conflict is no longer malignant (Volkan, 1992).

Let us return, by way of ending, to a more familiar part of the landscape, one with which this book has mainly been occupied: the small group-analytic group for patients run along Foulkesian lines. It seems to us that what the new wave of radical thinkers referred to in this chapter have in common is a wish to integrate the old dichotomies of thought – individual and group, self and other, creative and destructive forces, mind and society – and replace them with a more holistic conception of group analysis based on a pattern of deep and broad communication which crosses the old boundaries separating 'inside' and 'outside'. On the face of it, none of this is fundamentally different from classical Foulkesian thinking. Yet there are some important differences. For one thing, new terminologies and languages are evolving, attached to new concepts and theories, which must eventually influence practice. For another, there is a celebration of diversity and culture in group analysis, which was unheard of in Foulkes's day, and an acknowledgement of the importance of power in groups.

Foulkes was primarily a clinician. Today his method has found wide application to diverse populations, both clinical and non-clinical. Freud baulked at the use of psychoanalysis as a tool for changing society. He castigated Trigant Burrow for what he saw as his grandiose aspiration to influence the world by means of the analytic process. But the tide could not be stemmed. Group analysts today are converging on the stage set by the social theorists of the Frankfurt School in the 1930s: the application of their method to achieve a better society.

> 'Begin at the beginning,' the King said gravely, 'and go on till you come to the end: then stop.'   Lewis Carroll, *Alice in Wonderland*

Glossary

The condenser phenomenon – The group amplifies and concentrates the interactions of the group members and expresses them in shared symbols and metaphors, which act as condensers.

Dialogue – 'The rhythmic and reciprocal proto-conversation of each development is reproduced in an analytic dialogue . . . It is through the continuous rehearsal of: my action – your reaction – pause – my response, that differentiation and growth takes place' (Pines, 1996).

Ego-training in action – A group-analytic conception of therapy. By way of the challenges and opportunities which the group process affords, the group member is guided into processes in which the neurotic discharge of tension is transformed into constructive ego-building and strengthening communication.

Empathy and resonance – Empathy describes a deep internal understanding and feeling linking one group member to another. Resonance refers to one's own unique response to the feelings of another in the group.

Inter-subjectivity – The task in the group to speak about oneself and to listen to others increases the range of responsiveness to oneself and to others.

Location – The concept describes how any event in the group involves the total network of interrelations and intercommunications. What manifestly occurs is the 'figure', the rest is the 'ground' of the configuration (Gestalt) in the group. The process of location corresponds, roughly, to the work which brings this configuration in the group to light. (Foulkes, 1964).

Malignant mirroring – This denotes an uncontrollable attractive–destructive interaction between group members (Zinkin, 1983).

The matrix – The matrix is a metaphor for the operational basis for interpersonal and intrapersonal relationships in the group. The individual is compared to a nodal point in a field of interaction, in which conscious and unconscious reactions meet. In this way, each group member affects and is being affected, by the web of communication which constitutes the matrix.

Another perception of the matrix defines it as a process rather than a system or network: 'a process that is continuously replicating and potentially transforming patterns of inter-subjective narrative themes that organise the experience of being together.' (Stacey, 2001). Barbara Dick and Andrew Powell see the matrix as a 'psychophysical structure', both pre-existing and dynamically evolving through the group's procedures (Dick, 1993; Powell, 1994).

Mirroring – Group members see rejected and split-off aspects of themselves in another, long before they are able to re-integrate them within the self.

Translation – This denotes the sum total of the group conductor's verbal interventions, such as drawing attention, linking, confronting, interpreting. These interventions translate from primary process language, from the symptomatic and symbolic meaning, to thinking and understanding. It is the group-analytic equivalent of making the unconscious conscious.

Bibliography

FAMOUS GROUP ANALYSTS AT WORK : DR GLOMBOWSKI CONSULTS HIS TEXTBOOKS TO PROVE THAT THE GROUP IS INTELLECTUALIZING

We have chosen, from the considerable number of articles and books which have been written about group-analytic psychotherapy and the various fields of study and practice which impinge on it, some which have captured our interest over the years, and which we hope will similarly interest the reader. We have divided the bibliography for each chapter into two sections – firstly, those references which are cited in the text, followed by a list of articles or books on the particular topic of that chapter, intended as a signpost to more specialized reading. Where pioneers in the field are mentioned, such as Pratt, Wender and Lewin, we have simply listed one or two of their classic publications for the historically minded reader to turn to if so inclined. By way of conclusion, we have added a section which lists

271

some of the key texts on group analysis and group psychotherapy which have been published either as books or as chapters in books.

Chapter 1: The social and cultural basis of group analysis

References

Foulkes SH (1948) Introduction to Group-analytic Psychotherapy, p.29. London: William Heinemann Medical Books Ltd.

Mennell S (1992) Norbert Elias: an introduction, p.3. Dublin: University College Dublin Press.

Pines M (1981) The frame of reference of group psychotherapy. International Journal of Group Psychotherapy 31(3): 275–85.

van der Kleij G (1982) About the Matrix. Group Analysis 15(3): 219–34.

Further reading

Adorno TW, Frenkel-Brunswick E, Levinson DJ, Sanford RN (1950) The Authoritarian Personality. New York: Harper.

Agazarian YM, Peters R (1981) The Visible and Invisible Group: Two Perspectives on Group Psychotherapy and Group Process. London: Routledge and Kegan Paul.

Agazarian YM (1997) Systems Centred Therapy for Groups. New York: The Guildford Press.

Ahlin G (1995). The interpersonal world of the infant and the foundation matrix for the groups and networks of the person. Group Analysis 28(1): 5–20.

Bion W (1985) Container and contained. In: A Colman and M Geller (eds) Group Relations Reader 2. Washington, DC: AK Rice Institute.

Brown DG (1985). Bion and Foulkes: basic assumptions and beyond. In: M Pines (ed) Bion and Group Psychotherapy. London: Routledge and Kegan Paul.

Bowlby J (1969) Attachment (Vol. 1, Attachment and Loss). London: Hogarth Press.

Dalal F (1998) Taking the Group Seriously: Towards a Post-Foulkesian Group Analytic Theory. Jessica Kingsley: London and Philadelphia

Dalal F (2001) The social unconscious: a post-Foulkesian perspective. Group Analysis 34(4): 539–55.

Durkin H (1964) The Group in Depth. New York: International Universities Press.

Durkin H (1983) Some contributions of general systems theory to psychoanalytic group psychotherapy. In M Pines (ed) The Evolution of Group Analysis. London: Routledge and Kegan Paul.

Elias N The Civilizing Process (1939) 1st English edition: Vol. 1, The History of Manners (1978). Vol. 2, State Formation and Civilization (1982) Oxford: Blackwell.

Fairbairn WRD (1952) Psychoanalytic Studies of the Personality. London: Tavistock/ Routledge.

Fromm E (1970) The Crisis of Psycho-analysis. Harmondsworth: Penguin.

Goldstein K (1939) The Organism: A Holistic Approach to Biology. New York: American Book Company.

Harwood I (1992) Group psychotherapy and disorders of the self. Group Analysis 25(1): 19–26.

Hearst LE (1993) Our historical and cultural cargo and its vicissitudes in group analysis. Group Analysis 26(4): 389–405.

Holmes J (1993) John Bowlby and Attachment Theory. London and New York: Routledge.

Harwood I, Pines M (eds) (1998) Self Experiences in Groups; Intersubjective and Self Psychological Pathways to Human Understanding. London: Jessica Kingsley.

Hopper E (1997) Traumatic experience in the unconscious life of groups: a fourth basic assumption. 21st SH Foulkes Annual Lecture. Group Analysis 30(4): 439–70.

Hopper E (2001) The social unconscious: theoretical considerations. Group Analysis 34(1): 9–27.

James CD (1994) 'Holding' and 'containing' in the group and society. Chapter 5 in: D Brown and L Zinkin (eds) The Psyche and the Social World: Developments in Group-Analytic Theory. London and New York: Routledge.

Karterud S (1998) The group self, empathy, intersubjectivity and hermeneutics. A group analytic perspective. In: I Harwood and M Pines (eds) Self Experiences in Groups; Intersubjective and Self Psychological Pathways to Human Understanding. London: Jessica Kingsley.

Kohut H (1977) The Restoration of the Self. New York: International Universities Press.

Lacan J (1977) Ecrits: A Selection. Trans. Alan Sheridan. London: Tavistock.

Marcuse H (1955) Eros and Civilisation. Boston: Beacon Press.

Marrone M (1994) Attachment theory and group analysis. Chapter 10 in D Brown and L Zinkin (eds) The Psyche and the Social World: Developments in Group-Analytic Theory. London and New York: Routledge.

Mennell S (1997) A sociologist at the outset of group analysis: Norbert Elias and his sociology. Group Analysis 30(4): 489–514.

Pines M (1976) The contribution of SH Foulkes to group-analytic Psychotherapy. In: LW Wolberg and ML Aronson (eds) Group Therapy: An Overview. New York: Stratton Intercontinental, pp.9–29.

Rothe S (1989) The Frankfurt School: An influence on Foulkes's group analysis? Group Analysis 22(4): 405–15.

Skynner ACR (1981) An open-systems, group-analytic approach to family therapy. In: AS Gurman, DP Kniskern (eds) Handbook of Family Therapy. New York: Brunner/Mazel.

Volkan VD (2001) Transgenerational transmissions and chosen traumas: an aspect of Large-Group identity. Group Analysis 34(1): 79–97.

Wertheimer M (1912) Experimentelle Studien uber das Sehen von Bewegung. Z. Psychol. 61: 161–265.

Winnicott DW (1965) The Maturational Process and the Facilitating Environment. London: Hogarth Press.

Chapter 2: A century of group therapy

References

Freud S (1921) Group Psychology and the Analysis of the Ego. Standard Edition 18, London: Hogarth Press.

Freud S (1926) letter to Trigant Burrow 14 November 1926. Quoted in: J Campos (1992) Burrow, Foulkes and Freud: An Historical Perspective. Lifwynn Correspondence 2(2–9): 8.

Marsh LC (1933) An experiment in group treatment of patients at Worcester State Hospital. Mental Hygiene 17: 396–416.

Pratt JH (1907) The class method of treating consumption in the homes of the poor. Journal of the American Medical Association 49: 755–9.

Read Sir Herbert (1949) Review of The Neurosis of Man. In: The Tiger's Eye, quoted in 'Comments on Burrow'. Lifwynn Correspondence (1992) 2(1): 11.

Further reading

Adler A (1938) Social Interest: A Challenge to Mankind. London: Faber and Faber.

Argelander H (1972) Gruppenprozesse: Wege zur Anwendung der Psychoanalyse in Behandlung, Lehre und Forschung. Reinbek: Rowohlt.

Bion W (1961) Experiences in Groups. London: Tavistock Publications.

Bridger H (1992) Northfield Revisited. Chapter 3 in M Pines (ed) Bion and Group Psychotherapy. London: Routledge.

Burrow T (1927) The group method of analysis. Psychoanalytic Review 10: 268–80.

Burrow T (1928) The basis of group-analysis, or the analysis of the reactions of normal and neurotic individuals. British Journal of Medical Psychology 8: 198–206.

Campos J (1992) Burrow, Foulkes and Freud: An Historical Perspective. Lifwynn Correspondence 2(2–9).

De Maré P (1972) Perspectives in Group Psychotherapy: A Theoretical Background. London: George Allen and Unwin.

Dreikurs R (1959) Early experiments with group psychotherapy. A historical review. American Journal of Psychotherapy 13: 882–91.

Ettin MF (1992) Chapter 3: The invention of modern group treatment at the turn of the twentieth century; Chapter 4: The growth spurt of group psychotherapy. In: Foundations and Applications of Group Psychotherapy: A Sphere of Influence. Boston: Allyn and Bacon.

Ezriel H (1950) A psycho-analytic approach to group treatment. British Journal of Medical Psychology 23: 59–74.

Foulkes SH (1946) Group analysis in a military neurosis centre. Lancet, vol. 1, 2 March: 303–13.

Freud S (1921) Group Psychology and the Analysis of the Ego. Standard Edition Vol. 18. London: Hogarth Press.

Greenberg IA (ed) (1975) Psychodrama: Theory and Therapy. London: Souvenir Press.

Harrison T (2000) Bion, Rickman, Foulkes and the Northfield Experiments: Advancing on a Different Front. London: Jessica Kingsley.

Heigl-Evers A, Heigl F (1995) Psychosocial compromise formation: understanding defence and coping in group analysis. Group Analysis 28(4): 483–92.

Jones M (1953) The Therapeutic Community: A New Treatment Method in Psychiatry. New York: Basic Books.

Lazell EW (1921) The group treatment of dementia praecox. Psychoanalytic Review 8: 168–79.

Le Bon G (1896) La Psychologie des Foules, Paris. The Crowd: A Study of the Popular Mind. London: Benn (1947)

Lewin K, Lippitt R, White RK (1939) Patterns of aggressive behaviour in experimentally created 'social climates'. Journal of Social Psychology 10: 271–99.

Lewin K (1947) Frontiers in group dynamics: concept, method and reality in social science. Social equilibria and social change. Human Relations 1: 5–41.

Main T (1946) The Hospital as a Therapeutic Institution. Bulletin of the Menninger Clinic 10: 66–90.

Marsh LC (1935) Group therapy in the psychiatric clinic. Journal of Nervous and Mental Diseases 82: 381–92.

Moreno JL (1953) Who Shall Survive? Foundations of Sociometry, Group Psychotherapy and Sociodrama, 2nd edition. Beacon, NY: Beacon House (Original work published in 1934).

Nichol B (undated) Early Development of Group Psychotherapy in Britain. Centre for Adult and Higher Education. University of Manchester. Occasional Papers No. 22.

Nye RA (1975) The Origins of Crowd Psychology: Gustave LeBon and the Crisis of Mass Democracy in the Third Republic. London and Beverley Hills: Sage Publications.

Pines M (1983) The Contribution of SH Foulkes to Group Therapy. Chapter 16 in: M Pines (ed) The Evolution of Group Analysis. London: Routledge and Kegan Paul.

Pratt JH (1906) Home Sanatorium Treatment of Consumption. Johns Hopkins Hospital Bulletin.

Rosenbaum M (1978) Group Psychotherapy: Heritage, History and the Current Scene. Chapter 1 in H Mullan and M Rosenbaum Group Psychotherapy: Theory and Practice. Free Press, New York: Macmillan.

Scheidlinger S (1994) An overview of nine decades of group psychotherapy. Hospital and Community Psychiatry 45(3): 217–25.

Schilder P (1936) The analysis of ideologies as a psychotherapeutic method. American Journal of Psychiatry 93: 601–14.

Schilder P (1939) Results and problems of group psychotherapy in severe neurosis. Mental Hygiene 23: 87–98.

Schindler R (1957/58) Grundprinzipien der Psychodynamic in der Gruppe. Psyche 11, 308.

Slavson SR (1964) A Textbook in Analytic Group Psychotherapy. New York: International Universities Press.

Wender L (1936) The dynamics of group psychotherapy and its application. Journal of Nervous and Mental Diseases 84: 54–60.

Whitaker DS, Lieberman M (1964) Psychotherapy through the Group Process. Chicago: Atherton Press.

Whitaker DS (1987). Connections between group-analytic and a group focal conflict perspective. International Journal of Group Psychotherapy 37: 201–18.

Wolf A, Schwartz EK (1962) Psychoanalysis in Groups. New York: Grune & Stratton.

Chapter 3: Planning an analytic group

References

Foulkes SH (1948) Introduction to Group-Analytic Psychotherapy: Studies of Social Interaction of Individuals and Groups, p.55–6. London: Interface.

Piper WE (1991) Brief group psychotherapy. Psychiatric Annals 21(7): 419–22.

Further reading

Balmer R (1993) Therapeutic factors in group analysis: meeting them in the block training setting. Group Analysis 26(2): 139–45.

Barnes B, Ernst S, Hyde K (1999) Growing a Group. Chapter 3 in: An Introduction to Groupwork: A Group-Analytic Perspective. London: Macmillan.

Hilpert RH (1995). The place of the training group analyst and the problem of personal group analysis in block training. Group Analysis 28(3): 301–11.

Home HJ (1983) The effect of numbers on the basic transference pattern in group analysis. In: M Pines (ed) The Evolution of Group Analysis. Routledge: London.

Kibel HD (1981) A conceptual model for short-term inpatient group psychotherapy. American Journal of Psychiatry 138: 74–80.

Klein RH (1993) Short-term group psychotherapy. Chapter in: HI Kaplan and BJ Sadock (eds) Comprehensive Group Psychotherapy, 3rd edition. Baltimore: Williams and Wilkins.

Knauss W, Rudnitzki G (1990) Block training in Heidelberg: historical and contemporary influences. Group Analysis 23: 367–75.

Lorentzen S, Herlofsen P, Karterud S, Ruud T (1995) Block training in group analysis: the Norwegian Program. International Journal of Group Psychotherapy 45(1): 73–89.

Lorentzen S, Kuriené A, Laurenaitis E, Lyngstad K, Petkuté E, Sørlie T, Zileniéné S (1998) Block training in group psychotherapy in the Baltic States. Group Analysis 31(3): 351–61.

Marrone M (1993) Analytic group therapy in block sessions: An experience in Milan. Group Analysis 26(2): 147–55.

Molnos A (1995) A Question of Time: Essentials of Brief Dynamic Psychotherapy. London: Karnac.

Reik H (1989) A changed time-structure: the effects on the analytic group. Group Analysis 22(3): 325–32.

Rogers C (2004) Working in different settings. Chapter 7 in: Psychotherapy and Counselling: A Professional Business. London: Whurr Publishers.

Chapter 4: Dynamic administration

References

van der Kleij G (1983) The setting of the group. Group Analysis 16(1): 75–80.

Further reading

Foulkes SH (1975) 'The conductor in action: Part I: as administrator. Chapter 6 in: Group-Analytic Psychotherapy: Method and Principles. London: An Interface Book.

Pines M, Hearst LE, Behr HL (1982) Group analysis (group analytic psychotherapy) pp.150–54. In: GM Gazda (ed) Basic Approaches to Group Psychotherapy and Counselling. 3rd edition. Springfield, IL: Charles C Thomas.

Yalom ID (1970) Creation of the group: time, size, preparation. In: The Theory and Practice of Group Psychotherapy. New York and London: Basic Books.

Chapter 5: The assessment interview

References

Garland C (1982) Group analysis: taking the non-problem seriously. Group Analysis 15(1): 4–14.

Further reading

Brown D (1991) Assessment and selection for groups. Chapter 4 in: J Roberts and M Pines (eds) The Practice of Group Analysis. London: Routledge.

Coltart N (1988) The assessment of psychological mindedness in the diagnostic interview. British Journal of Psychiatry 153: 819–20.

Foulkes SH (1964) Therapeutic Group Analysis. London: George Allen and Unwin, pp.22–3, 44–6, 243–5.

Foulkes SH (1975) Group-Analytic Psychotherapy: Method and Principles, pp.38–63. London: Gordon and Breach.

Salvendy J (1993) Selection and preparation of patients for group Psychotherapy. In: HI Kaplan and BJ Sadock (eds) Comprehensive Group Psychotherapy. Baltimore: Williams and Wilkins.

Chapter 6: The symptom in its group context

Further reading

Battegay R (1989) Group psychotherapy with depressives. Group Analysis 22: 31–8.

Brown D (1989) A contribution to the understanding of psychosomatic processes in groups. British Journal of Psychotherapy 6: 5–9.

Fiumara R, Zanasi M (1989) Depression of the group and depression in the group. Group Analysis 22(1): 49–57.

Greenberg M, Shergill SS, Szmukler G, Tantam D (2003) Narratives in Psychiatry. London: Jessica Kingsley.

Holmes J (ed) (1991) A Textbook of Psychotherapy in Psychiatric Practice. Edinburgh: Churchill Livingstone.

Horwitz L (1980) Group psychotherapy for borderline and narcissistic patients. Bulletin of the Menninger Clinic 44(2): 181–200.

Knauss W (1985) The treatment of psychosomatic illness in group-analytic psychotherapy. Group Analysis 18(3): 177–90.

Pines M (1975) Group therapy with 'difficult' patients. In: L Wolberg and M Aronson (eds) Group and Family Therapy: An Overview. New York: Stratton Intercontinental.

Resnik S (1999) Borderline personalities in groups. Group Analysis 32(3): 331–47.

Roth BE, Stone WN, Kibel HD (eds) (1990) The Difficult Patient in the Group. Madison: International Universities Press.

Schermer VL, Pines M (eds) (1999) Group Psychotherapy of the Psychoses: Concepts, Interventions and Contexts. London: Jessica Kingsley.

Schneider E (1996) Holding and caring: a borderline patient in a new psychotherapy group. Group Analysis 29(2): 123–34.

Smith J (1999) Five questions about group therapy in long-term schizophrenia. Group Analysis 32(4): 515–24.

Winther G, Sorensen T (1989) Group therapy with manic depressives: dynamic and therapeutic aspects. Group Analysis 22(1): 19–30.

Zulueta F de (1993) From Pain to Violence: The Traumatic Roots of Destructiveness. London: Whurr Publishers.

Zulueta F de, Mark P (2000) Attachment and contained splitting: a combined approach of group and individual therapy to the treatment of patients suffering from borderline personality disorder. Group Analysis 33(4): 486–500.

Chapter 7: The start of a new group

Further reading

Agmon S, Schneider S (1998) The first stages in the development of the small group: a psychological understanding. Group Analysis 31(2): 131–56.

Kadis AL, Krasner JD, Weiner MF, Winick C, Foulkes SH (1974) The first group session: reparation, procedure and structure. Chapter 6 in: Practicum of Group Psychotherapy, 2nd edition. New York: Harper and Row.

Kennard D (1993) The first session – an apparent distraction. Chapter 3 in: D Kennard, J Roberts and DA Winter, A Work Book of Group-Analytic Interventions. London and New York: Routledge.

Nitsun M (1989) Early development: linking the individual and the group. Group Analysis 22(3): 249–61.

Winter DA (1993) Turn taking in the early sessions. Chapter 4 in: D Kennard, J Roberts and DA Winter, A Work Book of Group-Analytic Interventions. London and New York: Routledge.

Chapter 8: A newcomer to the group

Further reading

Bacha C (1997) The stranger in the group: new members in analytic group psychotherapy. Psychodynamic Counselling 3(1): 7–23.

Yalom ID (1975) The monopoliser. Chapter 12 in: The Theory and Practice of Group Psychotherapy. New York and London: Basic Books.

Chapter 9: The group in action

References

Battegay RC (1977) The group dream. In: LR Wolberg and ML Aronson (eds) Group Therapy: An Overview. New York: Stratton Intercontinental.

Dalal F (2002) Race, Colour and the Process of Racialization, p.74. London: Brunner/Routledge.

Foulkes SH (1964) Therapeutic Group Analysis.London: George Allen and Unwin.

Foulkes SH (1975) Group-Analytic Psychotherapy: Method and Principles, pp.1–5. London: An Interface Book.

Ogden TH (1979) On projective identification. International Journal of Psychoanalysis 60: 357–73.

Pines M (1981) The frame of reference of group psychotherapy. International Journal of Group Psychotherapy 31(3): 275–85.

Schlapobersky J (1994) The language of the group. In: D Brown and L Zinkin (eds) The Psyche and the Social World: Developments in Group-Analytic Theory. London: Routledge.

Volkan V (1997) Blood Lines: From Ethnic Pride to Ethnic Terrorism. New York: Farrar, Straus and Giroux.

Zinkin L (1983) Malignant mirroring. Group Analysis 16(2): 113–26.

Further reading

Blackwell D (1994) The emergence of racism in group analysis. Group Analysis 27(2): 197–211.

Burman E (2001) Engendering authority in the group. Psychodynamic Counselling 7(3): 347–70.

Conlon I (1991) The effect of gender on the role of the conductor. Group Analysis 24(2): 187–200.

Dalal F (2002) Race, Colour and the Process of Racialisation. London: Brunner/Routledge.

Foss T (1994). From phobic inhibitions to dreams. Group Analysis 27(3): 305–18.

Foulkes SH (1968). On interpretation in group analysis. International Journal of Group Psychotherapy 18(4): 432–44.

Friedman R (2000) The interpersonal containment of dreams in group psychotherapy: a contribution to the work with dreams in a group. Group Analysis 33(2): 221–33.

König K (1991) Projective identification: transference type and defence type. Group Analysis 24(3): 323–31

Pines M (1993) Interpretation: why, for whom and when. Chapter 12 in D Kennard, J Roberts and DA Winter, A Work Book of Group-Analytic Interventions. London and New York: Routledge.

Rauchfleisch U (1995) Dreams as defence and coping strategies in group analysis. Group Analysis 28(4): 465–72.

Roitman M (1989) The concept of projective identification: its use in understanding interpersonal and group processes. Group Analysis 22(3): 249–60.

Spotnitz H (1973) Acting out in group psychotherapy. In: LA Wolberg and EK Schwartz (eds) Group Therapy: an Overview. New York: Thieme.

Stone WN, Whitman RM (1980) Observations on empathy in group psychotherapy. Chapter 12 in: LR Wolberg, and MR Aronson (eds) Group and Family Therapy. New York: Brunner/Mazel.

Storck, LE (1997) Cultural psychotherapy: a consideration of psychosocial class and cultural differences in group treatment. Group 21(4): 331–49.

Zinkin L (1989) The group as container and contained. Group Analysis 22(3): 227–34.

Chapter 10: Life events in the group

References

König K (1981) Angst und Persoehnlichkeit: Das Konzept vom steuernden Objekt und seine Anwendung. Goettingen: Medizinische Psychologie. Vandenhoek Ruprecht.

Winnicott DW (1965) The Family and Individual Development, p.15. London: Tavistock Publications.

Further reading

Berne E (1964) Games People Play. New York: Grove Press.

Rogers C (2004) Clinical Predicaments. Chapter 2 in: Psychotherapy and Counselling: a Professional Business. London: Whurr Publishers.

Sandison R (1991) The psychotic patient and psychotic conflict in group analysis. Group Analysis 24(1): 73–83.

Zulueta F de (1993) From Pain to Violence: The Traumatic Roots of Destructiveness. London: Whurr Publishers.

Chapter 11: Bringing therapy to an end

Further reading

Maar V (1989) Attempts at grasping the self during the termination phase of group-analytic psychotherapy. Group Analysis 22(1): 99–104.

Mullan H, Rosenbaum M (1978) The last group session: the departure. Chapter 11 in: Group Psychotherapy: Theory and Practice. New York: Free Press.

Powell A (1994) Ending is for life. Group Analysis 27(1): 37–50.

Wardi D (1989) The termination process in the group process. Group Analysis 22(1): 87–99.

Zinkin L (1994) All's well that ends well – or is it? Group Analysis 27(1): 15–24.

Chapter 12: Therapeutic pitfalls

Further reading

Ezriel H (1950) A psycho-analytic approach to group treatment. British Journal of Medical Psychology 23: 59–74.

Foulkes SH (1975) Group-Analytic Psychotherapy: Method and Principles, pp.124–9. London: An Interface Book.

König K (1991) Group-analytic interpretations: individual and group. Descriptive and metaphoric. Group Analysis 24(2): 111–15.

Pines M (1993) Interpretation: why, for whom and when. Chapter 12 in: D Kennard, J Roberts and DA Winter, A Work Book of Group-Analytic Interventions. London and New York: Routledge.

Wolf A, Schwartz EK (1962). Psychoanalysis in Groups. New York: Grune & Stratton.

Chapter 13: Challenging scenarios

References

Behr HL (2004) Commentary on 'Drawing the Isolate into the Group Flow' by L Ormont. Group Analysis 37(1): 76–81.

Foulkes SH (1948) Introduction to Group-Analytic Psychotherapy, p.169. London: William Heinemann Medical Books.

Foulkes E (1990) (ed) SH Foulkes's Selected Papers: Psychoanalysis and Group Analysis, p.291. London: Karnac.

Ormont LR (2004) Drawing the isolate into the group flow. Group Analysis 37(1): 65–76.

Yalom ID (1975) Problem patients: the monopolist. Chapter 12 in: Theory and Practice of Group Psychotherapy. New York: Basic Books.

Zinkin L (1983) Malignant mirroring. Group Analysis 16(2): 113–26.

Further reading

Arzoumanides Y (1993) Disillusionment with therapy. Chapter 9 in: D Kennard, J Roberts and DA Winter, A Work Book of Group-Analytic Interventions. London and New York: Routledge.

Kennard D (1993) A potential drop-out. Chapter 5 in: D Kennard, J Roberts and DA Winter, A Work Book of Group-Analytic Interventions. London and New York: Routledge.

Knauss W (1999) The creativity of destructive fantasies. Group Analysis 32(3): 397–411.

Lyndon P (1994) The Leader and the Scapegoat: a dependency group study. Group Analysis 27(1): 95–104.

Maccoby H (1982) The Sacred Executioner. London: Thames and Hudson.

Nitsun M (1996) The Anti-Group: Destructive forces in the group and their creative potential. London: Routledge.

Roberts J (1991) Destructive phases in groups. Chapter 8 in: J Roberts and M Pines (eds) The Practice of Group Analysis. London: Routledge.

Roberts J (1993) Threatened premature termination of therapy. Chapter 8 in: D Kennard, J Roberts and DA Winter, A Work Book of Group-Analytic Interventions. London and New York: Routledge.

Scheidlinger S (1982) On scapegoating in group psychotherapy. International Journal of Group Psychotherapy 32: 131–43.

Tantam D (1984) A prophet in the group. Group Analysis 17(1): 44–57.

Chapter 14: The group analyst in trouble

Further reading

Anderson L (1994) The experience of being a pregnant group therapist. Group Analysis 27(1): 75–85.

Lesnik B (2003) Some observations from a group 'inherited' from a deceased therapist. Group Analysis 36(1): 55–72.

Mullen PE, Pathe M (2000) Stalkers and their Victims. Cambridge: Cambridge University Press.

Rogers C (2004) Events in the Therapist's Life. Chapter 1 in: Psychotherapy and Counselling: a Professional Business. London: Whurr Publishers.

Sharpe M (1991) Death and the Practice. Chapter 12 in: J Roberts, M Pines (eds) The Practice of Group Analysis. London: Routledge.

Chapter 15: The Large Group

References

Foulkes SH (1964) Therapeutic Group Analysis, pp.187–206. London: George Allen and Unwin.

Foulkes SH (1975) Problems of the large group from a group-analytic point of view. Chapter 1 in: L Kreeger (ed) The Large Group: Dynamics and Therapy London: Constable.

Shaked J (2003) The large group and the political process. Chapter 9 in: S Schneider, M Weinberg (eds) The Large Group Re-Visited: The Herd, Primal Horde, Crowds and Masses. London: Jessica Kingsley.

Springmann R (1975) Psychotherapy in the large group. In: L. Kreeger (ed) The Large Group. London: Constable.

Wilke G (2003) Chaos and order in the large group. Chapter 5 in: S Schneider, M Weinberg (eds) The Large Group Re-Visited: The Herd, Primal Horde, Crowds and Masses. London: Jessica Kingsley.

Further reading

De Maré P (1975) The politics of large groups. Chapter 3 in: L Kreeger (ed) The Large Group: Dynamics and Therapy. London: Constable.

De Maré P (1989) The history of Large Group phenomena in relation to group-analytic psychotherapy: the history of the Median Group. Group 13: 173–97.

De Maré P, Piper R, Thompson S (1991) Koinonia: From Hate, Through Dialogue, to Culture in the Large Group. London: Karnac.

Kreeger L (ed) (1975) The Large Group. London: Constable.

Island TK (2003) The large group and leadership challenges in a group-analytic training community. Chapter 13 in: S Schneider, M Weinberg (eds) The Large Group Re-Visited: The Herd, Primal Horde, Crowds and Masses. London: Jessica Kingsley.

Maxwell B (2000) The Median group. Group Analysis 33(1): 35–47.

Pisani R (2000) The Median group in clinical practice: an experience of eight years. Group Analysis 33(1): 77–90.

Schneider S, Weinberg M (eds) (2003) The Large Group Re-Visited: The Herd, Primal Horde, Crowds and Masses. London: Jessica Kingsley.

Turquet P (1975) Threats to identity in the large group. Chapter 3 in: L. Kreeger (ed) The Large Group. London: Constable.

Chapter 16: All in the same boat: homogeneous groups

References

Foulkes SH (1948) Part 3, Selection by Contrast, p.61. In Introduction to Group-Analytic Psychotherapy. London: Maresfield Reprint (1983).

Pratt JH (1907) The class method of treating consumption in the homes of the poor. Journal of the American Medical Association 49: 755–9.

Further reading

Barnes B, Ernst S, Hyde K (1999) Differences in groups: heterogeneity and homogeneity. Chapter 7 in: An Introduction to Groupwork: A Group-Analytic Perspective. New York: Macmillan Press.

Behr HL (1997) Group work with parents. Chapter 7 in: KN Dwivedi (ed.) Enhancing Parenting Skills: A Guide for Professionals Working with Parents. Chichester: John Wiley and Sons.

Evans S, Chisholm P, Walshe J (2001) A dynamic psychotherapy group for the elderly. Group Analysis 34(2): 287–98.

Hudson I, Richie S, Brennan C, Sutton-Smith D (1999) Consuming passions: groups for women with eating disorders. Group Analysis 32(1): 37–51.

Kibel HD (1981) A conceptual model for short-term in-patient group psychotherapy. American Journal of Psychiatry 138: 74–80.

Rice CA, Rutan JS (1987). Inpatient Group Psychotherapy. A Psychodynamic Perspective. New York: Macmillan.

Reading B, Weegmann M (2004) Group Psychotherapy and Addiction. London: Whurr Publishers.

Valbak K (2003) Specialized psychotherapeutic group analysis: how do we make group analysis suitable for 'non-suitable' patients? Group Analysis 36(1): 73–86.

Van der Kolk BA (1993) Groups for patients with histories of catastrophic trauma. Chapter 16 in: A Alonso, HI Swiller, Group Therapy in Clinical Practice. Washington and London: American Psychiatric Press.

Willis S (1999) Group analysis and eating disorders. Group Analysis 32(1): 21–33.

Woods J (2003) Group therapy for adolescents who have abused. Chapter 6 in: Psychoanalytic Therapy with Victims/Perpetrators of Sexual Abuse. London: Jessica Kingsley.

Wright S (2000) Group work. In: B Lask and R Bryant-Waugh (eds) Anorexia Nervosa and Related Eating Disorders, 2nd edition. London: Psychology Press.

Yalom ID (1983) Inpatient Group Psychotherapy. New York: Basic Books.

Chapter 17: Groups for children and adolescents

Further reading

Behr HL (1982) The significance of teasing in group psychotherapy. In: M Pines, L Rafaelsen (eds) The Individual and the Group: Boundaries and Interrelations. Volume 2: Practice. New York and London: Plenum Press.

Behr HL (1988) Group analysis with early adolescents: some clinical issues. Group Analysis 21(2): 119–33.

Behr HL (2003) Psychodynamic groups for children and adolescents. Chapter 8 in: ME Garralda, C Hyde (eds) Managing Children with Psychiatric Problems, 2nd edition. London: BMJ Books.

Berkovitz IH (ed) (1995) Adolescents Grow in Groups. New York: Jason Aronson.

Dwivedi KN (1993) Group Work with Children and Adolescents. London: Jessica Kingsley.

Evans J (1998) Active Analytic Group Therapy for Adolescents London: Jessica Kingsley.

Foulkes SH, Anthony EJ (1965) Group-analytic psychotherapy for children and adolescents. Chapter 8 in Group Psychotherapy: The Psychoanalytic Approach, 2nd edition. London: Penguin Books.

MacLennan BW, Dies KR (1992) Group Counseling and Psychotherapy with Adolescents, 2nd edition. New York: Columbia University Press.

Riester AE, Kraft IA (eds) (1986) Child Group Therapy: Future Tense. American Group Psychotherapy Association Monograph Series 3. New York: International Universities Press.

Slavson SR, Schiffer M (1975) Group Psychotherapies for Children. New York: International Universities Press.

Woods J (1996) Handling violence in child group therapy. Group Analysis 29(1): 81–98.

Chapter 18: Family therapy: a group-analytic perspective

References

Foulkes SH (1975) Group-Analytic Psychotherapy: Methods and Principles. London: Interface, Gordon and Breach, reprinted Karnac 1986

Haley J (1976) Problem-Solving Therapy. San Francisco: Jossey-Bass.

Hoffman L (1981) Foundations of Family Therapy. New York: Basic Books.

Minuchin S, Fishman C (1981) Family Therapy Techniques, Cambridge MA: Harvard University Press.

Palazzoli MS, Cecchin G, Pratao G, Boscolo L (1978) Paradox and Counter-Paradox. New York: Jason Aronson.

Skynner ACR (1979) Reflections on the family therapist as family scapegoat. Journal of Family Therapy 1: 7–22.

Further reading

Behr HL (1994) Families and group analysis. Chapter 11 in: D Brown, L Zinkin (eds) The Psyche and the Social World. London: Routledge.

Behr HL (1996) Multiple family group therapy: a group-analytic perspective. Group Analysis 29(1): 9–22.

Behr HL (2001) The importance of being father: a tribute to Robin Skynner. Journal of Family Therapy 23(3): 327–33.

Byng Hall J (1995) Rewriting Family Scripts: Improvisation and Systems Change. London: Guilford Press.

Schlapobersky JR (ed) (1987) Selected Papers of Robin Skynner vol. I. Explorations with Families: Group Analysis and Family Therapy. London: Methuen.

Skynner ACR (1981) An open-systems, group-analytic approach to family therapy. In: AS Gurman, DP Kniskern (eds) Handbook of Family Therapy. New York: Brunner/Mazel.

Chapter 19: The application of group analysis to non-clinical settings

References

Rance C (2003) Commentary on article by Marlene Spero. Group Analysis 36(3): 338.

Spero M (2003) A working conference on professional and management dilemmas working in and with organisations. Group Analysis 36(3): 324–35.

Stacey RD (2001) Complex Responsive Processes in Organisations, Learning and Knowledge Creation. London: Routledge.

Wilke G, Freeman S (2001) How to be a Good Enough GP: Surviving and Thriving in the New Primary Care Organisations. Abingdon: Radcliffe Medical Press.

Further reading

Cooklin A (1999) Changing Organisations. Clinicians as Agents of Change. London: Karnac.

Nitsun M (1998) The organisational mirror: a group-analytic approach to organisational consultation. Part 1 Group Analysis 31(3): 245–67. Part 2 Group Analysis 31(4): 505–18.

Obholzer A (1997) Institutions in a changing world. In: ER Schapiro (ed) The Inner World in the Outer World. London: Karnac.

Schwartz G (1980) Conflict resolution as a process. Chapter 8 in: Trygve Johnstad (ed.) Group Dynamics and Society: A Multinational Approach. Published by the European Institute for Transnational Studies in Group and Organisational Development. Cambridge, MA: Oelgeschlager, Gunn and Hain.

Whitaker DS (1992) Transposing learnings from group psychotherapy to work groups. Group Analysis 25(2): 131–49.

Chapter 20: The supervision of group therapy

Further reading

Foulkes SH (1964) Teaching, study and research. Chapter 20 in: Therapeutic Group Analysis. London: George Allen and Unwin Ltd.

Gustafson JP (1980) Group therapy supervision: critical problems of theory and technique. Chapter 17 in: LR Wolberg, ML Aronson, Group and Family Therapy. New York: Brunner/Mazel.

Halperin DH (1981) Issues in the supervision of group psychotherapy: countertransference and the group supervisor's agenda. Group 5(3): 24–32.

Moss E (1995) Group supervision: focus on countertransference. International Journal of Group Psychotherapy 45(4): 537–48.

Rosenthal L (1999) Group supervision of groups: a modern analytic perspective. International Journal of Group Psychotherapy 49(2): 197–213.

Schoenholtz-Read J (1996) The supervisor as gender-analyst: feminist perspectives on group supervision and training. International Journal of Group Psychotherapy 46(4): 479–501.

Sharpe M, Blackwell D (1987) Creative supervision through student involvement. Group Analysis 20(3): 195–208.

Sharpe M (ed) (1995) The Third Eye. London: Routledge.

Chapter 21: The group analyst as a professional

References

Rogers C (2004) Psychotherapy and Counselling: a Professional Business. London: Whurr Publishers.

Wilke G, Freeman S (2001) How to be a Good Enough GP: Surviving and Thriving in the New Primary Care Organisations. Abingdon: Radcliffe Medical Press.

Further reading

Clarkson P (2000) Working with Ethical and other Moral Dilemmas in Psychotherapy. London and Philadelphia: Whurr Publishers.

Cordess C (ed) (2001) Confidentiality and Mental Health. London: Jessica Kingsley.

Kibel HD (1987) Contributions of the group psychotherapist to education in the psychiatric unit: teaching through group dynamics. International Journal of Psychotherapy 37(1): 3–29.

Gazda GM, Mack S (1982) Ethical practice guidelines for groupwork practitioners. Chapter 3 in: GM Gazda (ed) Basic Approaches to Group

Psychotherapy and Group Counselling, 3rd edition. Springfield, IL: Charles C Thomas.

Sharpe M (1991) Administration of the practice. Chapter 13 in: J Roberts, M Pines (eds) The Practice of Group Analysis. London: Routledge.

Chapter 22: The changing landscape of group analysis

References

Apprey M (2001) Group process in the resolution of ethnonational conflicts: the case of Estonia. Group Analysis 34(1): 99–113.

Blackwell RD (2003) Colonialism and globalisation: a group-analytic perspective. Group Analysis 36(4): 445–63.

Brown DA (2001) Contribution to the understanding of the social unconscious. Group Analysis 34(1): 29–38.

Dalal F (1998) Taking the Group Seriously: Towards a Post-Foulkesian Group-Analytic Theory. London: Jessica Kingsley.

Dalal F (2001). The social unconscious: a post-Foulkesian perspective. Group Analysis 34(4): 539–57.

De Maré PB (1972) Perspectives in Group Psychotherapy: A Theoretical Background. London: George Allen and Unwin.

Ettin M (2001) A psychotherapy group as a sociopolitical context: the case of the 'silent majority'. Group Analysis 34(1): 39–54.

Fonagy P (2003) Psychoanalysis today. World Psychiatry 2(2): 73–80.

Hopper E (1997) Traumatic experience in the unconscious life of groups: a fourth basic assumption. Group Analysis. 30(4): 439–70.

Hopper E (2001) The social unconscious: theoretical considerations. Group Analysis 34(1): 9–27.

Hopper E (2003) The Social Unconscious: Selected Papers. London: Jessica Kingsley.

Karterud S (2000) On the scientific foundations of group analysis: commentary on article by Ralph Stacey. Group Analysis 33(4): 514–18.

Lorentzen S (2000) Assessment of change after long-term psychoanalytic group treatment: presentation of a field study of outpatients from private psychiatric practice. Group Analysis 33(3): 373–96.

Mendelssohn de F (2000) The aesthetics of the political in group-analytic process – the wider scope of group analysis. Group Analysis 33(4): 438–58.

Nitsun M (1996) The Anti-Group: Destructive forces in the group and their creative potential. London: Routledge.

Stacey RD (2000) Reflexivity, self-organisation and emergence in the group matrix. Group Analysis 33(4): 501–14.

Stacey RD (2003) Complexity and Group Processes: A Radically Social Understanding of Individuals. Hove: Brunner/Routledge.

Volkan VD (2001)Transgenerational transmissions and chosen traumas: an aspect of Large Group identity. Group Analysis 34(1): 79–97.
Volkan VD (1992) Ethnonationalistic rituals: an introduction. Mind and Human Interaction 4(1): 3–19.

Further reading

Auchincloss EL, Michels R (2003) A reassessment of psychoanalytic education: controversies and changes. International Journal of Psychoanalysis 84: 387–403.
Blackwell RD (2002) The politicisation of group analysis in the 21st Century. Group Analysis 35(1): 105–18.
Brown DA (1994) Self-development through subjective interaction. In: D Brown, L Zinkin (eds) The Psyche and the Social World: Developments in Group-Analytic Theory. London: Routledge.
Hearst LE, Sharpe M (1991) Training for and trainees in group analysis. Chapter 10 in: J Roberts, M Pines (eds) The Practice of Group Analysis. London: Routledge.
Hearst LE, Behr HL (1995) Training in group analysis: institutional dilemmas. Group Analysis 28(4): 407–12.
Karterud S (1992) Reflections on group-analytic research. Group Analysis 25: 353–64.
Karterud S (1996) The hospital as a therapeutic text. Therapeutic Communities 17: 125–9.
Karterud S (1998) The group self, empathy, intersubjectivity and hermeneutics. A group-analytic perspective. In: IH Harwood, M Pines (eds) Self Experiences in Group: Intersubjective and Self Psychological Pathways to Human Understanding. London: Jessica Kingsley.
Kennard D, Roberts J, Winter D (eds) (1993) A Workbook of Group-analytic Interventions. London: Routledge.
Mittwoch A (2001) Our place in the world of science: what is at stake? Group Analysis 34(4): 431–48.
Nitzgen D (2001) Training in democracy, democracy in training: notes on group analysis and democracy. Group Analysis 34(3): 331–47.
Pines M (1998) What should a psychotherapist know? (Chapter 8) Coherency and disruption in the sense of the self (Chapter 12) in: M Pines Circular Reflections: Selected Papers on Group Analysis and Psychoanalysis. London and Philadelphia: Jessica Kingsley.
Piper WE (1993) Group psychotherapy research. In: HI Kaplan and BJ Sadock (eds) Comprehensive Group Psychotherapy. Baltimore: Williams and Wilkins.
Roth A, Fonagy P (1996) What Works for Whom? A Critical Review of Psychotherapy Research. New York and London: Guildford Press.
Schneider S (1993) Group psychotherapy under the threat of war: The Gulf Crisis. Group Analysis 26(1): 99–108.
Schulte P (2000) Holding in mind: intersubjectivity, subject relations and the group. Group Analysis 33(4): 531–44.

Stern DN (1985) The Interpersonal World of the Infant. New York: Basic Books.
Stone EG (2001) Culture, politics and group therapy: identification and voyeurism. Group Analysis 34(4): 501–14.
Tsegos Y (1995) Further thoughts on group-analytic training. Group Analysis 28(3): 313–26.
Weegmann M (2001) Working intersubjectively: what does it mean for theory and therapy? Group Analysis 34(4): 515–30.
Whitaker DS (1992) Making research a part of group therapeutic practice. Group Analysis 25(4): 433–48.

Glossary

References

Dick B (1993) The group matrix as a Holomovement and Quantum Field. Group Analysis 26(4): 469–80.
Foulkes SH (1964) Therapeutic Group Analysis, p.81. London: George Allen & Unwin.
Pines M (1996) Dialogue and selfhood. Group Analysis 29(3): 327–41.
Powell A (1994) Towards a Unifying Concept of the Group Matrix. In: D Brown and L Zinkin (eds) The Psyche and the Social World. London: Routledge.
Stacey R (2001) Complexity and the group matrix. Group Analysis 34(2): 235.
Zinkin L (1983) Malignant mirroring. Group Analysis 16(2): 113–26.

Books on group-analytic psychotherapy

Barnes B, Ernst S, Hyde K (1999) An Introduction to Groupwork: A Group-Analytic Perspective. London: Macmillan.
Brown D, Zinkin L (eds) The Psyche and the Social World: Developments in Group-Analytic Theory. London: Routledge.
Foulkes E (ed) (1990) Selected Papers of S.H. Foulkes: Psychoanalysis and Group Analysis. London: Karnac.
Foulkes SH (1948) Introduction to Group-Analytic Psychotherapy. London: Heinemann. Maresfield reprint, 1984.
Foulkes SH (1964) Therapeutic Group Analysis. London: Allen and Unwin; reprinted London: Karnac (1984).
Foulkes SH, Anthony EJ (1965) Group Psychotherapy: The Psychoanalytic Approach, 2nd edition. London: Penguin Books.
Foulkes SH (1975) Group-Analytic Psychotherapy: Method and Principles. London: Gordon and Breach.

Heigl-Evers A (1978) Konzepte der Analytischen Gruppentherapi. Gottingen: Vandenhoek und Ruprecht.

Karterud S (1999) Gruppe Analyse og psykodynamisk gruppepsykoterapi. Oslo: Pax Forlag.

Kennard D, Roberts J, Winter DA (1993) A Workbook of Group-Analytic Interventions. London and New York: Routledge.

Pines M (1983) The Evolution of Group Analysis. London and New York: Routledge and Kegan Paul.

Pines M (1998) Circular Reflections: Selected Papers on Group Analysis and Psychoanalysis. London and Philadelphia: Jessica Kingsley.

Pines M, Rafaelsen L (1982) (eds) The Individual and the Group: Boundaries and Interrelations. Volume 1: Theory. Volume 2: Practice. New York: Plenum Press.

Roberts J, Pines M (1991) (eds) The Practice of Group Analysis. London: Tavistock / Routledge.

Thompson S (1999) The Group Context. London: Jessica Kingsley.

Chapters on group analysis in general texts

Behr HL, Hearst LE, van der Kleij GA (1985) Die Methode der Gruppenanalyse im Sinne von Foulkes. In: P Kutter (ed) Methoden und Theorien der Gruppenpsychotherapie: Psychoanalytische und tiefenpsychologische Perspektiven. Stuttgart: Frommann-Holzboog.

Pines M, Hearst LE (1993) Group analysis. In: HI Kaplan and BJ Sadock (eds) Comprehensive Group Psychotherapy, 3rd edition. Baltimore: Williams and Wilkins.

Pines M, Hutchinson S (1993) In: A Alonso and HI Swiller (1993) Group Therapy in Clinical Practice. Washington and London: American Psychiatric Press.

Pines M, Hearst LE, Behr HL (1982) Group analysis (group analytic psychotherapy). In: GM Gazda (ed) Basic Approaches to Group Psychotherapy and Counselling, 3rd edition. Springfield, IL: Charles C Thomas.

Schlapobersky J, Pines M (2000) Group methods in adult psychiatry. In: MG Gelder, JJ Lopez-Ibor, N Andreasan (eds) The New Oxford Textbook of Psychiatry. Oxford: Oxford University Press.

General texts on group psychotherapy

Alonso A, Swiller HI (1993) Group Therapy in Clinical Practice. Washington and London: American Psychiatric Press.

Ettin MF (1992) Foundations and Applications of Group Psychotherapy: A Sphere of Influence. Boston: Allyn and Bacon.

Gazda GM (1982) (ed) Basic Approaches to Group Psychotherapy and Counselling, 3rd edition. Springfield, IL: Charles C. Thomas.

Grotjahn M. (1977) The Art and Technique of Group Therapy. New York: Jason Aronson.

Kaplan HI, Sadock BJ (1993) Comprehensive Group Psychotherapy, 3rd edition. Baltimore: Williams and Wilkins.

Mullan H, Rosenbaum M (1978) Group Psychotherapy: Theory and Practice. New York: Free Press.

Rutan JS, Stone WN (1993) Psychodynamic Group Psychotherapy. New York: Guilford Press.

Scheidlinger S (1980) Psychoanalytic Group Dynamics: Basic Readings. New York: International Universities Press.

Schermer VL, Pines M (eds) (1994) Ring of Fire: Primitive Affects and Object Relations in Group Psychotherapy. London and New York: Routledge.

Shaffer JBP, Galinsky MD (1989) Models of Group Therapy and Sensitivity Training, 2nd edition. Princeton, NJ: Prentice-Hall.

Whitaker DS, Lieberman MA (1964) Psychotherapy Through the Group Process. Chicago: Aldine.

Whiteley JS, Gordon J (1979) Group Approaches in Psychiatry. London: Routledge and Kegan Paul.

Yalom ID (1995) Theory and Practice of Group Psychotherapy, 4th edition. New York: Basic Books.

Index

Numbers in *italics* refer to entries in the Bibliography.

Lightning Source UK Ltd.
Milton Keynes UK
UKOW03f1205070714

234691UK00001B/6/P